P9-DMQ-614

THE POWER
OF SOUL

*The Way to Heal, Rejuvenate,
Transform, and Enlighten All Life*

Dr. Zhi Gang Sha

ATRIA BOOKS

New York   London   Toronto   Sydney

Heaven's Library
Toronto

A Division of Simon & Schuster, Inc.
1230 Avenue of the Americas
New York, NY 10020

Toronto, ON

Copyright © 2009 by Heaven's Library Publication Corp. and Dr. Zhi Gang Sha

All rights reserved, including the right to reproduce this book
or portions thereof in any form whatsoever. For information
address Atria Books Subsidiary Rights Department,
1230 Avenue of the Americas, New York, NY 10020

The information contained in this book is intended to be educational and not
for diagnosis, prescription, or treatment of any health disorder whatsoever.
This information should not replace consultation with a competent health-care professional.
The content of the book is intended to be used as an adjunct to a rational and
responsible health-care program prescribed by a health-care practitioner.
The author and publisher are in no way liable for any misuse of the material.

First Atria Books hardcover edition January 2009

ATRIA BOOKS and colophon are trademarks of Simon & Schuster, Inc.

Heaven's Library and Soul Power Series are trademarks of Heaven's Library Publication Corp.

For information about special discounts for bulk purchases, please contact Simon & Schuster
Special Sales at 1-800-456-6798 or business@simonandschuster.com.

Designed by Davina Mock-Maniscalco

Manufactured in the United States of America

1   3   5   7   9   10   8   6   4   2

Library of Congress Cataloging-in-Publication Data
Sha, Zhi Gang.
The power of soul : the way to heal, rejuvenate, transform, and enlighten all life /
Zhi Gang Sha.—1st Atria Books hardcover ed.
p.   cm.—(Soul power series)
Includes bibliographical references.
1. Spiritual life.   2. Spiritual healing.   I. Title.
BL624.S47553   2009
204'.4—dc22   2008034433

ISBN-13: 978-1-4165-8910-5
ISBN-10:   1-4165-8910-4

*This book is dedicated to all humanity on Mother Earth
and all souls in all universes.*

This book reveals soul over matter, which is the power of soul.

The power of soul can be summarized in one sentence:

Soul can heal; boost energy, stamina, vitality, and immunity;
prevent sickness; rejuvenate; prolong life; and transform
every aspect of life, including relationships and finances;
as well as reach enlightenment.

*I love my heart and soul
I love all humanity
Join hearts and souls together
Love, peace and harmony
Love, peace and harmony*

*I am a servant of you and every reader.
I am a servant of all humanity and all souls.*

Thank you for the opportunity to serve and to reveal and share soul secrets, wisdom, knowledge, and practices to heal, rejuvenate, transform, and enlighten all life for humanity and all souls.

Contents

List of Figures

Soul Power Series

THE PURPOSE OF life is to serve. I have committed my life to this purpose. Service is my life mission.

My total life mission is to transform the consciousness of humanity and all souls in the universe and enlighten them, in order to create love, peace, and harmony for humanity, Mother Earth, and all universes. This mission includes three empowerments.

My first empowerment is to teach *universal service* to empower people to be unconditional universal servants. The message of universal service is:

I serve humanity and the universe unconditionally.
You serve humanity and the universe unconditionally.
Together we serve humanity and all souls in the universe
  unconditionally.

My second empowerment is to teach *healing* to empower people to heal themselves and heal others. The message of healing is:

I have the power to heal myself.
You have the power to heal yourself.
Together we have the power to heal the world.

My third empowerment is to teach *the power of soul,* which includes soul secrets, wisdom, knowledge, and practices, and to transmit Divine Soul Power to empower people to transform every aspect of their lives and enlighten their souls, hearts, minds, and bodies.

The message of Soul Power is:

> *I have the Soul Power to transform my consciousness and*
> *every aspect of my life and enlighten my soul, heart,*
> *mind, and body.*
> *You have the Soul Power to transform your consciousness*
> *and every aspect of your life and enlighten your soul,*
> *heart, mind, and body.*
> *Together we have the Soul Power to transform consciousness*
> *and every aspect of all life and enlighten humanity and*
> *all souls.*

To teach the power of soul is my most important empowerment. It is the key for my total life mission. The power of soul is the key for transforming physical life and spiritual life. It is the key for transforming and enlightening humanity and every soul in all universes.

The beginning of the twenty-first century is the transition period into a new era for humanity, Mother Earth, and all universes. This era is named the Soul Light Era. The Soul Light Era began on August 8, 2003. It will last fifteen thousand years. Natural disasters—including tsunamis, hurricanes, cyclones, earthquakes, floods, tornados, hail, blizzards, fires, drought, extreme temperatures, famine, and disease—political, religious, and ethnic wars, terrorism, proliferation of nuclear weapons, economic challenges, pollution, vanishing species, and other such upheavals are part of this transition. In addition, millions of people are suffering from depression, anxiety, fear, anger, and worry. They suffer from pain, chronic conditions, and life-threatening illnesses.

Humanity needs help. The consciousness of humanity needs to be transformed. The suffering of humanity needs to be removed.

The books of the Soul Power Series are brought to you by Heaven's Library and Atria Books. They reveal soul secrets and teach soul wisdom, soul knowledge, and soul practices for your daily life. The power of soul can heal, prevent illness, rejuvenate, prolong life, and transform consciousness and every aspect of life, including relationships and finances. The power of soul is vital to serving humanity and Mother Earth during this transition period. The power of soul will awaken and transform the consciousness of humanity and all souls.

In the twentieth century and for centuries before, *mind over matter* played a vital role for healing, rejuvenation, and life transformation. In the Soul Light Era, *soul over matter*—Soul Power—will play *the* vital role to heal, rejuvenate, and transform all life.

There are countless souls on Mother Earth—souls of human beings, souls of animals, souls of other living things, and souls of inanimate things. *Everyone and everything has a soul.*

Every soul has its own frequency and power. Jesus had miraculous healing power. We have heard many heart-touching stories of lives saved by Guan Yin's[1] compassion. Mother Mary's love has created many heart-moving stories. All of these great souls were given Divine Soul Power to serve humanity. In all of the world's great religions and spiritual traditions, including Buddhism, Taoism, Christianity, Judaism, Hinduism, Islam, and more, there are similar accounts of great spiritual healing and blessing power.

I honor every religion and every spiritual tradition. However, I am not teaching religion. I am teaching Soul Power, which includes soul secrets, soul wisdom, soul knowledge, and soul practices. Your soul has the power to heal, rejuvenate, and transform life. An animal's

---

1. Guan Yin is known as the Bodhisattva of Compassion and, in the West, as the Goddess of Mercy.

soul has the power to heal, rejuvenate, and transform life. The souls of the sun, the moon, an ocean, a tree, and a mountain have the power to heal, rejuvenate, and transform life. The souls of healing angels, ascended masters, holy saints, Taoist saints, Hindu saints, buddhas, and other high-level spiritual beings have great Soul Power to heal, rejuvenate, and transform life.

Every soul has its own standing. Spiritual standing, or soul standing, has countless layers. Soul Power also has layers. Not every soul can perform miracles like Jesus, Guan Yin, and Mother Mary. Soul Power depends on the soul's spiritual standing in Heaven. The higher a soul stands in Heaven, the more Soul Power that soul is given by the Divine. Jesus, Guan Yin, and Mother Mary all have a very high spiritual standing.

Who determines a soul's spiritual standing? Who gives the appropriate Soul Power to a soul? Who decides the direction for humanity, Mother Earth, and the universes? The top leader of the spiritual world is the decision-maker. This top leader is the Divine. The Divine is the creator and manifester of all universes.

In the Soul Light Era, all souls will join as one and align their consciousness with divine consciousness. At this historic time, the Divine has decided to transmit the Divine's soul treasures to humanity and all souls to help humanity and all souls go through Mother Earth's transition.

Let me share two personal stories with you to explain how I reached this understanding.

First, in April 2003 I held a Power Healing workshop for about one hundred people at the Land of Medicine Buddha in Soquel, California. As I was teaching, the Divine appeared. I told the students, "The Divine is here. Could you give me a moment?" I knelt and bowed down to the floor to honor the Divine. (At age six, I was taught to bow down to my tai chi masters. At age ten, I bowed down to my qi gong masters. At age twelve, I bowed down to my kung fu masters. Being Chinese, I learned this courtesy throughout my childhood.) I explained to the students, "Please understand that this is the way I honor the Divine, my spiritual fathers, and my spiritual mothers. Now I will have a conversation with the Divine."

I began by saying silently, "Dear Divine, I am very honored you are here."

The Divine, who was in front of me above my head, replied, "Zhi Gang, I come today to pass a spiritual law to you."

I said, "I am honored to receive this spiritual law."

The Divine continued, "This spiritual law is named the Universal Law of Universal Service. It is one of the highest spiritual laws in the universe. It applies to the spiritual world and the physical world."

The Divine pointed to the Divine. "I am a universal servant." The Divine pointed to me. "You are a universal servant." The Divine swept his hand in front of the Divine. "Everyone and everything is a universal servant. A universal servant offers universal service unconditionally. Universal service includes universal love, forgiveness, peace, healing, blessing, harmony, and enlightenment. If one offers a little service, one receives little blessing from the universe and from me. If one offers more service, one receives more blessing. If one offers unconditional service, one receives unlimited blessing."

The Divine paused for a moment before continuing. "There is another kind of service, which is unpleasant service. Unpleasant service includes killing, harming, taking advantage of others, cheating, stealing, complaining, and more. If one offers a little unpleasant service, one learns little lessons from the universe and from me. If one offers more unpleasant service, one learns more lessons. If one offers huge unpleasant service, one learns huge lessons."

I asked, "What kinds of lessons could one learn?"

The Divine replied, "The lessons include sickness, accidents, injuries, financial challenges, broken relationships, emotional imbalances, mental confusion, and disorder." The Divine emphasized, "This is how the universe operates. This is one of my most important spiritual laws for all souls in the universe to follow."

After the Divine delivered this universal law, I immediately made a silent vow to the Divine:

> _Dear Divine,_
>
> _I am extremely honored to receive your Law of Universal Service. I make a vow to you, to all humanity, and to all souls in all universes that I will be an unconditional universal servant. I will give my total GOLD [gratitude, obedience, loyalty, devotion] to you and to serving you. I am honored to be your servant and a servant of all humanity and all souls._

Hearing this, the Divine smiled and left.

My second story happened three months later, in July 2003 while I was holding a Soul Study workshop near Toronto. The Divine came again. I again explained to my students that the Divine had appeared, and asked them to wait a moment while I bowed down 108 times and listened to the Divine's message. On this occasion, the Divine told me, "Zhi Gang, I come today to choose you as my direct servant, vehicle, and channel."

I was deeply moved and said to the Divine, "I am honored. What does it mean to be your direct servant, vehicle, and channel?"

The Divine replied, "When you offer healing and blessing to others, call me. I will come instantly to offer my healing and blessing to them."

I was deeply touched and replied, "Thank you so much for choosing me as your direct servant."

The Divine continued, "I can offer my healing and blessing by transmitting my permanent healing and blessing treasures."

I asked, "How do you do this?"

The Divine answered, "Select a person and I will give you a demonstration."

I asked for a volunteer with serious health challenges. A man named Walter raised his hand. He stood up and explained that he had liver cancer, with a two-by-three-centimeter malignant tumor that had just been diagnosed from a biopsy.

Then I asked the Divine, "Please bless Walter. Please show me how you transmit your permanent treasures." Immediately, I saw the Divine send a beam of light from the Divine's heart to Walter's liver. The beam shot into his liver, where it turned into a golden light ball that instantly started spinning. Walter's entire liver shone with beautiful golden light.

The Divine asked me, "Do you understand what software is?"

I was surprised by this question but replied, "I do not understand much about computers. I just know that software is a computer program. I have heard about accounting software, office software, and graphic design software."

"Yes," the Divine said. "Software is a program. Because you asked me to, I transmitted or downloaded my Soul Software for Liver to Walter. It is one of my permanent healing and blessing treasures. You asked me. I did the job. This is what it means for you to be my chosen direct servant and channel."

I was astonished. Excited, inspired, and humbled, I said to the Divine, "I am so honored to be your direct servant. How blessed I am to be chosen." Almost speechless, I asked the Divine, "Why did you choose me?"

"I chose you," said the Divine, "because you have served humanity for more than one thousand lifetimes. You have been very committed to serving my mission through all of your lifetimes. I am choosing you in this life to be my direct servant. You will transmit countless permanent healing and blessing treasures from me to humanity and all souls. This is the honor I give to you now."

I was moved to tears. I immediately bowed down 108 times again and made a silent vow:

> *Dear Divine,*
>
> *I cannot bow down to you enough for the honor you have given to me. No words can express my greatest gratitude. How blessed I am to be your direct servant to download your permanent healing and blessing treasures to humanity and all souls! Humanity and all souls will receive your huge blessings through my service as your direct servant. I give my total life to you and to humanity. I will accomplish your tasks. I will be a pure servant to humanity and all souls.*

I bowed again. Then I asked the Divine, "How should Walter use his Soul Software?"

"Walter must spend time to practice with my Soul Software," said the Divine. "Tell him that simply to receive my Soul Software does not mean he will recover. He must practice with this treasure every day to restore his health, step by step."

I asked, "How should he practice?"

The Divine gave me this guidance: "Tell Walter to chant repeatedly: *Divine Liver Soul Software heals me. Divine Liver Soul Software heals me. Divine Liver Soul Software heals me. Divine Liver Soul Software heals me.*"

I asked, "For how long should Walter chant?"

The Divine answered, "At least two hours a day. The longer he practices, the better. If Walter does this, he could recover in three to six months."

I shared this information with Walter, who was excited and deeply moved. Walter said, "I will practice two hours or more each day."

Finally, I asked the Divine, "How does the Soul Software work?"

The Divine replied, "My Soul Software is a golden healing ball that rotates and clears energy and spiritual blockages in Walter's liver."

I again bowed to the Divine 108 times. Then I stood up and offered three Soul Softwares to every participant in the workshop as divine gifts. Upon seeing this, the Divine smiled and left.

Walter immediately began to practice as directed for at least two hours every day. Two and a half months later, a CT scan and MRI showed that his liver cancer had completely disappeared. At the end of 2006 I met Walter again at a signing in Toronto for my book *Soul Mind Body Medicine*. In May 2008 Walter attended one of my events at the Unity Church of Truth in Toronto. On both occasions, Walter told me that there was still no sign of cancer in his liver. For nearly five years, his Divine Soul Download healed his liver cancer. He was very grateful to the Divine.

This major event of being chosen as a direct divine servant happened in July 2003. As I mentioned, a new era for Mother Earth and the universe, the Soul Light Era, began on August 8, 2003. The timing may look like a coincidence, but I believe there could be an underlying spiritual reason. Since July 2003 I have offered divine transmissions to humanity almost every day. I have offered more than ten divine transmissions to all souls in all universes.

I share this story with you to introduce the power of divine transmissions or Divine Soul Downloads. Now, let me share the commitment that I made in *Soul Wisdom,* the first book of my Soul Power Series, and that I have renewed in every one of my books since:

**From now on, I will offer Divine Soul Downloads
in every book I write.**

Divine Soul Downloads are permanent divine healing and blessing treasures for transforming your life. There is an ancient saying: *If you want to know whether a pear is sweet, taste it.* If you want to know the power of Divine Soul Downloads, experience it.

Divine Soul Downloads carry divine frequency with divine love, forgiveness, compassion, and light. Divine frequency transforms the frequency of all life. Divine love melts all blockages, including energy and spiritual blockages, and transforms all lives. Divine forgiveness brings inner peace and inner joy. Divine compassion boosts energy, stamina, vitality, and immunity. Divine light heals, prevents sickness, rejuvenates, and prolongs life.

A Divine Soul Download is a new soul created from the heart of the Divine. The Divine Soul Download transmitted to Walter was a Soul Software. Since then, I have transmitted several other types of Divine Soul Downloads, including Divine Soul Transplants.

A Divine Soul Transplant is a new divine soul of an organ, a part of the body, a bodily system, cells, DNA, RNA, the smallest matter in cells, or the spaces between cells. When it is transmitted, it replaces the recipient's original soul of the organ, part of the body, system, cells, DNA, RNA, smallest matter in cells, or spaces between cells. A new divine soul can also replace the soul of a home or a business. A new divine soul can be transmitted to a pet, a mountain, a city, or a country to replace their original souls. A new divine soul can even replace the soul of Mother Earth.

Everyone and everything has a soul. The Divine can download any soul you can conceive of. These Divine Soul Downloads are permanent divine healing, blessing, and life-transforming treasures. They can transform the lives of anyone and anything. Because the Divine created these soul treasures, they carry Divine Soul Power, which is the greatest Soul Power among all souls. All souls in the highest layers of Heaven will support and assist Divine Soul Downloads. Divine Soul Downloads are the crown jewel of Soul Power.

Divine Soul Downloads are divine presence. The more Divine Soul Downloads you receive, the faster your soul, heart, mind, and body will be transformed. The more Divine Soul Downloads your home or business receives, and the more Divine Soul Downloads a city or country receives, the faster their souls, hearts, minds, and bodies will be transformed.

In the Soul Light Era, the evolution of humanity will be created by Divine Soul Power. Soul Power will transform humanity. Soul Power will transform animals. Soul Power will transform nature and the environment. Soul Power will assume the leading role in every field of human endeavor. Humanity will deeply understand that *the soul is the boss*.

Soul Power, including soul secrets, soul wisdom, soul knowledge, and soul practices, will transform every aspect of human life. Soul Power will transform every aspect of organizations and societies. Soul Power will transform cities, countries, Mother Earth, all planets, stars, galaxies, and all universes. Divine Soul Power, including Divine Soul Downloads, will lead this transformation.

I am honored to have been chosen as a divine servant to offer Divine Soul Downloads to humanity, to relationships, to homes, to businesses, to pets, to cities, to countries, and more. In the last few years, I have already transmitted countless divine souls to humanity and to all universes. I repeat to you now: **I will offer Divine Soul Downloads within each and every book of the Soul Power Series.** Clear instructions on how to receive these Divine Soul Downloads will be provided in the next section, "How to Receive the Divine Soul Downloads Offered in the Books of the Soul Power Series," as well as on the appropriate pages of each book.

I am a servant of humanity. I am a servant of the universe. I am a servant of the Divine. I am extremely honored to be a servant of all souls. I commit my total life and being as an unconditional universal servant.

I will continue to offer Divine Soul Downloads for my entire life. I will offer more and more Divine Soul Downloads to every soul. I will offer Divine Soul Downloads for every aspect of life for every soul.

I am honored to be a servant of Divine Soul Downloads.

Human beings, organizations, cities, and countries will receive more and more Divine Soul Downloads, which can transform every aspect of their lives and enlighten their souls, hearts, minds, and bodies. The Soul Light Era will shine Soul Power. The books in the Soul Power Series will spread Divine Soul Downloads, together with Soul Power—soul secrets, soul wisdom, soul knowledge, and soul practices—to serve humanity, Mother Earth, and all universes. The Soul Power Series is a pure servant for humanity and all souls. The Soul Power Series is honored to be a total GOLD² servant for the Divine, humanity, and all souls.

The final goal of the Soul Light Era is to join every soul as one in love, peace, and harmony. This means that the consciousness of every soul will be totally aligned with divine consciousness. There will be difficulties and challenges on the path to this final goal. Together we will overcome them. We call all souls of humanity and all souls in all universes to offer unconditional universal service, including universal love, forgiveness, peace, healing, blessing, harmony, and enlightenment. The more we offer unconditional universal service, the faster we will achieve this goal.

The Divine gives the Divine's heart to us. The Divine gives the Divine's love to us. The Divine gives Divine Soul Downloads to us. Our hearts meld with the Divine's heart. Our souls meld with the Divine's soul. Our consciousnesses align with the Divine's consciousness. We will join hearts and souls together to create love, peace, and harmony for humanity, Mother Earth, and all universes.

> *I love my heart and soul*
> *I love all humanity*
> *Join hearts and souls together*

---

2. Total GOLD means total gratitude, total obedience, total loyalty, and total devotion to the Divine.

Love, peace and harmony
Love, peace and harmony

Love all humanity. Love all souls. Thank all humanity. Thank all souls.

Thank you. Thank you. Thank you.

Zhi Gang Sha

How to Receive the Divine Soul Downloads Offered in the Books of the Soul Power Series

THE BOOKS OF the Soul Power Series are unique. For the first time in history, the Divine is downloading his soul treasures to readers as they read these books. Every book in the Soul Power Series will include Divine Soul Downloads that have been preprogrammed. When you read the appropriate paragraphs and pause for a minute, divine gifts will be transmitted to your soul.

In April 2005, the Divine told me to "leave Divine Soul Downloads to history." I thought, "A human being's life is limited. Even if I live a long, long life, I will go back to Heaven one day. How can I leave Divine Soul Downloads to history?"

In the beginning of 2008, as I was editing the paperback edition of *Soul Wisdom,* the Divine suddenly told me: "Zhi Gang, offer my downloads within this book." The Divine said, "I will preprogram my downloads in the book. Any reader can receive them as he or she reads the special pages." At the moment the Divine gave me this direction, I understood how I could leave Divine Soul Downloads to history.

Preprogrammed Divine Soul Downloads are permanently stored within this book and every book in the Soul Power Series. If people read this book thousands of years from now, they will still receive the Divine Soul Downloads. As long as this book exists and is read, readers will receive the Divine Soul Downloads.

Allow me to explain further. The Divine has placed a permanent blessing within certain paragraphs in these books. These blessings allow you to receive Divine Soul Downloads as permanent gifts to your soul. Because these divine treasures reside with your soul, you can access them twenty-four hours a day—as often as you like, wherever you are—for healing, blessing, and life transformation.

It is very easy to receive the Divine Soul Downloads in these books. After you read the special paragraphs where they are preprogrammed, close your eyes. Receive the special download. It is also easy to apply these divine treasures. After you receive a Divine Soul Download, I will immediately show you how to apply it for healing, blessing, and life transformation.

You have free will. If you are not ready to receive a Divine Soul Download, simply say *I am not ready to receive this gift*. You can then continue to read the special download paragraphs, but you will not receive the gifts they contain. The Divine does not offer Divine Soul Downloads to those who are not ready or not willing to receive the Divine's treasures. However, the moment you are ready, you can simply go back to the relevant paragraphs and tell the Divine *I am ready*. You will then receive the stored special download when you reread the paragraphs.

The Divine has agreed to offer specific Divine Soul Downloads in these books to all readers who are willing to receive them. The Divine has unlimited treasures. However, you can receive only the ones designated in these pages. Please do not ask for different or additional gifts. It will not work.

After receiving and practicing with the Divine Soul Downloads in these books, you could experience remarkable healing results in your physical, emotional, mental, and spiritual bodies. You could receive incredible blessings for your love relationships and other relationships. You could receive financial blessings and all kinds of other blessings.

Divine Soul Downloads are unlimited. There can be a Divine Soul Download for anything that exists in the physical world. The reason for this is very simple. *Everything has a soul.* A house has a soul. The Divine can download a soul to your house that can transform its energy. The Divine can download a soul to your business that can transform your business. If you are wearing a ring, that ring has a soul. If the Divine downloads a new divine soul to your ring, you can ask the divine soul in your ring to offer divine healing and blessing.

I am honored to have been chosen as a servant of humanity and the Divine to offer Divine Soul Downloads. For the rest of my life, I will continue to offer Divine Soul Downloads. I will offer more and more of them. I will offer Divine Soul Downloads for every aspect of every life.

I am honored to be a servant of Divine Soul Downloads.

What to Expect After You Receive Divine Soul Downloads

Divine Soul Downloads are new souls created from the heart of the Divine. When these souls are transmitted, you may feel a strong vibration. For example, you could feel warm or excited. Your body could shake a little. If you are not sensitive, you may not feel anything. Advanced spiritual beings with an open Third Eye can actually see a huge golden, rainbow, or purple light soul enter your body.

These divine souls are your yin companions[3] for life. They will stay with your soul forever. Even after your physical life ends, these

---

3. A yang companion is a physical being, such as a family member or pet. A yin companion is a soul companion without a physical form.

divine treasures will continue to accompany your soul into your next life and all of your future lives. In these books, I will teach you how to invoke these divine souls anytime, anywhere to give you divine healing or blessing in this life. You also can invoke these souls to leave your body to offer divine healing or blessing to others. These divine souls have extraordinary abilities to heal, bless, and transform. If you develop advanced spiritual abilities in your next life, you will discover that you have these divine souls with you. Then you will be able to invoke these divine souls in the same way in your future lifetimes to heal, bless, and transform every aspect of your life.

It is a great honor to have a divine soul downloaded to your own soul. The divine soul is a pure soul without bad karma. The divine soul carries divine healing and blessing abilities. The download does not have any side effects. You are given love and light with divine frequency. You are given divine abilities to serve yourself and others. Therefore, humanity is extremely honored that the Divine is offering the Divine's downloads. I am extremely honored to be a servant of the Divine, of you, of all humanity, and of all souls to offer Divine Soul Downloads. I cannot thank the Divine enough. I cannot thank you, all humanity, and all souls enough for the opportunity to serve.

Thank you. Thank you. Thank you.

Foreword to the Soul Power Series

I HAVE ADMIRED DR. Zhi Gang Sha's work for some years now. In fact, I clearly remember the first time I heard him describe his soul healing system, Soul Mind Body Medicine. I knew immediately that I wanted to support this gifted healer and his mission, so I introduced him to my spiritual community at Agape. Ever since, it has been my joy to witness how those who apply his teachings and techniques experience increased energy, joy, harmony, and peace in their lives.

Dr. Sha's techniques awaken the healing power already present in all of us, empowering us to put our overall well-being in our own hands. His explanation of energy and message, and how they link consciousness, mind, body, and spirit, forms a dynamic information network in language that is easy to understand and, more important, to apply.

Dr. Sha's time-tested results have proven to thousands of students and readers that healing energies and messages exist within specific sounds, movements, and affirmative perceptions. Weaving in his own personal experiences, Dr. Sha's theories and practices of working directly with the life-force energy and spirit are practical, holistic, and profound. His recognition that Soul Power is most important for every aspect of life is vital to meeting the challenges of twenty-first-century living.

The worldwide representative of his renowed teacher, Dr. Zhi Chen Guo, one of the greatest qi gong masters and healers in the world, Dr. Sha is himself a master of ancient disciplines such as tai chi, qi gong, kung fu, the *I Ching,* and feng shui. He has blended the soul of his culture's natural healing methods with his training as a Western physician, and generously offers his wisdom to us through the books in his Soul Power Series. His contribution to those in the healing professions is undeniable, and the way in which he empowers his readers to understand themselves, their feelings, and the connection between their bodies, minds, and spirits is his gift to the world.

Through his Soul Power Series, Dr. Sha guides the reader into a consciousness of healing not only of body, mind, and spirit, but also of the heart. I consider his healing path to be a universal spiritual practice, a journey into genuine transformation. His professional integrity and compassionate heart are at the root of his being a servant of humankind, and my heartfelt wish for his readers is that they accept his invitation to awaken the power of the soul and realize the natural beauty of their existence.

Dr. Michael Bernard Beckwith
Founder, Agape International Spiritual Center

Foreword to
The Power of Soul

D R. SHA BRINGS a unique view of the soul that is most needed as we enter the twenty-first century. As a student of mysticism as well as of holistic medicine, I found that Dr. Sha's 2006 book, *Soul Mind Body Medicine,* immediately resonated with me. My first reaction was, "We had it backward! Of course, the soul is the determiner." Indeed, in allegorical literature, the story of Pinocchio emphasizes the fact that the puppeteer (the soul) controls the puppet (the boy). When the boy does not follow his conscience, or soul, his nose grows.

After immersing myself in several of Dr. Sha's books, I had the privilege of attending his Soul Healing and Enlightenment retreat in Quebec in June 2008. That experience was a powerful reawakening of my lifelong belief that our primary purpose in life is to help others. In particular, Dr. Sha's Soul Songs are powerful tools for experiencing the power of soul.

Dr. Sha received a universal law from the Divine: *Universal service includes universal love, forgiveness, peace, healing, blessing, harmony, and enlightenment.* My insight for many years has been that love is the desire to help others. Indeed, I sense that our most essential instinct is to assist others. Unfortunately, some individuals have not felt nurtured enough to allow this instinct to blossom. On the other hand, the acts of nurturing, serving, and helping others bring most individuals more satisfaction, inner harmony, and peace than any other activity. Nothing in life is more important. Dr. Sha emphasizes this transcendent nature of all beings with practical approaches that assist us in dissolving karma, empowering us to shape our destiny and our entire life.

The soul is generally considered to be our unique, individual consciousness, the inner essence that survives the death of the human body. The dominant consensus among neuroscientists is that the mind, or consciousness, is the domain of the brain. Within the past century, the relationship of mind and body has become the major scientific focus. Mind-body medicine has evolved as a "new" field of study.

Emotions are generally considered to arise from the interaction of mind and body. Scientifically, the soul is considered to be a "belief" that shapes attitudes and behavior. How sad that science has ignored the real determiner of life and happiness! We are most fortunate that Dr. Sha has now opened this magic door for us.

In the last hundred years, increasing evidence has accumulated showing that the mind is a nonlocal aspect of consciousness. Clairvoyance, distance healing, and prayer healing have gained increasing respect in the field of healing. Holistic medicine was officially created in 1978 in order to emphasize the need for addressing the spiritual needs of patients. From that time until the present, the major theme has been *body, mind,* and *spirit,* with spirit essentially representing the various aspects of soul.

Beliefs, behavior, and emotions have been the major themes in this evolution of medical thought. But these themes have not explored or touched our ultimate divine essence, the soul. Mystics have written extensively of their experiences, which are often beautiful examples of the beginning of enlightenment. However, I was not aware of any spiritual being who has provided a specific blueprint for enlightenment—until I met Dr. Sha!

Now we have a new doorway to the power of soul—one of appreciation, devotion, and above all, of unconditional love at its most powerful. The soul is our major guide. Its power is limitless. The soul is the door to divine light, to assisting us in creating and experiencing enlightenment. The ancient wisdom of such foundational texts as the *Yoga Sutras of Patanjali* and the *Tao Te Jing*, as well as that of the great philosophers and mystics, has now been transformed into a universal approach to all of life—and Dr. Sha, assisted by Soul Power and Divine Soul Downloads, is the transformer.

I must mention again the Soul Songs and chants! I have practiced meditation, chants of OM, and many other chanting techniques. We are giant piezoelectric crystals—receiving, storing, and sending electromagnetic energy. Many of Dr. Sha's Soul Songs are by far the most powerful examples of direct soul connection that I have experienced. They are a significant creation and manifestation of the power of soul.

As Dr. Sha writes within this marvelous book:

> *The power of soul can be summarized in one sentence:*
> *Soul can heal; boost energy, stamina, vitality, and immunity;*
> *prevent sickness; rejuvenate; prolong life; and transform*
> *every aspect of life, including relationships and finances;*
> *as well as reach enlightenment.*

Dr. Sha's book opens the door for everyone to experience the power of soul—the ultimate journey of the soul. I hope you will receive as much joy, healing, blessing, and transformation from it as I have!

C. Norman Shealy, M.D., Ph.D.
Professor of Energy Medicine and President Emeritus
Holos University Graduate Seminary
Producer, *Medical Renaissance*

How to Read This Book

$\mathcal{J}$N EVERY BOOK of my Soul Power Series, I reveal soul secrets and teach soul wisdom, soul knowledge, and soul practices. Secret and sacred wisdom and knowledge are important. *Practice is even more important.* Since ancient times, serious Buddhist, Taoist, qi gong, and kung fu practitioners have spent hours and hours a day in practice. Their dedication empowers them to develop and transform their frequency, their consciousness, and their purification further and further. In the modern world, successful professionals in every field similarly spend hours a day for months and years to practice. Their commitment empowers them to develop and transform their power and abilities further and further.

Every book in my Soul Power Series offers new approaches to healing, rejuvenation, and life transformation. Along with the teachings of sacred wisdom and knowledge, I also offer Divine Soul Downloads as a servant, vehicle, and channel of the Divine. I am honored to serve you through these books. However, *the most important service offered in these books is the practices.* This is especially true of this book, *The Power of Soul.* In this book I lead you in dozens of practices. If you spend four or five minutes to do each practice, I fully understand that it will take you some time to finish all of them. Do a few practices today. Tomorrow do another few practices. Do a few more the day after tomorrow. The practices are vital. If you do not do them, how can you experience their power and benefits? If you do not experience their power and benefits, how can you fully understand and absorb the teaching?

My message to you is that as you read this book, make sure you do not miss the practices. I deliberately guide you in this book to do spiritual practices using the power of soul for healing, prevention of sickness, prolonging life, and transforming every aspect of life, including relationships and finances. Reading this book is like being at a workshop with me. When you go to a workshop and the teacher leads you in a meditation or practice, you do not run off to do something else, do you?

Do not rush through this book. Do every practice that I ask you to do. You will receive ten, fifty, a hundred times the benefit that you would receive if you simply read through the book quickly. Especially, to receive Divine Soul Downloads does not mean you receive their benefits. You must invoke them and practice to experience and receive divine healing and blessing. Remember also that going through this book just once is not enough. My advanced students go through my books many times. Every time they read and do the practices, they reach more and more "aha" moments. They receive more and more remarkable healing, purification, and life transformation results.

These are important messages for you to remember as you read this book. I wish each of you will receive great healing, rejuvenation, purification, and life transformation by doing the practices in this book. Receive the benefit of *soul over matter*, which is the power of soul.

Practice. Practice. Practice.

Experience. Experience. Experience.

Benefit. Benefit. Benefit.

Hao! Hao! Hao!

Thank you. Thank you. Thank you.

Introduction

MILLIONS OF PEOPLE worldwide are searching for spiritual secrets, wisdom, knowledge, and practices to transform and enlighten their lives. Throughout history, there have been many great teachers, including buddhas, holy saints, Taoist saints, healing angels, archangels, Indian gurus, Tibetan lamas, and others from many traditions and cultures. They have offered great teachings to humanity. They have explored the ability of spiritual power to transform human life. I honor all of these great teachers.

In this book, you will learn what Soul Power is, the significance of Soul Power, how to develop your Soul Power, and how to apply Soul Power for healing, prevention of sickness, rejuvenation, prolonging life, life transformation—including transformation of relationships and finances—and enlightenment of your soul, heart, mind, and body.

This book also reveals the true secrets of how Jesus, Mary, Shi Jia Mo Ni Fuo (the Chinese name for Shakyamuni, the founder of Buddhism), Guan Yin (the Chinese name for Avalokiteshvara, the Bodhisattva of Compassion or Goddess of Mercy), buddhas, and all major saints were able to receive great Soul Power from the Divine and the universe. They are great examples for us. In fact, every human being and every soul has the potential to receive the same Soul Power these great saints received from the Divine. But there is a requirement to receive this level of Divine Soul Power: *you must offer unconditional universal service to humanity and all souls.* To serve is to receive. The more you serve, the greater the Soul Power the Divine will give you.

The Divine created a spiritual law. Serve humanity. Awaken humanity. Transform the consciousness of humanity and all souls. Enlighten humanity and all souls. Only in this way can your spiritual standing be uplifted. Only in this way can you receive Divine Soul Power, one step at a time. *Power is given.* True Soul Power is given by the Divine.

On August 8, 2003, the Divine held a major soul conference in Heaven. That day marked the end of the previous fifteen-thousand-year era, whose two major spiritual leaders, Niu Wa Niang Niang and Yuan Shi Tian Zun, were uplifted to the divine realm. A new divine committee with twelve members was formed in Heaven to lead the new era that began on that day. This new era will also last for fifteen thousand years. It is called the Soul Light Era. In the Soul Light Era, the final destiny is to join every soul as one, by transforming the consciousness of humanity and all souls to align with divine consciousness, in order to enlighten all humanity and all souls.

How can we transform all consciousness to divine consciousness and enlighten all humanity and all souls? The process requires seven major steps.

The first step is to offer *soul healing,* to remove the suffering of humanity and all souls. This is the teaching of the Soul Power Series: **Heal the soul first; then healing of the mind and body will follow**. Humanity suffers at the physical, emotional, mental, and spiritual levels. In the human realm, there are thousands of different sicknesses. In the soul realm, there are countless sicknesses. A human being needs healing for the physical, emotional, mental, and spiritual bodies. An organization needs healing for harmony and success. A city and a country need healing for balance. The whole world needs healing and peace.

I honor all healing modalities. What I am sharing with humanity is soul healing. Soul healing is applying the power of soul to heal humanity, animals, Mother Earth, and all universes. Soul healing can carry Divine Soul Power to heal.

When people are suffering, it is very hard to create love, peace, and harmony for humanity, Mother Earth, and all universes. In order to create love, peace, and harmony, we have to offer soul healing to remove the suffering of humanity and all souls.

Every human being has a soul. Every system, every organ, every cell, every DNA and RNA has a soul. Soul has the power to heal itself. Soul has the power to heal mind and body. In this book, I will show you how to apply Soul Power to self-heal. You can also apply Soul Power to heal others. You can apply Soul Power to offer group healing. You can apply Soul Power to do remote healing. This book will teach you how.

The second step is *soul prevention of sickness*. This is the teaching of the Soul Power Series: **Prevent sicknesses of the soul first; then prevention of sicknesses of the mind and body will follow.** Soul can prevent sickness at the physical, emotional, mental, and spiritual levels. *The Yellow Emperor's Classic of Internal Medicine*, the authoritative book in traditional Chinese medicine, states: *The best doctor is one who can treat sickness before it occurs, instead of after it appears.* Prevention is so important. Prevent sickness and stop sickness at its initial stage. Transform sickness back to the normal, healthy condition. Restore the normal and healthy functioning of the body's systems, organs, and cells.

In the physical world, there are many approaches to prevention of sickness. We honor each of them. I am teaching soul prevention of sickness. This book will deliver the soul secrets, wisdom, knowledge, and practices to empower you to do soul prevention of sickness for your physical, emotional, mental, and spiritual bodies.

The third step is *soul rejuvenation*. Ancient Taoism has great secrets for rejuvenation. Ancient Buddhism and Confucianism also have great secrets. Gurus, lamas, and other holy beings from all kinds of spiritual realms hold great secrets for rejuvenation. I honor all of them. In this book, I will teach soul secrets, wisdom, knowledge, and practices for rejuvenation. This is the teaching of the Soul Power Series: **Rejuvenate the soul first; then rejuvenation of the mind and body will follow.**

The fourth step is *soul transformation* for every aspect of life, including relationships and finances. This is the teaching of the Soul Power Series: **Transform the soul first; then transformation of consciousness and every aspect of life will follow.**

The fifth step is *soul enlightenment*. This is the teaching of the Soul Power Series: **Enlighten the soul first; then enlightenment of the mind and body will follow.** Soul enlightenment is the first step on the enlightenment journey. To reach soul enlightenment, one needs great purification. On the soul enlightenment journey, one needs to remove selfishness, attachments, ego, struggles for power, and more, in order to become a pure, humble servant for humanity and the Divine. This book will deliver the soul secrets, wisdom, knowledge, and practical treasures to prepare you for your soul enlightenment journey. I will offer Divine Soul Downloads to purify your soul and transform your life.

After soul enlightenment comes mind enlightenment, which is more difficult to reach. It requires even more purification and commitment to be an unconditional universal servant for humanity and the Divine.

After mind enlightenment, you can move to body enlightenment. You have to heal all sicknesses at the physical, emotional, mental, and spiritual levels. You have to prevent sickness, rejuvenate your soul, mind, and body, and enjoy long, long life. To have long life, one must be a pure channel as a servant for humanity and the Divine.

The sixth step is to *enlighten all humanity*. It takes our greatest effort to purify and enlighten the souls, hearts, minds, and bodies of every human being. Everyone can be transformed to become pure channels to serve humanity and the Divine. In July 2003 I was chosen as a servant of humanity and the Divine. Shortly after this occurred, I was given a major divine task to offer soul healing and enlightenment service to humanity. Together with my Certified Master Teachers and Healers and Certified Divine Master Teachers and Healers, I offer Soul Healing and Enlightenment retreats worldwide. The purpose of these retreats is to enlighten the souls, hearts, minds, and bodies of humanity. At these retreats, we offer the highest divine blessing to enlighten humanity. In fact, at these retreats the Divine enlightens humanity.

Soul enlightenment is the final destiny of one's spiritual journey. To enlighten humanity is the Divine's direction for service to humanity. To enlighten humanity is to uplift the soul standing of every human being. Whoever receives soul enlightenment first will receive the benefits of soul enlightenment first. These benefits are to:

- purify your soul
- radiate the true love within your heart
- remove your selfishness, ego, and attachments
- gain Soul Power to heal suffering of your physical, emotional, mental, and spiritual bodies and balance your soul, heart, mind, and body
- attain inner peace and inner joy
- remove blockages in your relationships and finances
- uplift your soul standing in Heaven to be closer to the divine realm
- realize that the true purpose of life is to serve humanity and all souls, transform their consciousness, and enlighten them

In this book, I will share the important soul secrets, wisdom, knowledge, and practices of soul enlightenment.

The seventh and final step is to *enlighten all souls*. The spiritual world has two parts: the Light Side and the Dark Side. The Light Side includes holy saints, Buddhist saints, Taoist saints, Hindu saints, Tibetan lamas, Indian gurus, healing angels, archangels, ascended masters, and all great spiritual teachers. The Dark Side includes demons, monsters, ghosts, and more. Enlightening all souls includes enlightening the Dark Side.

The goal for the Soul Light Era is to accomplish the task of enlightening every soul in all universes, including both Light and Dark Sides. This is the biggest task that the Divine has given to humanity and all souls in all universes. It is a divine calling for humanity and all souls to move in this direction.

I have personally received a divine calling and blessing to create Soul Healing and Enlightenment Centers worldwide. Within every Soul Healing and Enlightenment Center, the Divine will create a Love Peace Harmony Center. The Divine will transmit his own Soul Power into each Love Peace Harmony Center. People will be able to sit in these divine healing centers to receive divine healing, blessing, and life transformation. Here is how the Divine created the first Love Peace Harmony Center:

On March 9, 2008, at 1:45 p.m. Mountain Daylight Time, while I was teaching an Opening Spiritual Channels workshop at the Boulder Broker Inn in Colorado, I received divine inspiration to create the first physical Love Peace Harmony Center in Boulder. I asked the Divine to create this center to offer divine healing, prevention of sickness, rejuvenation, and prolongation of life, as well as transformation of consciousness and every aspect of life, including relationships and finances. The Divine responded to my request and transmitted Divine Soul Power to Baba's Barn in Boulder. The Divine guided me to name this place a "Love Peace Harmony Center."

The Divine told me, "Dear my servant and servant of humanity, Zhi Gang, I love you. I have created this Love Peace Harmony Center because of your request. I have transmitted my soul healing and blessing power to it. Tell every student in this workshop [there were about one hundred participants] that they can come to this center with their loved ones. To all who enter, I as your beloved Divine will offer healing, blessing, and life transformation. Simply ask those who come to request: *Dear Divine, I love you. Please give me a healing for* _____ (make a silent request to me for your physical body, emotional body, mental body, or spiritual body). They can also request: *Dear Divine, could you bless* _____ (request silently) or *Dear Divine, please transform my relationship with* _____ *or my business* (request silently). After completing all of your requests, say: *I am extremely honored and blessed to receive divine healing, blessing, and life transformation. I am very grateful. Thank you.*

"Then sit in a meditative state. Close your eyes. Listen to my Soul Song *Love, Peace and Harmony* and receive my healing and blessing for your requests.

"My whole healing takes only fifteen to thirty minutes. At the end of the blessing, say *thank you* for the Divine Soul Healing Power. *Thank you. Thank you. Thank you.*"

This is how the first Divine Love Peace Harmony Center was formed. This is how you can receive divine healing, blessing, and life transformation in a special physical place.

This Love Peace Harmony Center carries divine presence. It is the first of many Love Peace Harmony Centers that will be formed worldwide. I wish you and your loved ones—I wish as many people as possible on Mother Earth—will receive this divine soul healing, blessing, and life transformation.

※

I received the seven-step process for transforming all consciousness to divine consciousness and enlightening all humanity and all souls from Divine Guidance. The purpose of this book and the entire Soul Power Series is to empower humanity to move in this divine direction, step by step. Each step is part of the sacred and secret teachings of this book. This book does not come from my logical mind. The entire book, like all of my books, comes from divine flow, which means I simply speak or flow out what I hear from the Divine. If some secrets or wisdom are not clear to me, I will have a direct conversation with the Divine for clarification. I am extremely honored to flow this book. I am extremely honored to be a servant of humanity and the Divine to accomplish this divine task.

To read this book is to experience divine healing, prevention of sickness, rejuvenation, prolongation of life, life transformation, and enlightenment. Divine flow carries divine love, forgiveness, compassion, and light. Divine love melts all blockages and transforms all life. Divine forgiveness brings inner joy and inner peace. Divine compassion boosts energy, stamina, vitality, and immunity. Divine light heals, prevents sickness, rejuvenates, prolongs life, transforms, and enlightens. Relax as you read this book. Open your heart and soul. Every moment, you are receiving divine blessings and life transformation.

This book will also offer eleven Divine Soul Downloads that every reader can receive. On the appropriate pages, I will tell you how to receive and apply these permanent divine soul treasures to heal, transform, and enlighten your life.

I am extremely honored to be a servant of every reader and all humanity. I am extremely honored to be a servant of all souls and the Divine.

> I love my heart and soul
> I love all humanity
> Join hearts and souls together
> Love, peace and harmony
> Love, peace and harmony

This book offers "The Way to Heal, Rejuvenate, Transform, and Enlighten All Life."

Thank you. Thank you. Thank you.

THE POWER
OF SOUL

1

Soul Basics

*F*OR MANY YEARS, I have traveled around the world to teach soul secrets, wisdom, knowledge, and practices. I always ask my students, "What is the soul?" Common answers include: *Soul is the inner being. Soul is the inner child. Soul is the spark of the Divine.* Some people say *soul is one drop of water in the vast ocean.* Others describe the soul as *the essence of one's life.* There are many different answers. Every answer has some significance and correctness for the concept of soul. I honor every answer but I would like to share my own insights on the fundamental wisdom of the soul.

What Is the Soul?

A human's soul is a golden light being. To see a soul, you must open your spiritual eye, which is named the Third Eye. Then you will see clearly that every human being has a golden light being inside his or her body. The soul can sit in different parts of the body. There are seven main areas where a human's soul can sit. These seven houses for the soul are located:

1. just above the genital area
2. between the genitals and the navel
3. at the level of the navel
4. in the heart chakra, which I call the Message Center
5. in the throat
6. in the head
7. just above the head, over the crown chakra

Where your soul sits is extremely significant for your spiritual journey. The significance is that the location of your soul represents your spiritual standing in Heaven. The higher your soul sits in your body, the higher your spiritual standing in Heaven.

A soul has to do Xiu Lian (pronounced *shew li-en*) in order to uplift its standing. Xiu Lian is an ancient spiritual term. "Xiu" means *purification*. "Lian" means *practice*. Xiu Lian represents the totality of the spiritual journey. It includes the cultivation and purification of your soul, heart, mind, and body. Neither you nor your soul can decide where your soul sits inside your body. This simply means that your spiritual standing is not determined by you or your soul's desires. The Akashic Records decide where your soul sits inside your body according to your spiritual standing. The Akashic Records are in a special place in Heaven; there, all of your lives are recorded, including all of your activities, behaviors, and thoughts. They also decide your spiritual standing in Heaven based on your life records.

If you offer good service, such as love, care, compassion, kindness, generosity, and purity, the Akashic Records record this good service. If you offer unpleasant service, such as killing, stealing, harming, and taking advantage of others, the Akashic Records also record this unpleasant service. There is a book in the Akashic Records for each person's soul. This book is dedicated to recording all of your services, good and unpleasant, in your present lifetime and all of your soul's previous lifetimes. Your soul also carries a copy of this record. A highly developed spiritual being can read this record directly, either from the

Akashic Records or from your soul. However, such spiritual beings are rare, as they must be given a spiritual order from the Divine to access this information. Not many beings in history have received this Divine Order to access the Akashic Records.

I cannot emphasize enough that where your soul sits inside your body is a vital factor for your spiritual journey. Today, many spiritual teachers talk about soul enlightenment. What exactly is soul enlightenment? The key to soul enlightenment is the soul's standing. To be enlightened, a soul must sit in the Message Center or higher. If your soul does not sit in these layers, you cannot be considered to have an enlightened soul. This teaching about the divine standard for soul enlightenment was given to me many years ago. Every year, I have two or more Soul Healing and Enlightenment retreats. In each one, the Divine enlightens every participant. The Divine has enlightened thousands of human beings in the last few years. In chapter 13, I will reveal the vital soul secrets, wisdom, knowledge, and practices of soul enlightenment.

I am extremely honored to be a servant of humanity and the Divine to offer divine soul enlightenment for humanity. The Divine gave me the task to offer soul enlightenment for all humanity. I am extremely humbled, honored, and blessed to offer divine soul enlightenment to humanity in my Soul Healing and Enlightenment retreats. I am simply a servant and vehicle of the Divine to offer the Divine's enlightenment to humanity. All credit belongs to the Divine. I am extremely honored to be a servant and vehicle. I cannot thank the Divine enough for choosing me to serve humanity and all souls in this way. Thank you, Divine, from the bottom of my heart.

Characteristics of the Soul

A human being has a character. Some people are very active. Some people are very quiet. Some people are very humorous. Some people are very serious. A soul has its own character. From my personal experience, I would like to share my insights on the main characteristics of the soul:

- Your soul (which I also call your body soul to distinguish it from other souls, such as the souls of your organs) is independent. A human being has a soul, mind, and body. They are separate but united. They are separate because they are independent. They are united because they reside in the same body and communicate with one another.

- Souls have consciousness and intelligence. They have awareness. They think. They analyze. They learn. They have likes and dislikes. One person may like to travel. Another may love food. You may like to read. Someone else may like sports. A soul has its own likes and dislikes, which it has developed over hundreds or even thousands of lifetimes. To help balance and harmonize your soul, mind, and body, it is important to know your soul's likes and dislikes.

- Souls have emotions. A soul can be happy, peaceful, sad, fearful, or upset.

- Souls have incredible wisdom. After you open your spiritual communication channels, you will be able to consult with your soul. You will be amazed to learn how much your soul knows. Your soul is one of your best consultants and guides.

- Souls have great memory. A soul can remember experiences from all of its lifetimes. For example, you may travel somewhere for the first time but clearly feel you are familiar with that place. You may feel like you were there before. Some places make you happy. Some places make you scared. You may have had past-life experiences in those places. You soul has memories of those experiences.

Therefore, you have special feelings at those particular places.

- Souls have flexibility. Walk toward a corner of your room. When you reach the corner, you will have nowhere else to go. You have to turn around to move farther. In life, many times you could be stuck in a situation like a corner. You *must* turn around to get unstuck and move farther. This teaches us to realize the importance of flexibility. There is a famous statement from ancient times: *hua you san shuo, qiao shuo wei miao.* The essence of this statement is: *There are three ways to say something. Find the best way in the moment.* This tells us there is flexibility in speaking every sentence. Therefore, there is flexibility in every aspect of life. Your beloved soul has profound wisdom, knowledge, and experience from hundreds of lifetimes. Your soul has great flexibility. Make sure you use the strength of your soul's flexibility to deal with your life.

- Souls communicate with other souls naturally. Your body soul communicates with other souls naturally. People often talk or dream about a soul mate. When you meet some people, you may instantly feel love. You may feel there is something special between you. The reason for this is that your souls were close in past lives. Your souls could have been communicating for many years before you met physically.

- Souls travel. When you are awake during the day, your soul remains inside your body. But when you are asleep at night, your soul may travel outside your body naturally. In fact, many souls do this. Where does the soul go? It goes where it loves to go. Your soul can visit your spiritual teachers to learn directly from them. It can also visit your old friends, or Heaven and other parts of the universe.

- Souls have incredible healing power. In this book, I will teach you how to apply Soul Power for healing, including self-healing, healing of others, group healing, and remote healing.
- Souls can help you prevent sickness. In this book, I will reveal the soul secrets of soul prevention of sickness.
- Souls can help you rejuvenate. In this book, I will share soul wisdom and practices for soul rejuvenation.
- Souls have incredible blessing capabilities. If you encounter difficulties and blockages in your life, simply ask your soul to help you: *Dear my soul, I love you, honor you, and appreciate you. Could you bless my life? Could you help me overcome my problems and difficulties? Thank you so much.* Invoke your own body soul in this way anytime, anywhere. Your soul can help you solve your problems and overcome your difficulties. Love your soul. Ask your soul to bless your life. Your soul will be delighted to assist you. You could be fascinated and amazed to see the changes in your life.
- Souls have incomprehensible potential powers. In this book, I will teach you how to develop the potential powers of your soul.
- Your soul connects with your mind. Your soul can teach your mind. Your soul can transmit its great wisdom to your mind.
- Your soul connects with your Heaven's Team, which includes your spiritual guides, teachers, angels, and other enlightened masters in Heaven.
- Your soul can store messages. Messages can be stored in your Message Center and in the souls of your body, systems, organs, cells, and more. After you develop the potential powers of your soul, you will be able to access those messages anytime and anywhere.

- Your soul is constantly searching for knowledge. Just as your mind is always learning, so too is your soul. Your soul can learn from other souls, particularly from your spiritual fathers and mothers. Your soul has the potential to learn divine wisdom and knowledge.

- Souls can protect your life. Your own soul can protect you. Other souls, including angels, saints, spiritual guides, enlightened teachers, and the Divine, can protect your life. They can help you prevent sickness, change a serious accident into a minor one, or help you avoid an accident completely.

- Souls can reward you as well as give you warnings. If the soul is happy with what you are doing, the soul can bless your journey. If the soul does not like what you are doing, it can make your life difficult. It could block your relationships or even make you sick.

- Your soul can predict your life. If you can communicate with your soul, your soul can tell you what is in store for you.

- Souls follow spiritual laws and principles. Your mind may not be aware of this, but your soul absolutely follows spiritual laws.

- Your soul is eternal.

- Many souls yearn to be enlightened. They want to offer good service in the form of love, care, compassion, sincerity, generosity, and kindness. That is why more and more people are searching for soul secrets, wisdom, knowledge, and practices. You are reading this book now. You may have a great desire to search more.

Relationships Among Soul, Mind, and Body

A human being has a soul, a mind, and a body. The body includes systems, organs, cells, cell units, DNA, and RNA. Mind is consciousness. Your body has consciousness. Every system, organ, cell, DNA, and RNA has consciousness. Your body has a soul. Every system, organ, cell, DNA, and RNA has a soul. Soul is a golden light being. If you have advanced spiritual abilities, you can see any of these souls, including the souls of DNA and RNA. They are different types of golden light beings.

Soul, mind, and body are separate but united as one inside the body. They work with each other. They communicate with each other. They harmonize and balance each other. For example, the liver, heart, spleen, lungs, and kidneys are the major yin organs. If one of them is sick, it will break the harmony among all of them.

Each major organ connects with the emotional body. The liver connects with anger. The heart connects with anxiety and depression. The spleen connects with worry. The lungs connect with grief and sadness. The kidneys connect with fear. Sickness in the physical body can create disharmony and imbalances in the emotional body.

Each organ has its own soul. The soul of the liver is named liver *hun*. The soul of the heart is named heart *shen*. The soul of the spleen is named spleen *yi*. The soul of the lungs is named lung *po*. The soul of the kidneys is named kidney *zhi*.

Every organ has its own soul, mind, and body. Every cell has its own soul, mind, and body. So does every DNA and RNA. To balance the souls, minds, and bodies of all your systems, organs, cells, DNA, and RNA is vital for life.

A human being has his or her own soul, mind, and body. This soul is the body soul. This mind is the consciousness of this being. This body includes all systems, organs, and cells. What are the relationships among them?

Generally speaking, human beings think they make decisions in their minds. They think they like or dislike someone or something. They think they want or do not want to do something. What I want to share with everyone is that your soul is involved in your decision making. Your soul shares its own likes and dislikes with your mind. If your mind's decision agrees with your soul's desire, things are smooth and successful. If your mind does not agree with your soul's desire, things are blocked.

I have experienced this divine wisdom for many years. The one-sentence secret for the relationships among soul, mind, and body is:

Soul is the boss.

In your company, your boss tells you to do something. When you follow his or her direction, things are smooth. If you do not follow your boss's direction, it could cause big problems. This does not mean your boss is always right. But even if your boss is not right, he or she does have the power to make decisions about your job. In the same way, a soul may not always be absolutely right, but the soul has the power to block your life.

This wisdom teaches us that it is important to communicate with your soul. Your soul has many lifetimes of experience. Generally speaking, your mind has experience from only one lifetime, your present one. Your soul knows much more than your mind. My teaching is to open your spiritual channels to communicate with your own soul. Listen to your soul's guidance. Follow your soul's desire. Your life could be much smoother and much more successful.

If you have disharmony among your soul, mind, and body, you could have poor health, unbalanced emotions, unpleasant relationships, and blockages in your finances. How to harmonize them? Let me show you a simple soul practice to balance soul, mind, and body.

Sit in a relaxed position and condition. Silently communicate with your soul, mind, and body like this:

Dear my soul, mind, and body, I love you all.
You may have some disharmony among yourselves.
You have the power to balance one another.
Do a good job.
Thank you.

Then, silently and repeatedly chant:

I love my soul, mind, and body. Balance and harmonize
my soul, mind, and body.
I love my soul, mind, and body. Balance and harmonize
my soul, mind, and body.
I love my soul, mind, and body. Balance and harmonize
my soul, mind, and body.
I love my soul, mind, and body. Balance and harmonize
my soul, mind, and body . . .

Practice three to five minutes per time, a few times a day. At the end of the practice, always say:

Hao! Hao! Hao!
Thank you. Thank you. Thank you.

Hao, pronounced "how," means "perfect," "wonderful," "balance," "harmonize," and "get well." It is an affirmation and a command.

The first *thank you* is to the Divine. The second *thank you* is to all of your spiritual fathers and mothers in Heaven. The third *thank you* is to your own soul, mind, and body. Gratitude is extremely important on the spiritual journey.

From this simple practice, you could receive remarkable healing for your physical, emotional, mental, and spiritual bodies. You could receive life transformation for your relationships and finances.

Why does this technique work? It works because you invoke and share love with your soul, mind, and body. You give a soul order to your soul, mind, and body to balance and harmonize themselves. The key reason it works is that *love melts all blockages and transforms all life*. Love has immeasurable power to remove all kinds of blockages. This soul order expresses the power of your soul for healing and transformation. I will reveal the most important soul secrets, wisdom, knowledge, and practices about soul orders in chapter 4.

The Purpose of Physical Life and Soul Life

Every human being has a purpose for life. Some people want to be scientists. Some people want to be doctors. Some people want to be artists. Some people want to be basketball players. Everyone has his or her own desires. Everyone loves doing something and dreams about doing it well.

If a person has a good profession, good relationships, a harmonized family, good health, and happiness, that person feels successful in physical life. Satisfaction in one's physical life is important. Many people have this kind of satisfaction. They are blessed.

Some people have this kind of physical success, yet they are not satisfied. They may feel that something is missing. They may feel empty. They may feel they are searching for something, but they do not know exactly what they are searching for. If this resonates with you, I believe you are searching for your soul journey.

Millions of people worldwide are already on their soul journey. They thirst for soul secrets, wisdom, knowledge, and practices. They want to know what the spiritual journey is and how to move forward on it. They want to be enlightened and learn how to reach enlightenment. In this book, I will share what the soul journey is, how to move forward on your soul journey, and how to reach soul enlightenment.

Soul enlightenment is the final destiny of one's soul journey. After you reach soul enlightenment, move further to mind enlightenment and body enlightenment. In chapter 13, I will deliver the soul secrets, wisdom, knowledge, and practices about soul enlightenment to you.

A human's physical life is limited. To live for one hundred years is great. To live longer than this is extraordinary. A human's soul life is unlimited. Soul life is eternal. I have a deep realization that the relationship between the physical journey and the spiritual journey can be summarized in a one-sentence secret:

The physical journey is to serve the soul journey.

If you offer great service to others; if you make others healthier and happier; if you help transform human consciousness; and if you contribute to love, peace, and harmony for humanity, Mother Earth, and the universes, you will accumulate great virtue. Virtue is the record of your services. Heaven records these services. Your great virtue from your good service will uplift your soul standing. Your future lives will be significantly blessed.

Your descendants, including your children, grandchildren, great-grandchildren, and beyond, will be tremendously blessed. There is a famous ancient spiritual statement:

Ancestor plants the tree. Descendants enjoy the shade.

On the other hand, if you offer unpleasant service, such as killing, harming, and taking advantage of others, Heaven also records these unpleasant services. These unpleasant services will profoundly influence your and your descendants' future lives. I will explain this wisdom further in chapter 2 on karma.

In conclusion, to have great success in physical life is wonderful, but it is not enough. To develop the soul's life is vital. To develop the soul's life is to reach soul enlightenment. To reach soul enlightenment is to uplift your soul standing in the spiritual world. The higher your soul standing is, the more abilities the Divine will give you to serve. The more you serve, the higher your spiritual standing will be. Finally, you will be a high-level spiritual being and will move closer and closer to the divine realm. Reaching the divine realm is the ultimate purpose of the spiritual journey.

On Mother Earth, there are many kinds of spiritual books, workshops, and seminars. In Heaven, there are also books, workshops, and seminars. In the physical world, spiritual teachers offer teaching. In Heaven, saints and the Divine offer teaching. In the divine realm, the Divine offers the teaching personally. The final goal of one's spiritual journey is to reach the divine realm. Now let me share another major one-sentence soul secret:

The higher the realm you reach in Heaven, the more profound teaching you can receive from Heaven and the more Soul Power you are given by Heaven to serve.

This is the true path for every spiritual being. Be sure you are aware of this soul wisdom.

Millions of people worldwide are searching for soul secrets, wisdom, knowledge, and practices. Their souls are yearning to uplift their standing in Heaven. This is why more and more people are moving on their spiritual journey and searching for soul enlightenment.

The ultimate goal of the Soul Light Era, the fifteen-thousand-year era that began on August 8, 2003, is to enlighten all humanity and all souls. We are at the dawn of this journey. Let us join hearts and souls together to follow this divine direction and move to achieve this final destiny of the Soul Light Era. We are honored to serve this divine mission. We are honored to reveal and share divine soul secrets, wisdom, knowledge, and practices to empower people to reach soul enlightenment.

Teach and spread soul secrets, wisdom, knowledge, and
*   practices.*
Do soul healing for the physical, emotional, mental, and
*   spiritual bodies.*
Transform and enlighten the souls, hearts, minds, and bod-
*   ies of humanity.*
Create love, peace, and harmony for humanity, Mother
*   Earth, and all universes.*
Hao! Hao! Hao!
Thank you. Thank you. Thank you.

What the Soul Can Do for Your Life

A human being has a soul, mind, and body. Your mind can do a lot for your life. Mind has the power to heal the body. Mind can create and manifest. Mind can transform consciousness and every aspect of life. Mind-body medicine and the mind-body connection are well known. They are examples of *mind over matter,* which is Mind Power. There has been a great deal of research that demonstrates the power of the mind. We honor the power of the mind, but the power of the mind is not enough.

The next step to serve humanity is *soul over matter,* which is Soul Power. "Soul over matter" means soul can make things happen. It includes soul healing, soul prevention of sickness, soul rejuvenation, soul prolongation of life, and soul transformation of every aspect of life, including relationships and finances. The final goal of soul over matter is to enlighten your soul, to enlighten all souls of humanity, and to enlighten all souls in all universes.

In this book, I will reveal and share with humanity the secrets of soul healing, soul prevention of sickness, soul rejuvenation, soul prolongation of life, soul transformation, and soul enlightenment. This book is the leading authority of my Soul Power Series. It transforms the universe of mind over matter to the universe of soul over matter.

The dawn of the Soul Light Era is a turning point for humanity, Mother Earth, and all souls. The power of mind over matter will move to the power of soul over matter. The Soul Power Series will empower humanity to use Soul Power to heal, transform every aspect of their lives, and enlighten their souls, minds, and bodies.

Soul over matter will transform every occupation. Soul over matter will transform people's views of Mother Earth and the universe. The Divine will show Divine Soul Power to humanity. Let me give you several examples.

As I described in the introduction, divine soul healing power has been transmitted to the first Love Peace Harmony Center in Boulder, Colorado. People can sit in this physical place and invoke this divine power. They can then receive remarkable results for healing and life transformation.

As another example, I have offered Divine Soul Downloads in teleconferences, workshops, radio programs, and television shows since July 2003. Thousands of heart-touching and moving stories have confirmed the power of these divine souls, beginning with Walter's story, which I shared in the opening section of this book.

The Divine has downloaded his healing power to more than seven hundred people since July 2003. These hundreds of Divine Healers have created remarkable healing results for humanity.

The Divine has created about one hundred Divine Writers in the last few years. Divine books, which are inspiring and profound, will be produced one after another.

As a final example, the Divine has offered thousands of karma cleansings, which I will explain further in the next chapter. Recipients have received extraordinary healing and transformation in every aspect of life. All of these examples confirm the power of soul.

Soul Power is the power of the twenty-first century. Soul Power is the power of the Soul Light Era. After reading this book and applying Soul Power by doing the soul practices and invoking Divine Soul Downloads, you could completely transform your thinking about healing, prevention of sickness, rejuvenation, prolonging life, life transformation, and enlightenment. Your consciousness could be completely transformed. Your view of the world could be completely transformed.

Soul over matter is the new divine direction for the entire Soul Light Era. The Divine made this decision on August 8, 2003. You can clearly see that the world is moving in this direction. Many more people are searching for soul secrets, wisdom, knowledge, and practices. Many more people are giving their love, care, compassion, forgiveness, peace, and harmony to others. Many more people are searching for the transformation of consciousness. Many more people want to become servants of humanity, Mother Earth, and the universes. The search for transformation of healing and consciousness and for soul wisdom has become a global movement of wave after wave. At this time, the Divine guided me to create the Soul Power Series of books. I am honored to offer these books to you and all humanity.

The books of the Soul Power Series will offer soul secrets, wisdom, knowledge, and practices to heal, prevent sickness, rejuvenate, prolong life, transform consciousness and every aspect of life, including relationships and finances, and enlighten your soul, heart, mind, and body.

The Divine guided me to flow these soul secrets, wisdom, knowledge, and practices. I give all the credit to the Divine and Heaven. I am only a servant of humanity, all souls, and the Divine. I am extremely honored to be this servant.

The essence of the guidance I received from the Divine for the Soul Power Series and the Soul Light Era is one sentence:

Soul over matter will transform humanity, Mother Earth,
and all universes.

The Soul Light Era

On August 8, 2003, the Divine appointed Yuan Shi Tian Zun, one of the top Taoist saints in history, to form a committee to lead a new era, the Soul Light Era. This highest divine committee has twelve members. In the committee's first meeting in Heaven, the Divine formally announced that the last era was ending. Niu Wa Niang Niang, the top spiritual leader of the last era in Jiu Tian (pronounced *joe ti-en*; "jiu" means *nine,* "tian" means *Heaven*), the nine layers of Heaven, had accomplished her task. She was uplifted to Tian Wai Tian, the Heaven beyond Heaven, which is the divine realm.

Souls who reside in Tian Wai Tian stop reincarnation. Souls who reside in Jiu Tian must continue to follow the spiritual law of reincarnation. Many great teachers from various spiritual traditions in history, including Jesus, Mary, Ar Mi Tuo Fuo (the Chinese name for Amitabha, an ancient buddha who is the leader of the Pure Land), Shi Jia Mo Ni Fuo (the Chinese name for Shakyamuni, the founder of Buddhism), Ling Hui Sheng Shi (the new name of Guan Yin, the Bodhisattva of Compassion), and Pu Ti Lao Zu (one of the top Taoist leaders), have all been souls in Jiu Tian. In the Soul Light Era, which will last fifteen thousand years, Jesus, Mary, buddhas, and other saints will continue to serve humanity to uplift their soul standing. Many of these saints will be uplifted to Tian Wai Tian. In fact, since August 8, 2003, six saints have already been uplifted from Jiu Tian to Tian Wai Tian, including a few of those I named above.

The ultimate goal of the Soul Light Era is:

To join every soul as one to reach universal soul enlightenment.

In Chinese, this ultimate goal is expressed as *wan ling rong he da yuan men.* "Wan" means *ten thousand,* which represents "all" or "every." "Ling" means *soul.* "Rong he" means *join as one.* "Da" means *big.* "Yuan men" means *enlightenment.*

In order to enlighten every soul, we have to enlighten our own souls first. Then enlighten the souls of our family members and loved ones. Then we enlighten the souls of our friends, neighbors, and colleagues. Next we enlighten the souls of all human beings in our city and country. Then we enlighten the souls of all humanity on Mother Earth. Finally, we enlighten all souls in all universes.

Everything has a soul. A human being has a soul. A bodily system has a soul. An organ has a soul. A cell has a soul. DNA and RNA have souls. An animal has a soul. A river has a soul. A tree has a soul. A mountain has a soul. A city has a soul. A planet has a soul. A star has a soul. A galaxy has a soul. A universe has a soul. To enlighten all souls is to enlighten all of them. This is a huge task. This is a divine calling and the divine direction.

I am honored to make a spiritual calling for the Divine to every reader, every soul of humanity, and every soul of all universes. Let us join hearts and souls together to offer our unconditional universal service to all humanity and all souls, in order to create love, peace, and harmony for humanity, Mother Earth, and all universes. Let us enlighten all humanity, all animals, all nature, and all universes.

In the beginning section of this book introducing the Soul Power Series, I shared how I became an unconditional universal servant. That was the calling the Divine made to me. I responded immediately. Three months later, I was chosen as a divine servant, vehicle, and channel. If you respond to this divine calling as an unconditional universal servant, you too will be chosen as a divine servant, vehicle, and channel at the appropriate layer and with the appropriate frequency.

If you commit as an unconditional universal servant, you must do it. You must show your commitment to the Divine. The Akashic Records record every activity, behavior, and thought of a human being. There is a renowned historical spiritual statement: *If you do not want people to know, do not do it. If you do it, you know, Heaven knows, Earth knows.*

On the spiritual journey, it is very important to make a vow to the Divine to show your commitment to serve. Major divine teachers, such as Jesus, Mary, Ar Mi Tuo Fuo, Shi Jia Mo Ni Fuo, Ling Hui Sheng Shi, Pu Ti Lao Zu, the Medicine Buddha, and many others, all made a big vow to the Divine to be an unconditional universal servant.

I would like to share a spiritual secret here. For advanced soul enlightenment on your soul journey, it is vital to make a vow to the Divine. To make a vow is to tell the Divine you are ready to be a total GOLD servant of the Divine and humanity. Total GOLD means total gratitude, total obedience, total loyalty, and total devotion to the Divine. You will bring the Divine's personal attention. When the Divine hears your big vow, the Divine will give you a task.

Remember, if you are ready to make a vow, do it. If you are not ready to make a vow, be sure you do *not* do it. After making a vow, the Divine and Heaven will give you a task in response to your vow. If you make a vow but you do not follow through, it will create major bad karma for your spiritual journey. Nobody wants this.

Make a vow to the Divine. Accept divine tasks and also realize that the Divine will give you spiritual tests. The Divine will test your commitment, persistence, ability to overcome difficulties and remove blockages, and your total GOLD.

This is a critical secret for every spiritual being to know. After making a vow to the Divine, you can be 100 percent sure that the Divine will give you a task and a test. Accomplish the task. Pass the test. Then your soul will be uplifted. Jesus, Mary, Shi Jia Mo Ni Fuo, Ar Mi Tuo Fuo, Guan Yin, Pu Ti Lao Zu, the Medicine Buddha, and many other great teachers all went through the process of making a vow to the Divine, passing divine tests, and accomplishing their divine tasks. Then they were uplifted by the Divine personally.

There is a famous statement about the spiritual journey: *Ren zai zuo. Tian zai kan.* In essence, this means: *Human beings are doing their work. Heaven is watching.* Therefore, as a spiritual being, you must know that if you make a vow, the Divine and Heaven *will* give you a task and test you. They *will* observe every aspect of your life. If you are committed to serving humanity and all souls, do not be scared. It is a vital secret to make a vow to tell Heaven and the Divine that you want to make a commitment to serve. Then they will give you your task and test you. The process could be very painful. But remember another renowned statement that also applies to the spiritual journey: *No pain, no gain.*

After passing spiritual testing and accomplishing divine tasks, your spiritual standing will be uplifted. Then continue to serve. Receive further testing and further tasks. Then receive further uplifting. The spiritual journey is a hard journey. It is also a painful journey. But finally, you will remove all selfishness, ego, and attachments to become a pure servant of humanity and all souls. When you reach this level, you gain inner joy and inner peace. Everything you touch will be a success. Whatever you think, will happen.

True spiritual power is beyond comprehension. You must reach advanced soul enlightenment to fully understand what I am saying. You will understand this teaching more and more as you read this book. You will experience it directly in your future spiritual journey. You may agree with me more and more. It does take time.

Now we are at the beginning of the Soul Light Era. This is a historic period. The Divine needs total GOLD servants. The Divine made a calling on August 8, 2003. I have hundreds of advanced students worldwide who have responded to this calling by making a vow to the Divine. More and more spiritual beings will respond to this special divine calling.

Nobody is forced to make a vow to the Divine. I am sharing a major spiritual secret with you and all people worldwide. It is your choice to respond or not.

In conclusion, to make a vow to the Divine to be an unconditional universal servant is vital for your spiritual journey. If you are ready, you can pause a moment and make a vow to the Divine as follows. This is just my suggestion for your reference. You can absolutely change the words. Just follow the essence of this suggestion.

> *Dear Divine,*
> *I am honored to make a vow to you and Heaven.*
> *I commit to being an unconditional universal servant to all humanity and all souls.*
> *I commit to being a total GOLD servant to you and humanity.*
> *Please give me your task and bless me to accomplish it.*
> *I am extremely honored.*
> *Thank you.*

If you decide to make a vow like this, what will happen when you do it? The Divine will appear at the moment you make this kind of vow. The leaders of the Akashic Records, including Yan Wang Ye and Jin Fa Sheng Shi, will also appear instantly. They will record your vow in your spiritual book in the Akashic Records. The Divine will give you a task. Then Heaven will wait for your accomplishment of the task. They will give you great spiritual support to facilitate your accomplishment of the divine task.

I offer the above teaching to explain further why this is a historic time. Mother Earth is in a transition period. All kinds of natural disasters, wars, and conflicts between religions and nations are happening worldwide. The Divine needs unconditional universal servants to stand out to serve humanity, to remove the suffering of humanity, and to create love, peace, and harmony for humanity, Mother Earth, and all universes. At this historic moment, make your vow to the Divine and Heaven. Commit yourself to being a divine servant. Then your spiritual journey will move a big step forward.

At least twice a year, I hold Soul Healing and Enlightenment re-treats. Their purpose is to offer soul healing and soul enlightenment for humanity. I welcome you to join me in one of my Soul Healing and Enlightenment retreats. I will offer the teaching with my Certi-fied Divine Master Teachers and Healers and my Certified Master Teachers and Healers. As a divine servant, vehicle, and channel, I will send a major Divine Order to enlighten the soul of every participant at the retreat. Soul enlightenment is the number-one task for the Soul Light Era. After reaching your own soul enlightenment, you can re-turn home to prepare the people around you for their soul enlighten-ment. You absolutely can reach soul enlightenment by yourself. However, I can be the servant and facilitator for your soul enlighten-ment journey. I am honored to be your servant.

> *Enlighten your soul.*
> *Enlighten the souls of your family members and loved ones.*
> *Enlighten society.*
> *Enlighten all souls of humanity.*
> *Enlighten Mother Earth.*
> *Enlighten all souls.*
> *Enlighten all universes.*

This is the divine task for the fifteen-thousand-year era that started on August 8, 2003. This is a divine calling. When you are ready, make a vow to the Divine to be an unconditional universal servant. Purify your soul, heart, mind, and body. Join hearts and souls together to accomplish this divine goal.

2

Karma

In history, Buddhists talk about karma. Christians talk about deeds. Taoists talk about *te* (pronounced "duh"). Other spiritual beings talk about virtue. These are different words for the same thing. Millions of people have heard about karma. Millions of people believe in karma. Millions of people desperately want to clear their own bad karma.

How important is karma for our lives? In the Soul Light Era, the Divine told me that I must offer karma teaching. The Divine gave me the honor of clearing the bad karma of human beings in July 2003, when I was chosen as a divine servant and a servant of humanity. But I do not actually clear karma. The Divine clears karma. The Divine chose me as the Divine's servant to offer divine karma cleansing to humanity. I have offered this divine service to thousands of people worldwide. Their stories are heart-touching and leave me speechless. They include recovery from life-threatening conditions such as liver cancer, paralysis due to stroke, heart attacks, genetic sicknesses in newborn babies, kidney failure, and many other conditions that doctors viewed as hopeless. People are in wonder, touched, and deeply moved by the life transformation from receiving the Divine's karma cleansing. People are very honored to receive great healing results. They come to thank me. I always reply instantly, "Please do not thank me. Thank the Divine. The Divine did the healing for you. I am your servant. I am the servant and vehicle of the Divine. I requested the Divine to offer healing to you."

Since the Divine chose me as the Divine's servant, vehicle, and channel, in every healing that I offer worldwide, the Divine is doing the healing. This is what the Divine told me on the day he chose me as the Divine's servant. Since then, this has always been the case. I cannot bow to and honor the Divine enough for being chosen as a servant of the Divine and a servant of humanity and all souls as well. All the credit belongs to the Divine. I am so happy to be a divine servant. I am extremely honored to offer divine creation to create Divine Healers, Divine Writers, Divine Editors, Divine Singers, Divine Music Composers, and more. I am extremely honored to offer countless Divine Soul Transplants to all humanity and all souls. I am extremely honored to offer divine karma cleansing to remove the spiritual debts of human beings and other souls.

What Is Karma?

Karma is the record of services. Karma is the term used in Buddhist teaching. Taoists use the term *te*. Christians use the term "deed." Many other spiritual beings use the term "virtue." Karma, *te,* deed, and virtue are the same thing but in different words. To understand karma is to understand all of these words.

Karma can be divided into good karma and bad karma. Good karma is the record of one's good services in all past lives and in this life. Good karma includes love, care, compassion, sincerity, honesty, generosity, kindness, purity, and all other kinds of good service. Bad karma is a record of one's unpleasant services, such as killing, harming, taking advantage, cheating, stealing, and all other kinds of unpleasant service.

Why We Have to Understand Karma

In April 2003 at the Land of Medicine Buddha in Soquel, California, I bowed to listen when the Divine came while I was teaching a workshop. The Divine delivered a major spiritual law, the Universal Law of Universal Service. I shared the complete process in the beginning section of this book on the Soul Power Series. With this spiritual law, the Divine completely explained karma issues. In summary, the Divine said:

> *Offer a little good service, receive a little blessing from the universe and me.*
> *Offer more good service, receive more blessing from the universe and me.*
> *Offer unconditional universal service, receive unlimited blessing from the universe and me.*

The Divine then taught me:

> *Offer a little unpleasant service, learn a little lesson from the universe and me.*
> *Offer more unpleasant service, learn bigger lessons from the universe and me.*
> *Offer huge unpleasant service, learn huge lessons from the universe and me.*

I asked the Divine, "What lessons will a person learn?"

The Divine replied, "The lessons include sickness, broken relationships, financial challenges, mental confusion, and emotional imbalances. They could be blockages in any aspect of life."

After listening to this spiritual law of universal service, I realized that this is how Heaven and the Divine operate Mother Earth and all universes. I immediately made a vow to be an unconditional universal servant for the Divine and humanity, as well as for all souls. Upon hearing my vow, the Divine smiled and left.

This personal story explains clearly how karma affects our lives. Good karma blesses your life. Bad karma creates all kinds of lessons and blockages in your life.

The Power of Karma: The Root Cause of Success and Failure in Every Aspect of Life

The Universal Law of Universal Service was delivered only a few years ago, just before the beginning of the Soul Light Era. However, this law is not a new teaching. Karma issues have been taught for thousands of years. The essence can be stated in one sentence, which I received as inspiration from divine teaching:

Karma is the root cause of success and failure in every aspect of life.

One's success depends on one's good service in previous lives and this life. One's blockages are due to one's unpleasant service in previous lives and this life. Your ancestors' karma also affects your life.

There are many great stories in history that illustrate that karma is the root cause of success and failure in every aspect of life. Allow me to share a few of them.

More than four thousand years ago in ancient China, Emperor Shun was the first major teacher in Chinese history of respect and honor for one's parents and others. Emperor Shun had a unique personality. Extremely modest, he never blamed anyone for any problems. If anything that was related to him turned out badly in his kingdom, he always took full responsibility and said it was his mistake. If his workers did not perform well, he always felt that he did not teach them well enough. Even though he was not treated well by his own family, he never complained. He focused on his own shortcomings and always gave his family love, compassion, and respect. He was a great example of a spiritual being with tremendous self-discipline.

His reign lasted a half-century, during which he accumulated great virtue for his country. His descendants prospered.

Commonly known as Confucius in the West, Kong Zi's whole life's teaching was to respect one's parents, to honor the principles and laws of one's country, and to be kind to others. To this day, he has had hundreds of descendants worldwide with extremely blessed lives. Many of them received honored titles and high positions in the imperial courts of China. Others had great financial and business success. Today the descendants of Kong Zi can be found in high government, academic, and business positions across Asia.

During the Han Dynasty, the emperors and their ministers used Confucius's and Mencius's (the western name for Meng Zi, the leading interpreter of Confucianism) teachings to structure education. Before the Han Dynasty, there were hundreds of teachings and theories about education. The government wanted to unite the country under one approach to educate all human beings in China. They chose the teachings of Confucius as the teaching for the whole country. Confucianism remained a foundation of Chinese culture from the Han Dynasty to the Qing Dynasty, a span of nearly two thousand years.

Confucius taught that the family, including a harmonized husband and wife, is the key for harmony and flourishing. How can a husband perform his duties and responsibilities well? How can a wife be a good wife? How should one deal with other family members— parents, children, brothers, and sisters? Each family member has his or her own responsibilities. Accomplishing one's own responsibilities and doing well in one's own tasks will help create a harmonized family. Then, as the ancient spiritual teaching states: *A harmonized family will bring flourishing.*

Confucius also taught about relationships in the workplace. How does one deal with and work under the leaders of any organization? In fact, Confucius also taught that across the whole country, everyone is a brother and sister. Think of the whole country as one big family. Unity and harmony in the whole family are very important.

The fundamental teachings of Confucius can be summarized as follows:

- Study and research the philosophy and practice of everything.
- Develop the wisdom and knowledge to understand everything in the universe.
- Practice honesty and sincerity to others.
- Purify and cultivate your heart.
- Purify and cultivate your body.
- Harmonize the family.
- Transform the country.
- Create a peaceful society and country.

This ancient teaching is ignored, or not taught enough, in modern-day schools. Modern teaching has emphasized the rational, the scientific, and the pragmatic more than the ethical, the moral, or the virtuous. However, students must be taught standards for being a kind being and a pure servant. Students must be given the wisdom that to serve others is a great honor. They need to understand the importance of offering love, forgiveness, peace, harmony, sincerity, and honesty to others. Lack of education about purifying the heart and soul leaves students with no standard in their hearts and minds for being a good person. When they grow up, selfishness, greed, struggles for power, and ego easily occupy their hearts and minds. Therefore, all kinds of problems arise easily.

The history of education in China gives us deep insight into the transformation of consciousness and purification of the heart. This process must start with babies and children. It must start from every family. In order to create love, peace, and harmony for humanity, Mother Earth, and all universes, purification of soul, heart, mind, and body must start with the individual and then proceed to every family member, to society, to the country, and finally to all humanity.

Shi Jia Mo Ni Fuo (the Chinese name for the founder of Buddhism, commonly known in the West as Shakyamuni or Gautama Buddha) emphasized purification of the heart. One of his most profound teachings is *ming xin jian xing.* "Ming" literally means *to purify or enlighten.* "Xin" means *heart.* "Jian" means *see.* "Xing" means *your true self,* which means your soul. *Ming xin jian xing* can be translated as: *purify and enlighten your heart to see your soul,* which is your true nature and your true self. Shi Jia Mo Ni Fuo also taught that to heal sickness, one must heal the heart first. He emphasized purification of the heart and soul in all of his teachings. In essence, he offers the same teaching as Confucius, but from a different perspective and with a different emphasis.

The flip side of the great good service that these ancient masters have offered is the flip side of the Universal Law of Universal Service: *If one offers much unpleasant service, one will learn very heavy lessons.* This is a spiritual law administered by the Akashic Records.

Again, let us observe Chinese history. There have been many dynasties and thousands of generals. Usually, the generals' descendants do not have blessed lives. Very often, the general's family does not even survive for three generations beyond him. Many descendants die from sickness or in disasters. Their children are often very poor and their daughters and granddaughters may turn to prostitution. What is the true reason for this? It is because the generals killed so many people in warfare. Among the thousands of generals in all the dynasties in Chinese history, it is difficult to find more than ten who have successful and blessed descendants.

One famous example of a general with successful descendants is Zi Yi Guo, a big general in the Tang Dynasty. He was very kind and accumulated great virtue. He was not a typical general who focused on killing enemies. He was very thoughtful and considerate. He sent orders not to harm civilians. As a result, he has had many, many generations of successful descendants.

General Cao Han, a general in the Song Dynasty, killed a lot of people without any care or concern. His daughter became a prostitute. His descendants did not last to the third generation. His entire lineage ended.

Cao Bing was another general in the Song Dynasty. He did not kill easily. He did not allow any of his soldiers to bother any farmers or other civilians. He was very serious about this. His descendants flourished for many, many generations.

These famous beings in history illustrate the universal law the Divine delivered to me in April 2003. If you serve well, you receive blessings. If you serve unpleasantly, you learn lessons. Serve well, be kind, and your descendants will be blessed and successful. Serve unpleasantly, kill and harm, and your descendants will be poor, in all kinds of bad situations, and your lineage may even end after a few generations.

There is a famous statement from ancient spiritual teaching: *Ancestor plants the tree. Descendants enjoy the shade.* If the ancestor harms, the descendants will learn a lesson. Some people may think this is not fair. If the ancestor made a mistake, why do the descendants have to suffer?

Actually, this law is very easy to understand. On Mother Earth, when you do a good job for humanity, you receive all kinds of awards from different societies and countries. You receive true love from humanity. If you kill a person, the police have to catch you and put you in jail to learn lessons. Otherwise you may continue to kill. Therefore, when you make mistakes, you must learn lessons in order to transform your life. In the spiritual world, if you made mistakes in previous lives, you will learn lessons in this life and your future lives. Your descendants will also learn lessons because they are your lineage. And so, just as they receive the benefits of your good service, they must carry the responsibility and learn the lessons for your unpleasant service.

This important spiritual law teaches humanity that when you offer good service to others, you will receive blessings for yourself, for your future lives, and for your descendants. If you offer unpleasant service to others, you will learn lessons in this life and future lives and so too will your descendants.

I have personally understood how karma affects many individuals. When I was a doctor in Asia, a twelve-year-old girl suddenly suffered a stroke. For six months she could not walk. In fact she could not even move her legs. I was invited to treat this girl with acupuncture. After about ten treatments, she was able to walk again. The medical diagnosis was simply that she had a blood clot in her brain. I am an M.D. from China myself. I totally honor conventional modern medicine. But I asked the Akashic Records for the true reason, for the root cause of the girl's stroke. The Akashic Records told me the spiritual reason, which is the true reason. The Akashic Records showed me that her grandfather, who was a banker, cheated many people of lots of money. This created bad karma that affected his granddaughter. The grandfather loved his granddaughter deeply. He may never have had any idea that his mistakes caused the lesson of such pain and suffering for his granddaughter.

This straightforward spiritual teaching is Divine Guidance for me to explain to you that many sicknesses, heartbreaks in relationships, and financial challenges are directly related with karma issues.

Cleansing Bad Karma

Bad karma is the spiritual debt one has accumulated for one's mistakes from all previous lives and this life. It includes killing, harming, taking advantage, cheating, stealing, and more. On Mother Earth, when you buy a house, you take out a mortgage from a bank. This mortgage is your debt to the bank. You pay every month for fifteen, twenty, or thirty years to clear your financial debt. In the spiritual realm, if you have bad karma, you may have to pay for many lifetimes to clear your spiritual debt.

On Mother Earth, money is the vehicle of exchange. If you have a debt, you offer money to pay off your debt. How do you pay off a spiritual debt? *Virtue* is spiritual money. If you have a spiritual debt, you must pay with virtue. Virtue is the record of services from all your lifetimes. Good virtue has spiritual value. Good virtue is earned by good service, including love, forgiveness, compassion, peace, sincerity, honesty, generosity, kindness, integrity, purity, and more. If you serve in these good ways, the Akashic Records will record these services. You are then given virtue.

Let me share an important soul secret: *Virtue can be measured by a high-level spiritual being.* Good virtue is given as dots and flowers of different colors—red, golden, rainbow, purple, and crystal dots and flowers. Ten small dots form a small flower. Ten small flowers form a big flower. Therefore, a flower carries more virtue than a dot. A big flower carries more virtue than a small flower. It is similar on Mother Earth, where we have denominations of money with different values—ten- and twenty-five-cent coins and paper currency of one, five, ten, twenty dollars, and so on.

When you offer good service to humanity and others, you are given different-colored dots. Groups of dots will form flowers. If you are doing great service, you can be given different sizes of flowers directly. This virtue expressed in dots and flowers will come down to your book in the Akashic Records and to your soul at the same time. When these dots and flowers come, the spiritual debt in your Akashic book will be paid, little by little. The dark records will be erased, little by little. If you offer a major service to humanity, you can receive huge flowers. Then your dark records, which are the mistakes you made in all past lives and this life, will be removed from your Akashic book. The lessons you were supposed to learn, which include sickness, broken relationships, financial challenges, and all other blockages in every aspect of your life, are canceled. Your spiritual debt is paid off.

There is only one way to clear your own bad karma: *Offer unconditional universal service.* The more you serve, the faster you will clear your karma. Prayer alone is not enough to clear your karma. You must offer service. You must make great efforts to clear your karma.

Let me share a profound new way to clear your karma in the Soul Light Era. This new soul secret is to sing the Soul Song "Love, Peace and Harmony." This Soul Song was given to me by the Divine in September 2005. Its lyrics are very simple:

> *I love my heart and soul*
> *I love all humanity*
> *Join hearts and soul together*
> *Love, peace and harmony*
> *Love, peace and harmony*

The first line, *I love my heart and soul,* is to purify your soul, heart, mind, and body. Heal the soul first; then healing of the mind and body will follow. This first line is a soul mantra to heal all of your sicknesses. It does take a lot of singing to restore your health from chronic and life-threatening conditions, but it definitely works. This soul mantra is so powerful that it is beyond one's comprehension. Love melts all blockages and transforms all life.

The second line, *I love all humanity,* is to offer service to humanity. Serve others! The Divine will give virtue for your service. This virtue will pay your spiritual debt. Lessons, blockages, and disasters due to bad karma will be removed. Sing *I love all humanity* from the bottom of your heart. This soul mantra will bring a soul healing wave to humanity, Mother Earth, and all universes. It could greatly benefit your karma cleansing. It may take many years to clear your karma in this way, but this is still one of the most powerful ways to clear your own karma.

The third line, *Join hearts and souls together,* is a divine calling. To call is to serve. This calling will create great virtue to clear your bad karma.

The fourth and fifth lines, *Love, peace and harmony,* state the goal of our service: to create love, peace, and harmony for humanity, Mother Earth, and all universes.

This Soul Song is simple, but it is a divine mantra for healing, life transformation, and soul enlightenment. It has great power for cleansing karma. You can visit my website to listen to this Soul Song. There I offer a few minutes of this Soul Song as a gift to humanity.

In March 2008 the Divine offered the soul of his Divine Soul Song "Love, Peace and Harmony" as a Soul Transplant gift to all humanity and all souls. Your soul, everyone's soul, and every soul in the universe have received this priceless permanent treasure for healing, rejuvenation, and life transformation. Here is how to practice to receive the benefits of this divine gift:

> *Dear soul, mind, and body of the Divine Soul Song, "Love,*
> * Peace and Harmony," downloaded to my soul,*
> *I love you, honor you, and appreciate you.*
> *Please heal my _____ (make a request for your physical*
> * body, emotional body, mental body, or spiritual*
> * body).*
> *Please purify my soul, heart, mind, and body.*
> *Please clear my bad karma.*
> *Please rejuvenate my soul, heart, mind, and body.*
> *Please transform my life, including my relationships and*
> * finances.*
> *Please enlighten my soul, heart, mind, and body.*
> *I am very grateful.*
> *Thank you.*

Then sing "Love, Peace and Harmony" for a few minutes with all your heart and soul.

The longer you sing, the better.

You may wonder. "Does this Soul Song really have the power to do this?" My answer is straightforward: *Yes, of course!* This Soul Song has power beyond words and thoughts. In order to explain this, I would like to share my personal story of how I received this Soul Song.

On Saturday, September 10, 2005, I visited the redwoods in Marin County, California, with three of my advanced students. One of them asked me, "Master Sha, could you ask the Divine for a song for your mission?" I replied, "Of course! I am delighted to ask for a song from the Divine." I raised my arm to Heaven and said, "Dear Divine, could you give me a Soul Song for our mission?" Instantly, a beam of rainbow light shot down from the Divine and went through my body from head to toe. I opened my mouth and these sounds came out:

> *Lu La Lu La Li*
> *Lu La Lu La La Li*
> *Lu La Lu La Li Lu La*
> *Lu La Li Lu La*
> *Lu La Li Lu La*

I had no idea what these sounds meant, but I knew they were in Soul Language, the universal language of all souls. I immediately asked the Divine for a translation, which was given to me in Chinese. Then, of course, I knew the exact meaning in English as well.

> *Wo ai wo xin he ling*
> *Wo ai quan ren lei*
> *Wan ling rong he mu shi sheng*
> *Xiang ai ping an he xie*
> *Xiang ai ping an he xie*
>
> *I love my heart and soul*
> *I love all humanity*
> *Join hearts and souls together*
> *Love, peace and harmony*
> *Love, peace and harmony*

Then I asked the Divine to give me a melody for these lyrics. Instantly, I received it. I was so excited to sing with my three students.

As we were singing, a little girl about two or three years old walked by. She was fascinated to listen to this first Divine Soul Song that I received. She broke out into a big smile and raised both arms above her head, shaking them, and making a very happy sound—*Yaaaay!!!* A few minutes later, she and her mother had walked a couple of hundred feet away. We continued to sing with great joy. The girl was walking farther and farther away. Suddenly, she stopped, turned around to face us, and raised both hands again, shaking both arms, and screamed *Yaaaay!!!* again.

My students and I sang together for more than an hour. We left the redwoods and went to a beach on the ocean. We were singing the whole time. Hungry, we went into town to have dinner at a crowded and popular restaurant. I kept singing. Three waitresses stopped their work and came to our table to listen to my singing. They stood there for a few minutes just listening, without moving or speaking. Finally, they asked me, "What are you singing?" I explained, "I am singing a Soul Song." They said, "It is beautiful! We never heard of a Soul Song before."

This story shares how I received my first Soul Song from the Divine. From that moment, I started to share this Soul Song in every workshop and class I have taught worldwide. Wherever I go, I sing this Soul Song. Wherever I teach, I teach this Soul Song. Wherever I have the opportunity, I share this Soul Song. I asked the Divine to download this Soul Song to all humanity and all souls. This Soul Song is in your heart and soul. It has offered remarkable healing and life transformation to humanity. I have hundreds of students worldwide who constantly play the CD of this Soul Song in their homes or offices to create divine feng shui.

I have taught my students that feng shui is important for life. Feng shui refers to the balance and movement of energy in a place. Feng shui literally means *wind water*. Wind is yang. Water is yin. Feng shui is yin-yang movement. At the same time, feng shui represents the condition of the soul. Many people study feng shui and adjust feng shui in homes and offices. Generally speaking, they are adjusting the energy. However, it is more important to adjust the *soul* of the home or office. Soul is the boss of life. Singing and playing a CD of the Divine Soul Song "Love, Peace and Harmony" constantly can offer healing, rejuvenation, and life transformation and create divine feng shui. I am extremely grateful that the Divine has given this priceless treasure to humanity.

Of course, there are many other ways to offer service to others, such as volunteer work. Offer your love, care, and compassion to others. Donate your money to fight poverty and hunger. Offer healing and teaching to people worldwide. Transform the consciousness of humanity and more. These are all ways to clear your own bad karma.

There is another special way to clear your karma. The Divine can clear your karma very quickly. In July 2003 the Divine asked me to offer karma cleansing for humanity. When I offer this karma cleansing service, I do not do the karma cleansing. The Divine does this service. As I described in the beginning section of this book, the Divine chose me as the Divine's servant in July 2003. The Divine told me, "You call me and I will heal. You call me and I will serve." The Divine offers all kinds of blessings, including Divine Soul Transplants and karma cleansings. I ask. The Divine blesses. I am extremely honored to be a servant of the Divine and humanity.

Increasing Good Karma by Offering Unconditional Universal Service

The purpose of life is to serve. In this section, I will discuss the best way to increase good karma, which is to offer unconditional universal service. Universal service includes seven aspects:

- universal love
- universal forgiveness
- universal peace

- universal healing
- universal blessing
- universal harmony
- universal enlightenment

UNIVERSAL LOVE

Universal love means to offer love to every human being and every soul in the universe. It is very easy to love a person you like. It is difficult to love a person you dislike. It is even more difficult to love your enemies. The teaching here is that you must love everyone. Love has incredible power for healing, rejuvenation, and life transformation.

I will share a story that happened in Toronto in 2004. In a workshop at the Learning Annex, I taught students how to apply love for healing. A senior lady suffered from serious arthritis. Her right knee was swollen. She could hardly walk. I told the workshop participants to focus on one area of their bodies that needed healing and to do a simple practice. Let me ask you to do this healing and life transformation practice by applying love with me for a few minutes.

Say *hello* with me:

> *Dear soul, mind, and body of my* _____ (choose one
>   organ or part of the body),
> *I love you.*
> *You have the power to heal yourself.*
> *Do a good job.*
> *Love has the power to heal you.*
> *Allow love to heal you.*
> *Thank you.*

Or for transforming relationships, for example, say *hello* like this:

> *Dear soul, mind, and body of* _____ (name one person),
> *I love you.*

Love has the power to transform our relationship.
Allow love to transform our relationship.
Thank you.

You can use this Say Hello formula to request any blessing you would like to receive from the power of love.

Then silently chant *love* for three minutes. Open your heart and soul to offer love sincerely to the organ, part of your body, or the other person—whatever you requested.

Close your eyes slightly. Sit up straight and chant with me now:

Love
Love
Love
Love
Love
Love
Love

. . .

Heal
Heal
Heal
Heal
Heal
Heal
Heal

. . .

Transform
Transform

Transform
Transform
Transform
Transform
Transform

. . .

After a few minutes of practice, you could be very surprised by the results. You are applying the Soul Power of *love, heal, transform.* If you do not feel any changes, it does not mean that the practice does not work. Do it a few more times. You could feel improvement. Sometimes it does take more time and practice to improve your condition.

Going back to the woman in my workshop with arthritis in her right knee, after a few minutes of this practice, she stood up and walked comfortably around the room. She was moved to tears. She said, "I have never before felt such a release from the arthritis in my knee."

Expanding the practice, you can use the same technique to offer love to heal others. For example, if a friend has back pain, you can practice like this:

> *Dear soul, mind, and body of the back of* _____ (name
>   your friend),
> *I love you.*
> *You have the power to heal yourself.*
> *Love has the power to heal you.*
> *Do a good job.*
> *Thank you.*

Then concentrate on your friend's back and silently chant:

Love
Love
Love
Love
Love
Love
Love

. . .

Heal
Heal
Heal
Heal
Heal
Heal
Heal

. . .

Thank you
Thank you
Thank you
Thank you
Thank you
Thank you
Thank you

. . .

You can use this technique to offer healing to anyone. You can do this remotely; your friend could be anywhere in the world. Soul Power is not limited by space or time.

This technique is so simple that it could be hard to believe. In ancient teaching, there is a famous statement: *If you want to know if a pear is sweet, taste it.* If you want to know if this technique works, experience it.

Now I am going to offer the first Divine Soul Download in this book. I will ask the Divine to offer a Divine Soul Transplant to every reader. This Divine Soul Transplant is named:

Divine Soul Transplant of Divine Love

It is a huge golden light soul that will be permanently downloaded to your soul. The Divine gave me the honor to transmit his souls in July 2003 as the Divine's servant, vehicle, and channel. Every time I offer Divine Soul Transplants, I have to make a sincere request and greatly honor the Divine. To transmit divine souls within a book, I have to preprogram the downloads with the Divine. Do not ask for anything different or more. It will not work.

Sit up straight. Put the tip of your tongue near the roof of your mouth. Relax. Open your heart and soul.

Prepare!

Divine Soul Transplant of Divine Love
Silent download!

Close your eyes for thirty seconds to receive this major divine soul treasure.

> *Hao! Hao! Hao!*
> *Thank you. Thank you. Thank you.*

We are extremely honored that the Divine offers the Divine's soul treasures to every reader. Congratulations on receiving this treasure! If this is your first time to receive a Divine Soul Transplant, I will say three times *Congratulations!* to you.

A divine soul carries divine love, forgiveness, compassion, light, and transformation. Divine love melts all blockages and transforms all life. Divine forgiveness brings inner peace and inner joy. Divine compassion boosts energy, stamina, vitality, and immunity. Divine light heals, prevents sickness, rejuvenates, prolongs life, and transforms consciousness and every aspect of life.

A divine soul is so powerful that you can instantly apply it for healing, rejuvenation, and life transformation. You have just received a divine soul of Divine Love. You can invoke this priceless treasure anytime and anywhere. Here is how to practice. Do it with me now:

> *Dear divine soul of Divine Love,*
> *I love you, honor you, and appreciate you.*
> *Please turn on.* (This is how to activate this permanent divine treasure that now resides in your body.)
> *Please give me a healing for* _____ (name the system, organ, part of the body, or condition for which you request a healing).

or

> *Please give me a blessing for my relationship with* _____ (name the person).

or

> *Please bless my business* (name the business) *and finances.*

Then relax and chant silently and repeatedly:

> *Divine Love soul heals me.*
> *Divine Love soul heals me.*

Divine Love soul heals me.
Divine Love soul heals me . . .

or

Divine Love soul blesses me.
Divine Love soul blesses me.
Divine Love soul blesses me.
Divine Love soul blesses me . . .

Chant for at least three to five minutes to experience the power of your Divine Love soul, the longer the better. For chronic and life-threatening conditions, chant for twenty to thirty minutes per time, for a total of at least two hours per day.

Recall that when I offered the first Divine Soul Download to a human being in July 2003, the recipient, Walter, suffered from liver cancer. He received a Divine Soul Software for Liver. He practiced more than two hours per day. Two and a half months later, he went to get a CT scan and MRI. There was no sign of the liver cancer. Three years later, in 2006, I met him again. He was still free of liver cancer. I was delighted to meet Walter a third time in 2008. After five years, he was still liver cancer–free. In the last few years, I have received hundreds of letters on my website that share remarkable healings from Divine Soul Downloads.

You must know that to receive a Divine Soul Download does not mean you will automatically recover. You must spend time practicing, as Walter did with dedication, by invoking the divine soul and chanting. The moment you start to chant, the divine soul will shine divine love, forgiveness, compassion, and light for healing, blessing, and life transformation. This soul of Divine Love can be used for healing, preventing sickness, rejuvenating, prolonging life, and transforming consciousness and every aspect of life, including relationships and finances. This soul of Divine Love is with you permanently. You may have family members with you in your life. They are your yang companions. This divine soul is your yin companion. Every Divine Soul Transplant you receive becomes your yin companion forever. They will be with your soul forever, even through all your future lives. That is the honor and blessing you and your soul have received. It is beyond words.

In fact, you can receive blessings from this divine soul by chanting *Divine Love soul heals me, Divine Love soul heals me, Divine Love soul heals me, Divine Love soul heals me* . . . when you are driving, walking, cooking, watching TV, showering, or during a short break.

There are two ways to chant: silently and aloud. Chanting silently vibrates the smaller cells and spaces in the body; it is yin chanting. Chanting aloud vibrates the bigger cells and spaces: it is yang chanting. Both ways are correct. You may choose to do one or the other or both.

You can chant *Divine Love soul rejuvenates my soul, mind, and body; Divine Love soul rejuvenates my soul, mind, and body; Divine Love soul rejuvenates my soul, mind, and body; Divine Love soul rejuvenates my soul, mind, and body* . . . Chanting like this can significantly benefit your rejuvenation.

You can also chant *Divine Love soul boosts my energy, stamina, vitality, and immunity; Divine Love soul boosts my energy, stamina, vitality, and immunity; Divine Love soul boosts my energy, stamina, vitality, and immunity; Divine Love soul boosts my energy, stamina, vitality, and immunity* . . . Chanting like this can build your energy foundation to benefit your entire life. A strong energy foundation is vital for everyone.

The soul of Divine Love has power without limitation. Apply it often to transform all life. At the end of each practice, always say (silently or aloud):

> *Hao! Hao! Hao!*
> *Thank you. Thank you. Thank you.*

I use the soul of Divine Love as the first example of how to apply divine souls for healing, rejuvenation, boosting energy, and transformation. You can use this wisdom to apply any divine soul you receive to heal, bless, and transform your life.

UNIVERSAL FORGIVENESS

Universal forgiveness means to offer forgiveness to all humanity and all souls. Forgiveness brings inner joy and inner peace. Think about your life. If you have a conflict with someone and you forgive that person, you are relieved. If someone forgives you, you are peaceful and appreciative. Let me share a spiritual practice to offer forgiveness:

> *Dear* _____ (name the person),
> *I love you.*
> *Please come.*
> *Let us practice forgiveness with each other.*

Then chant:

> *Universal forgiveness*
> *Universal forgiveness*
> *Universal forgiveness*
> *Universal forgiveness . . .*

Chant for at least three to five minutes, silently or aloud, the longer the better.

Forgiveness has power beyond imagination. Many people are sick because of an emotional imbalance. Emotional imbalances are often directly related to someone or something that bothers you and that you cannot let go of. Forgiveness can balance your emotions, which will help to heal your physical body as well. Just as your soul, heart, mind, and body are interconnected, your physical, emotional, mental, and spiritual bodies are interconnected also.

Now let me offer you a second Divine Soul Transplant:

Divine Soul Transplant of Divine Forgiveness

Sit up straight. Put the tip of your tongue near the roof of your mouth. Relax. Open your heart and soul.

Prepare!

Divine Soul Transplant of Divine Forgiveness
Silent download!

Close your eyes for thirty seconds to receive this major divine soul treasure.

> *Hao! Hao! Hao!*
> *Thank you. Thank you. Thank you.*

Thank you, Divine.

Now you have this second priceless divine treasure. This treasure can offer healing, prevention of sickness, rejuvenation, prolongation of life, and transformation of consciousness, relationships, finances, and more. Let us practice by applying this treasure:

> *Dear soul, mind, and body of* _____ (call someone with
>   whom you want to practice forgiveness),
> *I love you.*
> *Please come.* (The soul of the person you called will sub-
>   divide and one subdivided soul will come to you.)
> *Let us receive a blessing from the divine soul of Divine For-*
>   *giveness.*
> *We are grateful.*

Dear divine soul of Divine Forgiveness,
I love you, honor you, and appreciate you.
Please turn on.
Please bless _____ (name the person whose soul you
    called) *and me.*
We are very grateful.

Then chant silently or aloud:

Divine Forgiveness soul blesses us.
Divine Forgiveness soul blesses us.
Divine Forgiveness soul blesses us.
Divine Forgiveness soul blesses us . . .

Chant at least three to five minutes, silently or aloud, the longer
the better. Then close:

Hao! Hao! Hao!
Thank you. Thank you. Thank you.
Please return. (Return the subdivided soul of the person
    you called.)

The soul of Divine Forgiveness has already transformed thousands
of people's lives. This divine soul will transform millions of lives in the
future. You can send your soul of Divine Forgiveness to any person in
the world. For example, you may be in the United States and your
friend may be in Germany. Offer a blessing from this divine soul to
your friend like this:

Dear my divine soul of Divine Forgiveness,
I love you, honor you, and appreciate you.
Please go out to bless my friend in Germany.
Offer healing and blessing to him (or *her*).

I am deeply honored.
I am very appreciative.

The soul of Divine Forgiveness will come out from your Message Center and go to your friend in Germany to offer healing and blessing service. Chant *Divine Forgiveness soul blesses us* for three to five minutes, silently or aloud.

To close this remote blessing practice, call your soul of Divine Forgiveness back:

> *Dear my divine soul of Divine Forgiveness,*
> *Please return.*
> *I am very grateful*
> *Hao! Hao! Hao!*
> *Thank you. Thank you. Thank you.*

You can encourage your friend to receive this and other treasures by reading this book.

The soul of Divine Forgiveness will offer extraordinary service for humanity. We are extremely honored and blessed. You can use the same techniques that I shared in the previous section on universal love to receive benefits from this divine soul.

Give forgiveness.

Receive forgiveness.

Heal.

Prevent sickness.

Rejuvenate.

Prolong life.

Transform consciousness and every aspect of life.

Hao! Hao! Hao!

Thank you. Thank you. Thank you.

UNIVERSAL PEACE

Universal peace means to offer peace to all humanity, all races, all religions, all societies, all nations, and all universes. Forgiveness brings peace, which is the absence of conflict and ill will. Without universal peace, universal harmony is not possible. Universal peace is a must step to accomplish *wan ling rong he*—all souls joining as one.

Universal peace is a soul. Universal peace is a mantra. Its power is beyond imagination. Here is a simple practice for universal peace. Call the soul of anyone whom you would like to receive universal peace:

> *Dear soul of my friend* _____ (name your friend),
> *I love you.*
> *Please come to receive the blessing of universal peace.*
> *I am honored to serve you.*

Then chant *universal peace, universal peace, universal peace, universal peace* . . . for at least three to five minutes, the longer the better. Return the soul of your friend when you end the practice.

Now let me offer you a third Divine Soul Transplant:

Divine Soul Transplant of Divine Peace

Sit up straight. Put the tip of your tongue near the roof of your mouth. Relax. Open your heart and soul.

Prepare!

Divine Soul Transplant of Divine Peace
Silent download!

Close your eyes for thirty seconds to receive this major divine soul treasure.

Hao! Hao! Hao!
Thank you. Thank you. Thank you.

Thank you, Divine.

You can practice like this:

> *Dear souls of all nations, all races, all religions, and all so-*
> *cieties on Mother Earth,*
> *I love you.*
> *Please come to receive the blessing from my divine soul of*
> *Divine Peace.*
> *We are honored and blessed.*
>
> *Dear divine soul of Divine Peace,*
> *I love you, honor you, and appreciate you.*
> *Please turn on.*
> *Please offer a blessing for world peace.*
> *I am very grateful.*

Then chant:

> *Divine Peace soul creates peace for the world.*
> *Divine Peace soul creates peace for the world.*
> *Divine Peace soul creates peace for the world.*
> *Divine Peace soul creates peace for the world . . .*

Chant for at least three to five minutes, silently or aloud, the longer the better. Then close:

> *Hao! Hao! Hao!*
> *Thank you. Thank you. Thank you.*
> *Please return.*

UNIVERSAL HEALING

Millions of people worldwide are suffering from all kinds of sicknesses of the physical body, emotional body, mental body, and spiritual body. Soul has the power to self-heal. Universal healing has incredible abilities to heal. Here is a simple soul healing practice using universal healing:

Choose any part of your body that needs healing.

> *Dear soul, mind, and body of* _____ (name any part of
>   your body),
> *I love you.*
> *You have the power to heal yourself.*
> *Dear universal healing,*
> *I love you.*
> *You have the power to heal my* _____ (name the same
>   part of the body).
> *I am very grateful.*
> *Thank you.*

Then chant:

> *I have the power to heal myself.*
> *Universal healing has the power to heal me.*
> *I have the power to heal myself.*
> *Universal healing has the power to heal me.*
> *I have the power to heal myself.*
> *Universal healing has the power to heal me.*
> *I have the power to heal myself.*
> *Universal healing has the power to heal me . . .*

Chant for at least three to five minutes, silently or aloud, the longer the better. Close the practice as usual:

Hao! Hao! Hao!
Thank you. Thank you. Thank you.

Here is an example of a soul healing practice for the mental body using universal healing:

Dear soul, mind, and body of my mind and my ego,
I love you.
You have the power to heal yourselves.
You have the power to improve your concentration, focus,
    and clarity.
You have the power to release mind-sets, attitudes, and be-
    liefs that are not helpful to me or to others.
Dear universal healing,
I love you.
You have the power to heal my mind and my ego.
I am very grateful.
Thank you.

Then chant:

I have the power to heal myself.
Universal healing heals me.
I have the power to heal myself.
Universal healing heals me.
I have the power to heal myself.
Universal healing heals me.
I have the power to heal myself.
Universal healing heals me . . .

Chant for at least three to five minutes, silently or aloud, the longer the better. Close the practice as usual.

You can use this technique to heal any part of your physical, emotional, mental, or spiritual bodies. You can use this technique to prevent sickness, rejuvenate, prolong life, and transform your consciousness and any aspect of your life. For example, if you feel a cold is coming on, do the following soul prevention of sickness practice right away. In this practice we use the universal healing power of universal light:

Use both palms to tap your chest gently while saying:

> *Dear soul, mind, and body of my lungs,*
> *I love you.*
> *You have the power to prevent a cold.*
> *Do a good job.*
> *Thank you.*

> *Dear soul, mind, and body of my palms,*
> *I love you.*
> *You have the power to prevent a cold.*
> *Please tap my chest to prevent it.*
> *Do a good job.*
> *Thank you.*

> *Dear soul, mind, and body of universal light,*
> *I love you.*
> *You have the power to prevent a cold.*
> *Do a good job.*
> *Thank you.*

Then tap both palms on your chest gently and repeatedly and chant:

> *Universal light heals me.*
> *Universal light heals me.*
> *Universal light heals me.*
> *Universal light heals me . . .*

Tap and chant for at least three to five minutes, silently or aloud, the longer the better. Close the practice as usual.

UNIVERSAL BLESSING

The universe has all kinds of power to bless your life. Universal blessing itself is a mantra. It is also a universal calling. Chant *universal blessing* and you can receive extraordinary blessings. For example, to bless a business:

> *Dear soul, mind, and body of* _____ (name the business),
> *I love you.*
> *You have the power to improve yourself.*
> *Do a good job.*
> *Thank you.*

> *Dear universal blessing,*
> *I love you.*
> *You have the power to bless my business.*
> *I am very grateful.*
> *Thank you.*

Then chant:

> *Universal blessing blesses my business.*
> *Universal blessing creates great success for my business.*
> *Universal blessing blesses my business.*
> *Universal blessing creates great success for my business.*
> *Universal blessing blesses my business.*
> *Universal blessing creates great success for my business.*
> *Universal blessing blesses my business.*
> *Universal blessing creates great success for my business . . .*

Chant for at least three to five minutes, silently or aloud, the longer the better. Close the practice as usual.

Apply *universal blessing* for any aspect of your life. You will be amazed by this mantra and practice. I wish you will receive the greatest blessing from it.

UNIVERSAL HARMONY

To reach universal harmony, one must start with personal harmony, then move to family harmony, community harmony, city harmony, country harmony, Mother Earth harmony, all planets harmony, all stars harmony, all galaxies harmony, and finally, all universes harmony.

Now, let me offer you a fourth Divine Soul Transplant:

Divine Soul Transplant of Divine Harmony

Sit up straight. Put the tip of your tongue near the roof of your mouth. Relax. Open your heart and soul.

Prepare!

Divine Soul Transplant of Divine Harmony
Silent download!

Close your eyes for thirty seconds to receive this major divine soul treasure.

> *Hao! Hao! Hao!*
> *Thank you. Thank you. Thank you.*

Thank you, Divine.

You can practice like this for healing:

Dear my divine soul of Divine Harmony,
I love you, honor you, and appreciate you.
Please offer healing for _____ (name the organ or sick-
   ness to receive healing).
I am very honored and grateful.
Thank you.

Then chant:

Divine Harmony soul heals me.
Divine Harmony soul heals me.
Divine Harmony soul heals me.
Divine Harmony soul heals me . . .

Chant for at least three to five minutes, silently or aloud, the longer the better.

Here is a practice for family harmony:

Dear my divine soul of Divine Harmony,
I love you, honor you, and appreciate you.
Please harmonize all of my family members (name all of
   them you wish).
I am very honored and grateful.
Thank you.

Then chant:

Divine Harmony soul creates family harmony.
Divine Harmony soul creates family harmony.
Divine Harmony soul creates family harmony.
Divine Harmony soul creates family harmony . . .

Chant for at least three to five minutes, silently or aloud, the longer the better.

Here is another example to help harmonize all humanity:

> *Dear my divine soul of Divine Harmony,*
> *I love you, honor you, and appreciate you.*
> *Please harmonize all humanity.*
> *I am very honored and grateful.*
> *Thank you.*

Then chant:

> *Divine Harmony soul harmonizes all humanity.*
> *Divine Harmony soul harmonizes all humanity.*
> *Divine Harmony soul harmonizes all humanity.*
> *Divine Harmony soul harmonizes all humanity . . .*

Chant for at least three to five minutes, silently or aloud, the longer the better.

> *Hao! Hao! Hao!*
> *Thank you. Thank you. Thank you.*

UNIVERSAL ENLIGHTENMENT

Universal enlightenment is the ultimate goal in the fifteen-thousand-year Soul Light Era. The process is:

- enlighten a person's soul first
- enlighten a person's mind next
- enlighten a person's body
- enlighten all human beings
- enlighten all souls

This is the biggest task for the entire Soul Light Era. This is the divine direction and a divine calling. There will be many challenges to accomplishing this task. To reach soul enlightenment, we must transform the consciousness of humanity first. There are all kinds of teachings from many great teachers worldwide about transforming the consciousness of humanity. We take this step to prepare for soul enlightenment.

The major practice to prepare for and reach soul enlightenment is the deep purification of the soul, heart, and mind. Totally transform the consciousness of soul, heart, and mind. A simple yet powerful way to do this is to sing the second Divine Soul Song that I received, "God Gives His Heart to Me."

> *Lu la lu la la li*
> *Lu la lu la la li*
> *Lu la lu la li*
> *Lu la lu la li*
>
> *God gives his heart to me*
> *God gives his love to me*
> *My heart melds with his heart*
> *My love melds with his love*

On my website, you can listen to a sample of this Soul Song for several minutes. To chant this Soul Song is to completely meld your soul, heart, mind, and body with the Divine. You will receive great purification by chanting this Divine Soul Song. The power is immeasurable. You can apply it like this:

> *Dear Divine Soul Song, "God Gives His Heart to Me,"*
> *I love you, honor you, and appreciate you.*
> *You have the power to heal my* _____ (make your request).

You have the power to transform my life _____ (make
    your request).
You have the power to purify my soul, heart, mind, and
    body.
I am extremely honored and grateful.
Thank you.

Then sing this Soul Song.

Lu la lu la la li
Lu la lu la la li
Lu la lu la li
Lu la lu la li

God gives his heart to me
God gives his love to me
My heart melds with his heart
My love melds with his love

Sing for at least three to five minutes, silently or aloud, the longer the better.

※

In summary, universal service includes universal love, forgiveness, peace, healing, blessing, harmony, and enlightenment. Each one is a universal mantra. A mantra is a special sound and a special message that carries power for healing, blessing, and life transformation. There are many renowned ancient mantras, including:

- *Weng Ar Hong* (a Tibetan mantra)
- *Weng Ma Ni Ba Ma Hong* (Guan Yin's six-word mantra for enlightenment)

- *Na Mo Shi Jia Mo Ni Fuo* ("na mo" means *respect and honor;* Shi Jia Mo Ni Fuo is the founder of Buddhism)
- *Na Mo Ar Mi Tuo Fuo* (Ar Mi Tuo Fuo is the buddha who is the founder of *Ji Le Shi Jie,* the "World of Most Happiness," known in the West as the Pure Land)
- *Na Mo Guan Shi Yin Pusa* (Guan Yin is the Bodhisattva of Compassion)
- *Na Mo Yao Shi Fuo* (Yao Shi Fuo is the Chinese name of the Medicine Buddha)
- *Ling Guang Pu Zhao* (literally, soul light widely shines, or "Shining Soul Light")
- *Tao Fa Zi Ran* (literally, "tao" means *The Way,* "fa" means *method,* "zi ran" means *to be natural;* it can be translated as "Follow Nature's Way")

These ancient mantras have served millions of people worldwide through history. They are powerful and extraordinary. Universal love, universal forgiveness, universal peace, universal healing, universal blessing, universal harmony, and universal enlightenment are new mantras for the Soul Light Era. They too are extremely powerful. Practice more and more. You will receive remarkable results for healing, blessing, life transformation, and enlightenment.

How does a mantra work? A mantra carries Soul Power and sound vibration. When you chant a mantra, you are invoking enlightened souls such as the ones just listed. These souls will instantly appear before you. They will remove your energy blockages for healing. They will remove the blockages in your relationships. They will offer purification for your soul, heart, mind, and body. To chant a mantra is to invoke this Soul Power for healing, blessing, and life transformation.

Why do I offer such simple teaching to heal, bless, and transform your life? Why do I offer such simple techniques to enlighten your soul, heart, mind, and body? These techniques do not come from the realm of the mind. Mind over matter is great. But what I am offering is *soul over matter*.

Mind over matter means mind can make things happen, including healing, blessing, and life transformation. Soul over matter means soul has the power to do this also. I am not only offering soul over matter, I am offering Divine Soul Transplants, permanent soul treasures downloaded to you. These divine souls carry Divine Soul Power for healing, blessing, and life transformation. In all of history up to now, only some advanced spiritual leaders have received Divine Soul Downloads. This is definitely the first time in history that the Divine has decided to give his soul treasures to all humanity to heal, bless, and transform our lives. This is definitely the first time in history that humanity has the opportunity to receive and apply divine souls to heal, bless, and transform consciousness and every aspect of life, and to enlighten the soul, heart, mind, and body.

Why do I not explain complicated theories? Because it is not complicated! Healing, preventing sickness, rejuvenating, prolonging life, transforming consciousness and every aspect of life, including relationships and finances, and enlightening the soul, heart, mind, and body are not complicated. When you use Soul Power, you directly come to the point. Remember the essence of the teaching of this book:

- Heal the soul first; then healing of the mind and body will follow.
- Prevent sicknesses of the soul first; then prevention of sicknesses of the mind and body will follow.
- Rejuvenate the soul first; then rejuvenation of the mind and body will follow.
- Prolong the life of the soul first; then long life for the mind and body will follow.
- Transform the consciousness of the soul first; then transformation of the consciousness of heart, mind, and body will follow.

- Transform the soul of a relationship first; then transformation of the relationship will follow.
- Transform the soul of finances and a business first; then transformation of finances and the business will follow.
- Enlighten the soul first; then enlightenment of the heart, mind, and body will follow.

These one-sentence secrets are the secret and sacred divine teaching for the Soul Light Era. Make sure you master the techniques in this book and the other books of my Soul Power Series to heal, bless, transform, and enlighten your life.

>⋇<

I would like to explain clearly that I am flowing this book from the Divine. Every sentence, every word flows out from the Divine's heart. What I hear is what I share.

There is a most renowned statement in Taoist teaching: *Da tao zhi jian.* "Da" means *big.* "Tao" means *The Way.* "Zhi" means *extremely.* "Jian" means *simple.*

The Big Way is extremely simple. Do not search for complicated ways for healing, blessing, transformation, and enlightenment. The simplest way is the best way. What I am teaching and offering is the soul way—the divine soul way—for healing, blessing, transformation, and enlightenment. From A to B, make a straight line. Do not turn around and around to get from A to B. Enjoy divine simplicity and creativity in this book.

What is a Divine Soul Transplant? It is divine creation on the spot. The Divine preprogrammed these Soul Transplants in special paragraphs in this book and downloads them to you at the moment you read these paragraphs. Readers could receive these Divine Soul Transplants anytime, anywhere. This is divine creation. After receiving these divine soul treasures, you can instantly apply them for healing, purification, rejuvenation, transformation, and enlightenment.

Pause for a moment. Think about it. How simple the Divine has made it for us! I am honored to be a servant for humanity and the Divine. I do not take any credit for any healing, blessing, life transformation, or enlightenment that you may enjoy from the teachings, practices, and Divine Soul Downloads in this book. I completely give the honor and the credit to the Divine and Heaven. The divine souls offer divine healing, blessing, transformation, and enlightenment.

Many people worldwide have wondered throughout history, "Who is God and where is he?" The Divine created a way to download the Divine's permanent soul treasures to you as you read a book. That is divine creation and divine presence, isn't it? The Divine offers these priceless treasures to us as a gift. How honored and blessed we are!

Take this divine opportunity by using the divine treasures offered in this book to heal, prevent sickness, rejuvenate, prolong your life, transform your consciousness and every aspect of your life, and enlighten your soul, heart, mind, and body. The teaching is extremely simple. The techniques are extremely practical. The results could be very profound.

> *Learn it.*
> *Digest and absorb it.*
> *Practice it.*
> *Experience it.*
> *Benefit from it.*
> *Transform every aspect of your life.*
> *Enlighten your soul, heart, mind, and body.*
> *Enlighten all humanity.*
> *Enlighten Mother Earth.*
> *Enlighten all souls.*
> *Enlighten all universes.*
> *Hao!*

We *can* do it. We *must* do it.

Align our consciousness with divine consciousness. Every human being, every soul, let us join hearts and souls together to create love, peace, and harmony for humanity, Mother Earth, and all universes.

The Divine Soul Songs "Love, Peace and Harmony" and "God Gives His Heart to Me" are divine mantras. Divine Love, Divine Forgiveness, Divine Peace, and Divine Harmony, whose souls were given to you in this chapter, are also major divine mantras for healing, blessing, life transformation, and enlightenment. Each of these treasures has immense power to bless humanity, Mother Earth, and all universes. We are extremely honored that the Divine is downloading the Divine's soul treasures more and more in the Soul Light Era to transform the consciousness of humanity, to enlighten the souls, hearts, minds, and bodies of human beings, and to enlighten all souls. We are extremely honored and humbled. I am extremely blessed to be a servant of humanity and the Divine.

This chapter has revealed many soul secrets and offered divine soul treasures for healing, prevention of sickness, rejuvenation, prolonging life, transformation of life, and enlightenment. Apply these secrets and treasures to benefit your life.

Increase your good karma. Offer unconditional universal service. The blessings you will receive are unlimited.

Thank you, Divine.

Thank you, all humanity.

Thank you, Mother Earth.

Thank you, all universes.

Thank you, dear reader, for giving me the opportunity to share and serve.

Thank you. Thank you. Thank you.

3

Develop the Power of Soul

MIND HAS POWER to heal, bless, and transform life. Soul has greater power to heal, bless, and transform life. I wrote this book to share with and teach humanity the power of soul.

What Is the Power of Soul?

Every human being has a soul. Every system in the body, every organ, every cell, every cell unit, every DNA and RNA has a soul. Animals have souls also. An ocean has a soul. A tree has a soul. A star has a soul. A galaxy has a soul. Many people still wonder if a stone has a soul. The answer is *yes*. A stone has a soul. A few years ago, I saw a headline in a newspaper: "Does a business have a soul?" Of course! A business has a soul.

In ancient spiritual teaching, there is a famous statement: *Wan wu jie you ling*. "Wan" means *ten thousand*. It represents all or every. "Wu" means *thing*. "Jie" means *all*. "You" means *has*. "Ling" means *soul*. Wan wu jie you ling means *everything has a soul*.

Let me give you an example. If you have advanced Third Eye abilities, when you hold a piece of herb, you could be surprised to see a small golden light being in the herb. This small golden light being is the soul of the herb.

People talk about consciousness. Mind has a consciousness. Most people think that to transform consciousness is to transform the consciousness of the mind. It is great to transform the consciousness of mind, but it is not enough. The power of soul teaches us to transform the consciousness of soul.

A human being has a soul, heart, mind, and body. A heart and a mind exist when a person exists. When a person dies, the heart and the mind of that person disappear. The soul of the human being will go to the Akashic Records to register. After completing life in the physical world, the soul will stay in the Akashic Records for forty-nine days. Then the soul will be assigned to the next life. The soul could stay in Heaven for five, twenty, one hundred, three hundred, or five hundred years before reincarnating again. You may ask, "Is it better to stay in Heaven a shorter time or a longer time?" The answer is, "The longer you stay in Heaven, the better."

A soul has experienced one life after another. A soul lives life in the physical world within a physical body. The same soul also experiences life in the spiritual realm in a formless condition. Whether it is within a body or not, a soul is constantly learning, experiencing life, increasing wisdom and knowledge, and gaining more abilities to serve.

Each soul carries its own frequency. Each soul has its own consciousness. In chapter 1, I explained the characteristics of the soul. Each soul has its own desires, likes, and dislikes. Each soul has its own abilities to serve. This is easy to understand. Think about human beings. Human beings have different jobs because every human being has different abilities. The soul is the same. Some souls have great abilities in a certain field. Other souls have more abilities in other fields. Souls are just like human beings. They have different areas of expertise in their soul journeys. Just as there are human experts in various fields, there are soul experts in various fields. Just as a human being can develop his or her abilities, a soul can also develop its own abilities. A human being's life is short. A soul's life is eternal. Therefore, I am here to help you develop the potential power of the soul, which is the vital teaching of this book.

The Significance of the Power of Soul

The one-sentence secret about the power of soul is:

> *The power of soul is* soul over matter, *which means*
> *soul can heal; boost energy, stamina, vitality, and immunity;*
> *prevent sickness; rejuvenate; prolong life;*
> *and transform every aspect of life, including relationships*
> *and finances; as well as reach enlightenment.*

Soul Power can heal. This book will reveal how you can use Soul Power to heal yourself and to heal others. It will also reveal soul secrets for healing a group of people, even remotely for many people at the same time. In chapter 7, I will reveal the vital soul secrets for soul healing.

Soul Power can prevent sickness. In chapter 8, I will share the techniques for preventing soul sicknesses first. Then prevention of all sicknesses will follow.

Soul Power can rejuvenate and prolong your life. In chapter 9, I will reveal the vital soul secrets for this.

Soul Power can transform relationships and finances. In chapters 10 and 11, I will reveal the essential soul secrets to do this.

Soul Power can enlighten your soul. In chapter 13, I will share this very important soul wisdom and knowledge.

Soul over matter is the new direction in the twenty-first century for transforming consciousness and every aspect of life. Soul over matter can also transform every occupation. I will share one example. In February 2008 I was teaching and healing in Frankfurt, Germany. I offered Divine Soul Transplants of Divine Occupations to create divine professionals. I asked for a person who was willing to receive one of these Divine Soul Transplants as a demonstration. A woman volunteered and joined me. I asked her, "What is your profession?"

She replied, "I am an opera singer."

I said, "Can you sing an aria from an opera for us?"

She said, "I am delighted to sing for everyone."

Her singing was beautiful and powerful. Everyone gave her a big round of applause.

Then I said, "Could I offer a Divine Soul Transplant of Divine Opera Singer to you?"

She replied, "I would be honored to receive a divine soul of Divine Opera Singer."

I told her to close her eyes and prepare to receive. Then I raised my right hand to Heaven and said, "Dear Divine, I request a Divine Soul Transplant of Divine Opera Singer to her."

The Divine instantly responded to my request and downloaded a Divine Opera Singer soul to her. I told her to open her eyes and explained to her, "When you sing an aria again, you will be singing from your Divine Opera Singer soul."

She began to sing the same aria again. The vibration was obviously different and much more powerful. The wave of her sound swept over all two hundred of us in the room. When she finished, people cheered wildly. I asked everyone, "Have you felt the different vibration after the Divine Soul Transplant of Divine Opera Singer?" People were literally shouting their responses: *"Yeeeeeahhhh! Powerful! Extremely powerful!!! Amaaaaazing!!!"* Many of them requested immediately to receive their own Divine Soul Transplant for Divine Occupation.

We honor all professionals. The Divine creates *divine* professionals by transmitting the Divine's own souls for that profession. This is not a physical professional. For example, there are many singers. But only the Divine transmits divine souls to create Divine Singers. There are many music composers. The Divine has transmitted divine souls to create a Divine Music Composer. There are many writers. The Divine has transmitted divine souls to create about one hundred Divine Writers in the last four years. There are many healers. The Divine has transmitted divine souls to create more than seven hundred Divine Healers in the last five years.

Soul has the power to transform consciousness and every aspect of life. Divine souls carry divine creation and divine manifestation to transform consciousness and every aspect of life. Every Divine Soul Transplant *is* divine creation and divine manifestation.

Since July 2003 I have offered Divine Soul Transplants for countless souls. I continue to do so. Now I am offering Divine Soul Transplants in my books and on radio and television programs. Divine souls can accelerate the transformation of the consciousness of humanity and all souls.

To receive a divine soul is to be able to receive its benefits for healing and life transformation. However, you must invoke and practice with the divine soul. What you receive is what you should chant. For example, if you receive a Divine Healer soul, chant:

> *Divine Healer soul heals me.*
> *Divine Healer soul heals me.*
> *Divine Healer soul heals me.*
> *Divine Healer soul heals me . . .*

If you receive a Divine Artist soul, chant:

> *Divine Artist soul transforms my art.*
> *Divine Artist soul transforms my art.*
> *Divine Artist soul transforms my art.*
> *Divine Artist soul transforms my art . . .*

Divine creation and divine manifestation are unlimited. We are extremely honored that the Divine is creating the Divine's professionals worldwide. We are extremely blessed that the Divine is downloading divine souls to humanity to heal, bless, and transform our lives. We are extremely humbled that the Divine has sent an order to humanity to transform our consciousness in order to create love, peace, and harmony for humanity, Mother Earth, and all universes.

Thank you. Thank you. Thank you.

Sacred and Secret Practices for Developing the Potential Power of the Soul

At this moment, the Divine is telling me that most human beings now on Mother Earth have experienced more than six hundred lifetimes. Some of you have had more than a thousand lives. A very old soul could have had thousands of lives. In each lifetime, you could have had a different occupation. Therefore, your soul has had a great variety of life experiences and gained all kinds of wisdom, knowledge, abilities, and potential power.

Developing the potential power of your soul will greatly increase the wisdom, knowledge, and abilities available for your life. For example, I have many students who were not writers. After developing their soul potentials, they have become fluent writers. Many of my students were not healers. After developing their soul abilities, they have become powerful healers. You may not be a writer in this life. That does not mean you were not a writer in a past life. You may not be a healer in this life. That does not mean you were not a healer in a past life.

After developing the potential power of your soul, you can bring out abilities that you have not experienced in this life but which your soul experienced in previous lives. I have many students who were not singers. After developing their soul potentials, they have become beautiful singers. Our souls have extreme potential power and abilities that are waiting to be brought out.

If you understand this teaching on the potential power of the soul, you are ready for the wisdom, knowledge, and practical techniques for developing the potential power of your soul. Here's how to do it:

Sit up straight. Put your left hand over your chest with the palm facing your Message Center (heart chakra). Put your right hand in the prayer position with the fingers pointing upward. This hand position is a special signal to connect your soul with the Divine and the Soul World. I call it the Soul Light Era Prayer Position (figure 1). It focuses on your Message Center because that is the key energy center for the potential power of your soul.

Next you will use the mantra San San Jiu Liu Ba Yao Wu, which is Chinese for the sacred healing number 3396815. This mantra, pronounced *sahn sahn joe lew bah yow woo,* is a divine code for opening

Figure 1. Soul Light Era Prayer Position

your soul communication channels and unlocking all of the potential power of your soul. Chant 3396815 repeatedly as fast as you can. Do it with me now:

> San San Jiu Liu Ba Yao Wu
> San San Jiu Liu Ba Yao Wu
> San San Jiu Liu Ba Yao Wu
> San San Jiu Liu Ba Yao Wu

Chant faster and faster. Let go of any conscious intent to pronounce the individual words clearly. As you chant faster and faster—as fast as you can—suddenly, a special voice you have not heard before may flow out. This special voice is your soul voice speaking Soul Language. I taught this wisdom in my book *Soul Wisdom*,[1] with additional teachings in my book *Soul Communication*.[2] Thousands of people worldwide have used this technique to bring out their Soul Language. If you are a new student, bringing out your Soul Language is the first step in developing the potential power of your soul.

You can learn many profound secrets about Soul Language in *Soul Wisdom*. Most people can open their Soul Language very quickly. If your Soul Language does not open, go back to *Soul Wisdom*, the first book in my Soul Power Series. I offered Divine Soul Downloads in that book to empower every reader to open their Soul Language and to translate Soul Language. Opening and translating Soul Language are vital for developing the potential power of your soul.

The second step in developing the potential power of your soul is to turn your Soul Language to Soul Song. Soul Song is the song of your Soul Language. Soul Song is your personal soul mantra. It is the further development of Soul Language. Your Soul Song carries an even

---

1. Zhi Gang Sha, 2008, *Soul Wisdom,* New York/Toronto: Atria Books and Heaven's Library.
2. Zhi Gang Sha, 2008, *Soul Communication,* New York/Toronto: Atria Books and Heaven's Library.

higher frequency and vibration than your Soul Language carries. Soul Song is a pure and powerful connection with the Divine, the highest saints, and the highest realms. Therefore, Soul Song is vital for developing the potential power of your soul.

As long as you can speak your Soul Language, your Soul Language can easily be turned to Soul Song. This is a one-sentence secret. I love to share and teach one-sentence secrets. If you can summarize any wisdom in one sentence, you must have deeply understood and mastered that field. For example, the one-sentence secret for using mind power for healing is: *Visualize light*. The one-sentence secret for chanting is: *You* are *the mantra*. Now let me share a one-sentence secret to transform your Soul Language to Soul Song.

> *Dear soul, mind, and body of my Soul Language,*[3]
> *I love you, honor you, and appreciate you.*
> **Please turn my Soul Language into Soul Song.**
> *I am very grateful.*
> *Thank you.*

Then, right away, *sing* your Soul Language. Your Soul Language will instantly turn to Soul Song.

The third step in developing the potential power of your soul is to use your Soul Song to develop your hidden potential soul abilities. For example,

> **Dear my Soul Song, could you bring out my potential**
> **soul healing power?**

---

3. Soul Language has a soul. Soul Language has a mind. Soul Language has a body. In fact, everyone and everything has a soul, mind, and body. A soul is a light being. A mind is the consciousness of a being. A body of a being is made of tiny matter. A soul is a light being that is made of tiny matter.

I am very grateful.
Thank you.

Then sing a Soul Song. When you sing this time, your Soul Song will be different than it was when you sang before. It will bring out your hidden soul healing power. Sing for a few minutes, the longer the better. This is the one-sentence secret to bring out your hidden soul healing power.

After you bring out your potential soul healing power, you can invoke it and apply it.

Dear my Soul Song,
I love you, honor you, and appreciate you.
When you offer healing, please bring my full potential soul
*   healing power out to offer healing.*
I would like to offer healing to my ___ (make your re-
*   quest) or*
I would like to offer healing to ___ (name someone else).
I am very grateful.
Thank you.

Then sing a Soul Song to offer the soul healing you have requested. Your soul healing power will be significantly different.

Here is another example:

Dear my Soul Song,
I love you, honor you, and appreciate you.
Could you bring out my hidden potential soul writ-
***   ing abilities?***
I am very grateful.
Thank you.

Then sing a Soul Song. When you sing this time, your Soul Song will be different again. It will bring out your hidden soul writing power. Sing for a few minutes, the longer the better. This is the one-sentence secret to bring out your hidden soul writing power.

After you bring out your potential soul writing power, invoke it like this:

> *Dear my potential soul writing abilities,*
> *I love you, honor you, and appreciate you.*
> *Could you guide me to write?*
> *I am very grateful.*
> *Thank you.*

Then determine the title of what you would like to write. It may come from your logical mind. It may come from your soul's desire. It may come in a message that you hear, see, or know. Then what you hear is what you will write. This is exactly how I am writing this book now. What I hear from the Divine is what I am writing.

Doing soul writing in this way does benefit from further training and practice. If you cannot hear and flow out from your soul right away, do not be disappointed. Practice a few more times. This ability usually comes unexpectedly and sometimes not right away. It can come at any moment. Be delighted, not surprised, when it does. Be grateful to the Divine and to your own soul.

The fourth step in developing the potential power of your soul is Divine Soul Downloads. Through these permanent divine soul treasures, the Divine creates and transmits divine soul abilities. Take Divine Soul Song singing, for example. In order to become a Divine Soul Song Singer, one receives almost one hundred Divine Soul Downloads to transform major parts of the physical, emotional, mental, and spiritual bodies for singing.

Now I will give every reader another Divine Soul Download.

This is the fifth Divine Soul Download given in this book as a divine gift to every reader:

Divine Soul Transplant of Divine Voice

Everything has a soul. Your voice has a soul. This Divine Soul Transplant of Divine Voice will replace the original soul of your voice with a new divine soul. The original soul of the voice is usually one or two inches tall. The new divine soul of Divine Voice is about eighty to one hundred feet tall and ten to twenty feet wide. Generally speaking, these huge divine souls will shrink to fit in your body within one to four days after you receive them. The original soul of your voice will return immediately to the Divine's heart.

Sit up straight. Put the tip of your tongue near the roof of your mouth. Relax. Open your heart and soul.

Prepare!

Divine Soul Transplant of Divine Voice
Silent download!

Close your eyes for thirty seconds to receive this major divine soul treasure.

Hao! Hao! Hao!
Thank you. Thank you. Thank you.

Thank you, Divine.
Let's invoke this new gift and practice:

Dear my divine soul of Divine Voice,
I love you, honor you, and appreciate you.
Please offer a healing to my _____ (make your request) or
Please offer a blessing for _____ (make your request).

Then sing a Soul Song to bring out the Soul Power of your divine voice. You may instantly feel a major difference in your Soul Song.

The vibration, frequency, and light are of a higher level and quality. The healing and blessing power your Soul Song carries has been uplifted.

Divine Soul Downloads are the divine way to develop the potential power of your soul. You are given a new divine soul that is created specifically for you. This new divine soul carries Divine Soul Power that can instantly transform your soul, heart, mind, and body. Do not forget to invoke and practice with your permanent Divine Soul Downloads. They are pure divine servants. They are delighted to serve. Use these treasures to serve yourself and to serve others. Use them often. Use them well.

We cannot thank, we cannot honor the Divine enough for bringing these treasures to humanity and all souls at this time.

Thank you. Thank you. Thank you.

4

Soul Orders

PEOPLE UNDERSTAND AN order. In ancient China, when the emperor gave an order, every subject had to obey. In your family, when your young children do something wrong, you tell them, "Stop! Do not do this." You give your children an order; they will stop misbehaving. In an organization, the chief officer can give an order. "I made a decision. This is the direction in which I want to go." All of the subordinates have to follow the leader's wishes. A judge could give someone an order to do something or not do something. If the person does not follow the order, he could be fined or arrested and put in jail.

In this chapter, I am introducing new soul secrets and wisdom that have not been released before. These secrets and wisdom are about Soul Orders for healing, preventing sickness, rejuvenating, transforming life, and enlightening life. This is the first time the Divine has guided me to release these secrets and wisdom.

What Soul Orders Are and How to Give Them

A Soul Order is exactly that: an order given by a soul to do something that is good service, such as healing, preventing sickness, rejuvenating, transforming life, and enlightening life. A Soul Order can be given by your body soul. A Soul Order can be given by any of your inner souls, including the souls of your systems, organs, cells, cell units, DNA, and RNA.

A Soul Order can be given for self-healing. Say, for example, you have back pain. The back has a soul. The soul of your back can give an order to heal your back. Here's how you can do it:

> *Dear soul of my back,*
> *I love you, honor you, and appreciate you.*
> *You have the power to send an order to heal my back.*
> *Please send an order to heal my back.*
> *The order is:*
> *Soul of my back orders my back to heal.*

Then activate the order by chanting repeatedly:

> *Soul of my back orders my back to heal.*
> *Soul of my back orders my back to heal.*
> *Soul of my back orders my back to heal.*
> *Soul of my back orders my back to heal . . .*

Repeat this order for at least three to five minutes, silently or aloud, the longer the better.

Here is another example. If you have digestive problems, give a Soul Order like this:

> *Dear soul of my digestive system,*
> *I love you, honor you, and appreciate you.*
> *Give an order to the mind and body of my digestive system*
>   *to heal my digestive system.*

Then activate the order:

> *Soul of my digestive system orders my digestive system to heal.*
>
> *Soul of my digestive system orders my digestive system to heal.*
>
> *Soul of my digestive system orders my digestive system to heal.*
>
> *Soul of my digestive system orders my digestive system to heal . . .*

Repeat this order for at least three to five minutes, silently or aloud, the longer the better.

The human mind can give an order. We all know this. We all have done this. The soul secret I am revealing is to give a Soul Order. An organ's soul can give an order. A cell's soul can give an order. A DNA's soul can give an order. Here is another example.

If you have knee pain, you can give a direct Soul Order like this:

> *Souls of my knees order my knees to heal.*
> *Souls of my knees order my knees to heal.*
> *Souls of my knees order my knees to heal.*
> *Souls of my knees order my knees to heal . . .*

To send a Soul Order for healing and transformation, you can use any of the following major techniques:

- Any soul of your systems, organs, cells, DNA, and RNA can give a Soul Order to itself for healing and transformation.

For example:

> *Soul of my immune system orders my immune system to heal.*

Soul of my immune system orders my immune system to heal.

Soul of my immune system orders my immune system to heal.

Soul of my immune system orders my immune system to heal . . .

Or:

Soul of my liver orders my liver to heal.
Soul of my liver orders my liver to heal.
Soul of my liver orders my liver to heal.
Soul of my liver orders my liver to heal . . .

Or:

Souls of my lung cells order my lung cells to heal.
Souls of my lung cells order my lung cells to heal.
Souls of my lung cells order my lung cells to heal.
Souls of my lung cells order my lung cells to heal . . .

Or:

Souls of my kidney DNA and RNA order my kidney DNA and RNA to heal.

Souls of my kidney DNA and RNA order my kidney DNA and RNA to heal.

Souls of my kidney DNA and RNA order my kidney DNA and RNA to heal.

Souls of my kidney DNA and RNA order my kidney DNA and RNA to heal . . .

- A vital secret is that the soul of your heart is the boss for the souls of all your systems, other organs, cells, DNA, and RNA. Your heart soul can give a Soul Order to your systems, organs, cells, DNA, and RNA.

For example:

> *My heart soul orders my immune system to heal.*
> *My heart soul orders my immune system to heal.*
> *My heart soul orders my immune system to heal.*
> *My heart soul orders my immune system to heal . . .*

Or:

> *My heart soul orders my liver to heal.*
> *My heart soul orders my liver to heal.*
> *My heart soul orders my liver to heal.*
> *My heart soul orders my liver to heal . . .*

Or:

> *My heart soul orders my lung cells to heal.*
> *My heart soul orders my lung cells to heal.*
> *My heart soul orders my lung cells to heal.*
> *My heart soul orders my lung cells to heal . . .*

Or:

> *My heart soul orders my kidney DNA and RNA to heal.*
> *My heart soul orders my kidney DNA and RNA to heal.*
> *My heart soul orders my kidney DNA and RNA to heal.*
> *My heart soul orders my kidney DNA and RNA to heal . . .*

- Your soul (which I also call your body soul) is in turn the boss of your heart soul and of all the other souls in your body. Your body soul can give a Soul Order to any of your other inner souls.

For example:

> *My body soul orders my musculoskeletal system to heal.*
> *My body soul orders my musculoskeletal system to heal.*
> *My body soul orders my musculoskeletal system to heal.*
> *My body soul orders my musculoskeletal system to heal . . .*

Or:

> *My body soul orders my breast to heal.*
> *My body soul orders my breast to heal.*
> *My body soul orders my breast to heal.*
> *My body soul orders my breast to heal . . .*

Or:

> *My body soul orders my brain cells to heal.*
> *My body soul orders my brain cells to heal.*
> *My body soul orders my brain cells to heal.*
> *My body soul orders my brain cells to heal . . .*

Or:

> *My body soul orders my heart DNA and RNA to heal.*
> *My body soul orders my heart DNA and RNA to heal.*
> *My body soul orders my heart DNA and RNA to heal.*
> *My body soul orders my heart DNA and RNA to heal . . .*

These examples show how simple it is to use Soul Orders for healing. You can use Soul Orders to heal any organ, any part of your body, or any condition. Try it. Taste it. Experience it. Benefit from it. You could be amazed at the results. However, the power of Soul Orders goes far beyond what they can do for healing.

The Power of Soul Orders

A Soul Order can be used for healing. It can also be used for preventing sickness. It can even be used for rejuvenation and prolonging life. Ultimately, it can be used for transforming consciousness and every aspect of life.

How can you give a Soul Order for preventing sickness? It is not difficult at all. If you feel like you are coming down with a cold, give the following Soul Order.

> *Souls of my lungs order my lungs to prevent a cold.*
> *Souls of my lungs order my lungs to prevent a cold.*
> *Souls of my lungs order my lungs to prevent a cold.*
> *Souls of my lungs order my lungs to prevent a cold . . .*

Now let me show you how to send a Soul Order for rejuvenation:

> *My body soul orders my body to rejuvenate.*
> *My body soul orders my body to rejuvenate.*
> *My body soul orders my body to rejuvenate.*
> *My body soul orders my body to rejuvenate . . .*

Always practice for at least three to five minutes, the longer the better. If you are sensitive, you could be amazed that your whole body resonates and vibrates when the Soul Order is given.

Soul is the boss for mind and body. When your soul sends an order, your mind and body will follow. This is the power of soul. This is soul over matter. This is soul healing, soul rejuvenation, and soul transformation of your mind and body.

Here is how to send a Soul Order to transform your relationship with a person:

> *My body soul orders my heart and mind to transform my relationship with* _____ (name the person).
> *My body soul orders my heart and mind to transform my relationship with* _____.
> *My body soul orders my heart and mind to transform my relationship with* _____.
> *My body soul orders my heart and mind to transform my relationship with* _____ . . .

Next let me share the wisdom of how to give a Soul Order to transform your business:

> *Soul of my business orders my business to transform.*
> *Soul of my business orders my business to transform.*
> *Soul of my business orders my business to transform.*
> *Soul of my business orders my business to transform . . .*

This is the first time Soul Orders for healing, blessing, and life transformation have been introduced to humanity. Practice. Practice. Practice. Experience. Experience. Experience. You could have many "aha" moments that help you understand the power of Soul Orders better and better. I wish you will have your first "aha" moment very soon. I wish you will then have more and more "aha" moments.

Soul Standing Is Vital

I have just explained Soul Orders and given examples to guide you in giving Soul Orders for healing, preventing sickness, rejuvenating, and transforming life. Now I will explain the key to the power of Soul Orders.

In the physical world, different positions in a company have different levels of authority and responsibility. For example, in a bank the board of trustees makes the decisions for the direction of the bank. The president is in charge of operations. The vice presidents are in charge of different departments. Department heads have their own authorities and responsibilities. The structure of the government of a country is similar. The higher the position one has in a company or in a country, the more authority and responsibility one carries.

It is similar in the spiritual world. In the spiritual world, the Divine is the top leader. There are different committees that report to the Divine. There are different spiritual groups that gather in different parts of Heaven. Each group has its leader and assistant leaders. Each group has its founder and his or her lineage. The founder and lineage holders are in charge of that group. In the Soul Light Era, at this moment there is a Saints Committee in Jiu Tian, the nine layers of Heaven ("jiu" means *nine,* "tian" means *Heaven*), which is the realm our souls are in. This committee has twelve saints who were elected by the spiritual world and approved by the Divine. Every group in Heaven must listen to this committee, which acts just like the board of trustees of a bank.

Your body soul can give a Soul Order to your mind and body. It works! It works because your body soul is the boss of your other inner souls. If your soul stands higher than the soul of another human being, then when you send a Soul Order to heal that person, it works also. If your soul's standing is lower than another person's, then when you send a Soul Order to heal that person, generally speaking, it will not work. Therefore, to increase the power of your Soul Orders, your soul's spiritual standing must be uplifted.

Bible stories are amazing and heart-touching because Jesus was the chosen son of the Divine. He had a high-level spiritual standing. When he said, "You are healed," he was giving a Soul Order. He was the chosen servant of the Divine. When he spoke, the Divine healed.

How do you uplift your soul standing? The only way is to offer unconditional universal service. In chapter 2 about karma, I explained a great deal of the secret wisdom, knowledge, and practice of universal service. When you serve, the Divine will give you virtue. Serve unconditionally and the Divine will give you great virtue. Virtue will uplift your spiritual standing. Only virtue can uplift your spiritual standing. The higher your spiritual standing, the more Soul Power you are given. Then your Soul Orders will be more powerful.

Principles to Follow in Giving Soul Orders

To send a Soul Order, you must follow these major principles:

- Always send a positive order, one that shares love, forgiveness, compassion, and light.
- Never send a harmful order to others. This will only create bad karma for you.
- Generally speaking, do not send an order to others, because you may not be sure of your spiritual standing. In the spiritual world, there are two sides, Light Side and Dark Side. Each one has its layers of spiritual standing. Each one has its powers. Each one is given different tasks from the universe and the Divine. Sometimes they are united. Sometimes they are opposed. Sometimes they are in harmony. Sometimes they are fighting. If you send an order to a dark soul, that dark soul could have a higher spiritual standing in the Dark Side than you have in the Light Side. As a result, that dark soul could harm you.

If you clearly understand where your soul stands in the spiritual world, and if you are given divine authority to give special Soul Orders, then you could offer Soul Orders to help others. But make sure you are very clear about your soul standing and authority. If you are not clear, do *not* send a Soul Order to others. What you and everyone absolutely can do is send a Soul Order for yourself, as I have taught in this entire chapter.

In summary, Soul Order is a major soul treasure for the Soul Light Era. It can transform every aspect of your life. In this chapter, I release the secret wisdom and the practices. This soul treasure will serve you tremendously for healing, preventing sickness, rejuvenating, prolonging life, and transforming relationships and finances.

The techniques are so simple. The power is beyond comprehension.

Use it.

Practice it.

Benefit from it.

Thank you. Thank you. Thank you.

The first *thank you* is always for the Divine. The second *thank you* is for all your spiritual fathers and mothers in all layers of Heaven. The third *thank you* is for your own soul, mind, and body.

Soul Guidance for Your Spiritual Journey

A NEWBORN BABY NEEDS great care from its parents. A toddler needs to learn a lot from parents. In elementary school, children need lots of guidance from teachers and parents. Even adults need guidance. People with all kinds of difficulties in life seek out counselors—financial counselors, marriage counselors, psychologists, business consultants, life coaches, and more. Just about everybody needs guidance and training at some point. Guidance is important for life.

Just as a physical being needs lots of guidance for physical life, a spiritual being also needs lots of guidance. Soul guidance can be guidance for your physical life, emotional life, mental life, or spiritual life. To receive soul guidance, you must open your spiritual communication channels. You must have a physical spiritual master or Heaven's spiritual masters to guide you.

What Is Soul Guidance?

Soul guidance comes from your spiritual masters. You must find true spiritual masters. What is a true spiritual master? There is one standard of measurement. Your spiritual master must be a total GOLD and unconditional universal servant to offer universal love, forgiveness, peace, healing, blessing, harmony, and enlightenment. Your spiritual master must be a pure and kind teacher who has great compassion. A true spiritual teacher will guide you well. A false spiritual teacher will guide you in the wrong direction.

Your Heaven's spiritual guides can also guide you. After you open your spiritual channels, you can listen to their guidance. Buddhas, holy saints, and healing angels in Heaven find their students on Mother Earth. They offer their teachings to their physical students to guide them. Your Heaven's spiritual guides can converse with you or show you spiritual images to guide you. They also bless you and protect you. They give you great love, care, and compassion.

In your spiritual journey, you must also understand and pass spiritual testing. You must understand the purification process. If you cannot pass spiritual testing, you may not move further on your spiritual journey. Many spiritual students cannot pass their spiritual testing. They quit the spiritual journey halfway. It is a great pity.

Every spiritual being must go through serious spiritual testing. On my spiritual journey, when I was learning from my beloved spiritual master and adoptive father, Master and Dr. Zhi Chen Guo, in China, some people came to me to tell me that Master Guo was not the right teacher for me. I thought he was a great teacher. His healing techniques worked. He taught all of his students to purify the heart, transform the personality, and accumulate virtue to be a pure servant. I was determined to continue to learn from him and was not affected by these outside influences.

Later, I received spiritual testing from my spiritual guides in Heaven. For a few weeks in 1994, my Third Eye saw many images.

They also showed me that Master Guo was not the right teacher. They told me not to follow him. I knew that my teacher worked and studied tirelessly, put great effort into clinical research, showed great compassion and generosity to all of the patients who came to him, and cured many "incurable" cases. His deep wisdom had a profound impact on me. His techniques were incredibly effective. So I did not listen to this false guidance.

At that moment, I did not understand that I was being tested by Heaven. But because I did not listen to the false messages, I passed my test. I was very firm in continuing to follow my teacher's teaching. After my spiritual guides saw my loyalty and commitment to my teacher's journey, they blessed my spiritual journey with my teacher more and more. They also started to have soul conversations with me to directly teach me soul secrets, wisdom, knowledge, and practices. Finally, in July 2003, the Divine chose me as the Divine's servant and as a servant of humanity to offer divine healing, divine blessing, and divine creation through Divine Soul Downloads to serve humanity.

Essential Soul Guidance for the Spiritual Journey

Soul guidance is vital to transforming your life. Your physical spiritual master can guide you. Your spiritual fathers and mothers in Heaven can guide you. The Divine can guide you. To move further on your spiritual journey, it is very important for you to be very firm in your heart and mind that you want to be a total GOLD servant. When you make this decision, let no one and no soul influence you. If you do not have a total commitment to serve, it is very hard to move further on your spiritual journey. The Divine needs dedicated pure servants.

Let me offer you important soul guidance for your spiritual journey by sharing essential teachings on a few key topics.

1. WHY DO YOU WANT TO BE ON A SPIRITUAL JOURNEY?

Millions of people around the world are on a spiritual journey. If you are one of them, have you asked yourself why you want to be on a spiritual journey? You may think, "I want to have more love for myself and others." Others may think, "I want to transform my relationships." Others may think, "I want to help the poor, the sick, and the homeless." Others may think, "I want to enlighten my soul."

Let me share the key wisdom. The spiritual journey is the journey for the soul. If you want to be on the spiritual journey, you must first be aware right away that you will need to purify your soul and heart. You are transforming your soul and heart to be more loving, forgiving, compassionate, sincere, kind, generous, and grateful.

Your spiritual journey is not only for you and your soul. It is also a journey of service. You are on a path to serve others better and better, and more and more. You are on a path to transform others. You are serving the divine mission, which is to create love, peace, and harmony for humanity, Mother Earth, and all universes.

The key is to commit yourself to the path of service to others. Your soul wants to do this because the Divine made a law: to serve others is to uplift your soul's spiritual standing.

To uplift your spiritual standing is to move closer to the Divine, which is to move closer to the divine realm. Every soul desires this. Why? What are the benefits of having your soul stay in a higher realm?

The nearer you are to the Divine, the more secret and sacred teaching and wisdom you are given. You are also given greater divine abilities to heal, bless, and transform the lives of others. Jesus, Mary, renowned buddhas, and many great spiritual fathers and mothers on Mother Earth have already demonstrated their divine abilities because they are dedicated to serving humanity. Their souls stay in a very high position in Heaven. They are given divine wisdom and divine abilities to heal and transform others. Therefore, their service has resulted in many heart-touching stories. Millions of people honor the teachings and appreciate the healings, blessings, and love from these very high-level souls.

Therefore, the one-sentence secret about the spiritual journey is:

The purpose of the spiritual journey is to serve others.

The Divine gave me a spiritual law in July 2003, the Universal Law of Universal Service. This universal law states:

> *I am a universal servant.*
> *You are a universal servant.*
> *Everyone and everything is a universal servant.*
> *A universal servant offers universal service, including universal love, forgiveness, peace, healing, blessing, harmony, and enlightenment.*
> *If one offers a little service, one receives little blessing from the universe and from me.*
> *If one offers more service, one receives more blessing.*
> *If one offers unconditional service, one receives unlimited blessing.*

This Universal Law of Universal Service clearly states the purpose of one's spiritual journey and the results. The final destination of one's spiritual journey is to reach the divine realm. When one's soul reaches the divine realm, one will receive direct divine teaching and gain more wisdom and abilities from the Divine to serve humanity and all souls.

2. SPIRITUAL TESTING

If you are a spiritual being, the moment you commit to your spiritual journey, spiritual testing will start. It could come right away from your family. For example, if your spouse is not a spiritual being, he or she could create disharmony between the two of you. You may find you no longer have a common language, even if you did before. Your spouse will not understand or agree with many of the things you choose to do. Your spouse may feel that you are strange and difficult to understand. Family quarrels could start and happen one after another.

When you are on your spiritual journey, it could also happen right away that your close friends feel you are acting funny or strange. They feel you are different. They may feel alienated from you. They may tell you that you have been brainwashed by your spiritual teacher. They will start to influence you right away.

As I said before, if you are committed to be on the spiritual journey, you must understand that your purpose is to offer service to others. You must give unconditional love, forgiveness, compassion, care, kindness, and generosity to others. You cannot be selfish anymore. Therefore, your view of the world *has* changed. *You* have changed. Therefore, your spouse, your family members, your friends, and your colleagues at work could feel you are strange. You *are* changed. This is very understandable because your consciousness has transformed and is probably transforming further. Your family, friends, and colleagues now do not share the same consciousness as you. Therefore, arguments, quarrels, and all kinds of disagreements are very understandable.

How do you deal with these sudden changes? First of all, you must understand that the views and opinions of others are spiritual testing for you. Always be patient, loving, and compassionate with your family and friends. The Divine made a spiritual law. Every spiritual being who wants to move forward on the spiritual journey must be tested. The further you want to move, the more you will be tested. Testing can come from every aspect of life. Testing usually comes in the area of our most significant weaknesses. If you have selfishness, you will be tested in that area. If you have fear, you will be tested there. If you have ego, your ego will be tested. If your commitment to service is wavering, your commitment will be tested. No testing, no growth. No pain, no gain.

Think about school, from elementary school through graduate school. Testing happens year after year, one test after another. If you cannot pass your school tests, you cannot advance to a higher grade. It works the same way in the spiritual world. If you do not pass your spiritual tests, how can Heaven confirm your commitment to serve humanity? How can your soul standing be uplifted on your spiritual journey? How can you be enlightened? There is no second way. Therefore, testing is a must.

3. HOW TO PASS SPIRITUAL TESTING

The most important secret for passing spiritual testing is that you must have a very firm desire in your heart and mind. *I want to serve humanity. I want to give my love, care, compassion, forgiveness, generosity, kindness, and purity to others. I am committed to being a servant of humanity.* You should never think, "I give others too much." You should never think, "Why did I go out of my way to help? I must have gotten lost." After all, what is unconditional universal service? It is to serve without conditions. It is to serve without expectations. If you have this firm heart, you will be solid. No loving action is wasted. No forgiving action is wasted. No compassionate action is wasted. No service to others and humanity is wasted. The more you serve, the faster you will grow on your spiritual journey. You will overcome any challenges and pass any spiritual testing.

The second secret for passing spiritual testing is that you must chant divine mantras. Two divine mantras are vital to help you pass spiritual testing. One is "Love, Peace and Harmony" (see p. 33). The other is "God Gives His Heart to Me" (see p. 59). Any moment you feel challenged, any moment you feel emotional, any moment you doubt, any moment you feel strange, chant one of these divine mantras right away. Your thoughts and feelings will transform right away.

Remember, this is your spiritual journey. Nobody else can do it for you. You are in charge of your own spiritual journey. Of course, when you are struggling, it is very important to contact your spiritual teacher and the advanced spiritual beings whom you trust to give you guidance. Their help is vital to transforming your spiritual journey.

The third secret for passing spiritual testing is to have a regular spiritual practice. I suggest singing a Soul Song as many times per day as you can for as long as you can. Soul Song carries a soul healing wave. It carries love, care, and compassion. Soul Song is a spiritual calling, a treasure for the spiritual world. The moment you sing a Soul Song, you will receive a great response from the spiritual teachers and guides in Heaven. When they come, they know your struggle right away. They will send love and light instantly to transform your dark thoughts or behavior. Immediately, your spiritual journey will align with the divine path again.

I have personally sung many Soul Songs for my students and other individuals worldwide to bless their spiritual journeys and their healing, blessing, and life transformation. I welcome you to listen to my Soul Songs. They carry divine love and light to serve you.

The fourth secret for passing spiritual testing is to be grateful for the tests. Testing is a gift from the Divine and your spiritual fathers and mothers. Testing gives you the opportunity to eliminate your weaknesses and to replace darkness with love and light. Without testing, how could you purify your soul, heart, mind, and body? Without testing, how can the Divine know you are a total GOLD, unconditional universal servant? The only appropriate response to testing is *thank you*.

If you follow these four pieces of soul guidance, it will absolutely help your spiritual journey.

I wish your spiritual journey will move higher and higher.

Pass spiritual testing.

Uplift your spiritual standing.

Finally, your soul can reach the divine realm.

Thank you. Thank you. Thank you.

4. SERVE HUMANITY AND ALL SOULS UNCONDITIONALLY

It is easy to say, "Serve humanity and all souls unconditionally." It is difficult to do it. When you start to serve others, right away you may think, "I am spending too much time. This is taking too much effort. Is this worth it?" You may serve so hard and yet others do not pay attention. They are not appreciative. This could really make you wonder, "Should I continue to serve or not?"

Do not forget that everybody is on the spiritual journey. However, many people do not realize this. Many people do not have pure love, care, and kindness. Many people still think of themselves first. They are not ready to sacrifice themselves to serve others. They think their time should belong to their family or to themselves. Why spend so much time to do volunteer work? Why spend lots of time to chant mantras? Why spend hours to meditate? If they are not in the same condition as you, they do not understand, much less appreciate, that you are offering universal service through your volunteer work, chanting, and meditation.

The best approach is to explain directly to your family members, your loved ones, and your friends what you are doing. They may understand and support you. If they do not understand or even go against you, do not fight with them. Allow them time to understand. Do not lose your temper. Be soft. Be yin. If one person wants to fight but the other person remains completely quiet and soft, a fight will not happen. Fighting always happens when one side wants to fight and the other side fights back. This is not a solution for a spiritual being.

If you are a spiritual being, stand in a higher position. Understand that other people may not have the commitment that you have. Have patience and give them time to understand your heart. Give them love and compassion to transform them. Love melts all blockages and transforms all life. Forgiveness brings inner peace and inner joy. Compassion unites. If you carry love, forgiveness, and compassion, your spouse, family, and friends will understand you better and better. In time, your situation can be transformed to peace and harmony.

You made your commitment to offer unconditional service to others, to humanity, and to the universe. You cannot expect anyone else to do this. There is an ancient spiritual statement: *The teacher only teaches the ready ones.* Another renowned spiritual statement is: *When the student is ready, the teacher appears.* The best way to deal with your family members, friends, and colleagues is to be an example of a pure servant. Use your example to influence them and touch their hearts. At the same time, try to offer teaching to them. The Divine needs millions of pure servants and teachers for humanity. If everyone on Mother Earth were to offer love, peace, and harmony, Mother Earth would pass through her transition very quickly. Conflicts would be dissolved. Natural disasters would be reduced. Always remember: *Love melts all blockages and transforms all life. Forgiveness brings inner peace and inner joy.* Unconditional love and forgiveness are the golden keys to transforming humanity, Mother Earth, and all universes.

You spend time serving others, society, and humanity. You devote great effort to chanting and meditating and to sending your love to the universe. This time is not wasted. You will never get lost. Heaven and the Akashic Records record your service. The Divine knows in his heart that you are a pure servant. You are appreciated by the Divine. Lots of virtue is given to your soul. Your soul standing is uplifted. Every aspect of your present life and your future lives will be extremely blessed. You will flourish abundantly in every aspect of your life.

You serve. Heaven blesses you. The Divine honors you. We are honored to be a servant. We are extremely honored to be an unconditional universal servant.

5. TRANSFORM YOUR CONSCIOUSNESS

Generally speaking, when people talk about consciousness, they think it resides in the brain and mind. This is correct. But the teaching on consciousness that I offer in this book goes further.

Consciousness has three aspects: soul consciousness, mind consciousness, and body consciousness. Every system, every organ, every cell, every cell unit, every DNA and RNA, and every space between the cells has its own consciousness.

To transform consciousness is to transform all consciousness at every level of a human being. Furthermore, an organization has a consciousness. A city has a consciousness. A country has a consciousness. Mother Earth has a consciousness. A planet has a consciousness. A star has a consciousness. A galaxy has a consciousness. A universe has a consciousness.

To transform consciousness is to transform the universal consciousness. What is the universal consciousness? Universal consciousness is divine consciousness. Align every consciousness in all universes with divine consciousness. The Divine's consciousness is our consciousness. The Divine's heart is our heart. The Divine's soul is every soul in all universes. Meld our hearts with the Divine's heart. Meld our souls with the Divine's soul.

Let me lead you in a practice to transform your consciousness and universal consciousness together. The technique is extremely simple and practical. Its power is beyond words.

Chant and sing the Divine Soul Song "God Gives His Heart to Me," which is a divine mantra:

Lu la lu la la li
Lu la lu la la li
Lu la lu la li
Lu la lu la li

God gives his heart to me
God gives his love to me
My heart melds with his heart
My love melds with his love

When you chant and sing this divine mantra, you align your heart, your soul, and your consciousness with the Divine. Begin by saying *hello:*

Dear soul, heart, mind, and body of every human being on
Mother Earth,
Dear soul, heart, mind, and body of every animal on
Mother Earth,
Dear soul, heart, mind, and body of everything in nature,
Dear soul, heart, mind, and body of everyone and every-
thing in all universes,
I love you, honor you, and appreciate you.
Let us join hearts and souls together to chant the divine
mantra and Divine Soul Song, "God Gives His Heart
to Me"
To transform soul, heart, mind, body, and consciousness of
all humanity and all souls in all universes.
I am grateful and appreciative.
Thank you.

Then start to chant:

Lu la lu la la li
Lu la lu la la li
Lu la lu la li
Lu la lu la li

God gives his heart to me
God gives his love to me

My heart melds with his heart
My love melds with his love

Chant for as long as you can, as many times as you can. Every moment you chant, you are offering the biggest service to humanity and every soul in all universes. You will gain incredible virtue. Your life will be transformed further and further. The blessing you can receive is beyond comprehension.

This technique is so simple. Do you really get it? I wish that you do. The real secret is that when you chant, you *are* the Divine's heart. You *are* the Divine's soul. You *are* all humanity. You *are* all souls in all universes.

Humanity is one.

Mother Earth is one.

All universes are one.

All souls are one.

Divine is one.

Transform all souls, hearts, minds, bodies, and consciousnesses to divine consciousness.

Chant. Chant. Chant.

Practice. Practice. Practice.

Serve. Serve. Serve.

Transform. Transform. Transform.

Oneness. Oneness. Oneness.

Hao! Hao! Hao!

Thank you. Thank you. Thank you.

6. ENLIGHTEN YOUR SOUL

The purpose of one's soul journey is to reach soul enlightenment. Soul enlightenment means uplifting your soul standing to a special layer. Our souls are now in the Jiu Tian realm in Heaven. "Jiu" means *nine*. "Tian" means *heaven*. A soul in Jiu Tian, the "nine layers of Heaven," must reincarnate. There is a heaven above Jiu Tian, which is named Tian Wai Tian: literally, the "Heaven beyond Heaven." The Divine stays in his temple in Tian Wai Tian, which is the divine realm. A soul who reaches Tian Wai Tian stops reincarnation. The entire spiritual journey for every human being and every soul in all universes is to offer unconditional universal service in order to uplift your soul to Tian Wai Tian.

In chapter 13, I will share the secrets, wisdom, knowledge, and practical tools to reach soul enlightenment. If you wish, you can read chapter 13 now. It could be very beneficial. Or you can wait and read it later.

※

The Power of Soul is a soul book. It shares fundamental and advanced soul secrets, wisdom, knowledge, and practices with you. It also offers Divine Soul Downloads, which are permanent divine soul treasures, to you. The secrets and wisdom are shared within the words of this book. But there are hidden words within the book. Each time you read this book, relax. Open your heart and soul. "Aha" moments will come to you. The more times you read this book, the deeper the real-izations you will achieve and the further you will be inspired. Your commitment to unconditional universal service will be firmer and firmer in your heart and soul.

Many "aha" moments are waiting for you. Relaxing as you read this book is itself a soul meditation. Every sentence and every word in this book carries messages to serve your soul journey, as well as your healing, prevention of sickness, rejuvenation, life transformation, and enlightenment journeys.

May the teachings of this book serve you well.

Serve. Serve. Serve.
Love. Love. Love.
Heal. Heal. Heal.
Prevent. Prevent. Prevent.
Rejuvenate. Rejuvenate. Rejuvenate.
Transform. Transform. Transform.
Enlighten. Enlighten. Enlighten.
Hao! Hao! Hao!
Thank you. Thank you. Thank you.

6

Soul Intelligence, Wisdom, and Knowledge

PEOPLE UNDERSTAND INTELLIGENCE. People understand IQ. Some children have a high IQ. They are considered to be intelligent. Generally speaking, people think intelligence comes from the brain, which is correct but not complete.

Five thousand years ago, *The Yellow Emperor's Classic of Internal Medicine,* the authoritative book of traditional Chinese medicine, stated: *The heart houses the mind and soul.* This teaches us that the heart is directly related to intelligence. This is wisdom for every reader to consider in order to understand intelligence further.

This book teaches soul intelligence. A human being's soul has had hundreds of lifetimes. Your soul has been in many, many different occupations. In your past lives you could have been an author, a scientist, a teacher, a philosopher, a businessperson, a musician, an athlete, a leader of a country, a poet, a religious father, a doctor, a lawyer, or many other different occupations. In every life, your soul learned different wisdom and knowledge. Your soul gained further and further intelligence.

Your soul also learned lessons in all of its lifetimes. There is an ancient statement: *chi yi kui, zhang yi zhi.* This can be translated as: *Learn a lesson one time, gain wisdom one time.* This tells us that life is experience. In one life, you will learn many lessons and you will gain some wisdom from them. In hundreds of lifetimes, you will learn many more lessons but you will gain much more wisdom. Your soul will gain more and more intelligence.

A soul has intelligence in all its lifetimes. A soul has wisdom and knowledge in all its lifetimes. Your soul is the greatest resource for your intelligence. To realize this is the first step. To receive soul intelligence, wisdom, and knowledge to transform your life is the second step. To develop your soul intelligence, wisdom, and knowledge further is the third step.

Let me explain step by step.

The Soul Stores Intelligence, Wisdom, and Knowledge

There is a renowned story from ancient China. Malaria had spread over a big area of China. At that time, there was a lack of medicine and herbs. It was well known that the herb named Mao Er Chao was excellent for healing malaria. People rushed to get it from the ground to boil and drink it. The supply of this herb quickly ran out. A wise man said, "If we cannot find the herbs, speak the herbs." People started to chant: *I eat Mao Er Chao. I eat Mao Er Chao. Please heal me. Please heal me.* Just by doing this, people began to heal from malaria.

My beloved spiritual father, Master and Dr. Zhi Chen Guo, created Body Space Medicine, which is becoming more and more widespread in China and even in foreign countries. Body Space Medicine has served millions of people in China. It was credited with containing the SARS epidemic in China in 2003. The documentary film *Soul Masters* shows the essence of Body Space Medicine.

Master Guo teaches people to use the *message* (which is the soul) of herbs for healing. In Body Space Medicine, there are two herbs that are vital for healing all kinds of sickness. One is Gong Ying (dandelion). The other is Du Huo (angelica root). I have thousands of students who use the souls of these two herbs for soul healing by chanting *Gong Ying, Du Huo, Gong Ying, Du Huo. Gong Ying, Du Huo, Gong Ying, Du Huo.* People have received remarkable results by invoking the souls of these herbs in this way.

These two stories tell us that the soul, or message, of the herbs carries the healing power of the physical herbs. People can and have applied the message or soul of the herbs for healing and received great results. This is more evidence that the soul carries the power and the wisdom. The soul of the herb knows exactly what needs to be done for healing. We do not need to tell it what to do. The soul stores its own intelligence and has its own abilities to serve.

There are countless stories in the history of spiritual beings and spiritual traditions, including all religions and other traditions, about prayer. People pray to God, Jesus, Mary, buddhas, Taoist saints, holy saints, lamas, gurus, and more for healing and blessings.

There are countless stories of healings, blessings, and life transformations received. To pray is to ask a soul to heal, bless, and transform. Throughout history the results of prayer have told us that the soul has the power to serve. Time has proven that prayer works. Otherwise, how could prayer have lasted for thousands of years in history?

Prayer is great. Now the Divine has guided me to share with you and all humanity two new ways to receive spiritual blessings. One is Say Hello Healing. I shared this wisdom in my book *Soul Mind Body Medicine*.[4] The other is Soul Order, which I shared in chapter 4. These two new ways are the powerful soul secrets for receiving soul healing, prevention of sickness, blessing, rejuvenation, prolonging of life, transformation, and enlightenment.

The one-sentence secret of soul intelligence, wisdom, and knowledge is:

---

4. Zhi Gang Sha, 2006, *Soul Mind Body Medicine,* Novato: New World Library.

Soul carries power, intelligence, wisdom, and knowledge to
heal and transform life; what we need to do is ask.

Ask Soul Intelligence, Wisdom, and Knowledge to Transfer Power to Your Heart and Mind

We know that the soul has power. Our own soul has power. Holy saints, buddhas, healing angels, and all layers of spiritual fathers and mothers have their power to bless us. The simple and important wisdom is to directly ask your soul to bless your life and to deliver soul wisdom and knowledge to you. We can also ask all kinds of spiritual fathers and mothers to deliver their intelligence, wisdom, and knowledge to us. We can even directly ask the Divine to deliver wisdom and knowledge to us.

In April 2003, the Divine delivered the Universal Law of Universal Service to me. The Divine said that he is a universal servant. If the Divine is a universal servant, we are all universal servants. Every soul is a universal servant. A soul loves to serve. A soul loves to share. *The key is to ask.*

Let me first give you a few examples to review with you how to ask. Then in the rest of this chapter, I will give you practical tools for asking for soul intelligence, wisdom, and knowledge.

The first example:

> *Dear souls of my knees,*
> *I love you.*
> *You have the power to heal yourselves.*
> *Please heal my knees.*
> *Thank you.*

Then chant:

> *My knee souls heal my knees.*
> *My knee souls heal my knees.*

My knee souls heal my knees.
My knee souls heal my knees . . .

If you have a knee problem, chant for three to five minutes per time, three to five times per day, for healing your knee. If you have a serious or chronic knee problem, chant longer and more often—the longer the better. This is Say Hello Healing.

If you do not have a knee problem, how do you apply this wisdom? This is the way:

> *Dear souls of my knees,*
> *I love you.*
> *You have the power to prevent knee problems and rejuve-*
> *nate and prolong the life of my knees.*
> *Please do a good job.*
> *Thank you.*

Then chant:

> *My knee souls prevent my knee problems, rejuvenate and*
> *prolong the life of my knees.*
> *My knee souls prevent my knee problems, rejuvenate and*
> *prolong the life of my knees.*
> *My knee souls prevent my knee problems, rejuvenate and*
> *prolong the life of my knees.*
> *My knee souls prevent my knee problems, rejuvenate and*
> *prolong the life of my knees . . .*

Chant for three to five minutes per time, three to five times per day, for prevention of knee problems, and for rejuvenating and prolonging the life of your knees.

In the second example, I will again use the knees to deliver the wisdom. This example reviews what you have learned about Soul Orders. This is how to do it.

If you have a knee problem, send a Soul Order like this:

> *Dear souls of my knees,*
> *I send an order to you to heal my knees.*
> *Thank you.*

Then repeat:

> *My soul orders the souls of my knees to heal my knees.*
> *My soul orders the souls of my knees to heal my knees.*
> *My soul orders the souls of my knees to heal my knees.*
> *My soul orders the souls of my knees to heal my knees . . .*

At the end of the practice, show your great gratitude:

> *Thank you. Thank you. Thank you.*

Practice three to five minutes per time, three to five times per day, the more the better.

This Soul Order comes from your soul. In chapter 4, I gave you more wisdom and principles to follow for giving Soul Orders.

These two examples share the wisdom and practices of Say Hello Healing and Soul Order techniques. Soul has intelligence, power, and abilities. You can ask the soul for something. You can send an order from your soul. Either way, the soul will respond. The soul will serve.

Always remember gratitude and respect. Even when sending an order to the souls of your knees, do not forget to show your gratitude and respect. If you do not give sincere gratitude and respect to the souls of your knees, your knee souls will not listen to your order and will not serve you very well.

Expanding the wisdom from these two examples, you can offer healing, prevention, and rejuvenation to every part of your body in the same ways.

My third example is to transform every aspect of your life. Here is one way to do it:

> *Dear Divine Love soul and Divine Forgiveness soul* (permanent divine soul treasures that you received as you read chapter 2 on karma),
> *I love you, honor you, and appreciate you.*
> *Please heal and transform my* _____ (request any healing or life transformation you wish for any aspect of life, including relationships and finances).

Then chant, silently or aloud:

> *Divine Love soul and Divine Forgiveness soul heal and transform my* _____.
> *Divine Love soul and Divine Forgiveness soul heal and transform my* _____.
> *Divine Love soul and Divine Forgiveness soul heal and transform my* _____.
> *Divine Love soul and Divine Forgiveness soul heal and transform my* _____ . . .

Practice three to five minutes per time, three to five times per day, the more the better.

This third example is the divine way to heal and transform every aspect of life. The Divine gives the Divine's Soul Transplants to every reader for healing and life transformation. These divine soul treasures are priceless. We are honored and appreciative. We are speechless and our hearts are deeply touched.

How to Develop Soul Intelligence, Wisdom, and Knowledge

Every soul has power, intelligence, wisdom, and knowledge. Every soul can develop its power, intelligence, wisdom, and knowledge further and further. How? This section will give you the soul secrets for developing soul intelligence, wisdom, and knowledge.

BE A TOTAL GOLD SERVANT

To develop soul intelligence, there is only one vital one-sentence secret: *Serve humanity and all souls.*

The Divine serves. Every saint serves. Every spiritual father and mother serves. Every human being serves. Every soul serves.

There are different layers of service. Serve a little, serve more, or serve unconditionally. Different layers of service bring completely different results.

Serve a little. Gain a little soul intelligence and power.

Serve more. Gain more soul intelligence and power.

Serve unconditionally. Gain unlimited soul intelligence and power.

What is unconditional service to humanity and all souls? It is to remove all your selfishness, ego, attachments, and negative mind-sets and emotions. Your total heart and soul are dedicated to creating love, peace, and harmony for others, humanity, and all souls.

Heaven is most fair.

You are serving. Heaven is watching.

You are serving. Heaven is recording.

You are serving. Heaven is rewarding.

You are serving. Heaven is charging you with Heaven's light, liquid, and nutrients to boost your energy, stamina, vitality, and immunity.

You are serving. Heaven is healing your physical, emotional, mental, and spiritual bodies.

You are serving. Heaven is preventing sickness in all of your bodies.

You are serving. Heaven is rejuvenating and prolonging your life.

You are serving. Heaven is transforming every aspect of your life, including relationships and finances.

You are serving. Heaven is purifying your soul, heart, mind, and body.

You are serving. Heaven is increasing your soul intelligence, wisdom, and knowledge.

You are serving. Heaven is transferring soul power and abilities to bless and serve.

Most important:

You are serving. Heaven is uplifting your soul standing.

To uplift your soul standing is to reach soul enlightenment. There are different layers of soul enlightenment. Jesus, Mary, buddhas, Taoist saints, and all great teachers are continuing to serve, uplifting their soul standing one step after another. I will share the key soul secrets, wisdom, knowledge, and practices of soul enlightenment in chapter 13.

In order to help you increase your soul intelligence, wisdom, and knowledge, I will now reveal two major soul secrets for humanity: (1) the soul has a brain and (2) there are two secret soul centers in the body for soul intelligence, wisdom, and knowlege.

THE SOUL HAS A BRAIN

A human's soul is a golden light being. Within the soul, there are different parts. The soul has a brain. The soul has a heart. The soul has kidneys, liver cells, and lung DNA and RNA.

The soul's brain carries the soul's intelligence, wisdom, and knowledge from all lives. The soul's brain can develop its intelligence, wisdom, and knowledge further. There are two secret soul centers in the body for storing and developing soul intelligence, wisdom, and knowledge.

THE FIRST SECRET SOUL CENTER OF SOUL INTELLIGENCE, WISDOM, AND KNOWLEDGE

The first secret soul center is the Message Center. From the point at the middle of your sternum or breastbone (in traditional Chinese medicine, this is the Shan Zhong acupuncture point), go 2.5 *cun* inside your body. (The *cun* is a unit of measurement used in traditional Chinese medicine. One *cun* is defined as the width of the top joint of the thumb at its widest part. Although this varies from person to person, it is roughly equivalent to one inch.) That is the center of your Message Center, which is a fist-sized energy center. The Message Center is also known as the heart chakra.

The Message Center is one of the most important energy centers because it is the center for soul communication, Soul Language, healing, emotions, love, forgiveness, compassion, karma, life transformation, and soul enlightenment.

This first secret soul center of soul intelligence, wisdom, and knowledge stores all the messages from all your lifetimes. If your Message Center is highly developed, you can access all of the information from all of your previous lifetimes. Most important, you can access the soul intelligence, wisdom, and knowledge from all of your lifetimes.

How do you access this incredible warehouse? This is the way to do it:

> *Dear soul of my Message Center,*
> *I love you, honor you, and appreciate you.*
> *Could you deliver soul intelligence, wisdom, and knowledge to me?*

I am very grateful.
Thank you.

Then chant:

Soul of my Message Center delivers soul intelligence, wis-
dom, and knowledge to my heart and mind.
Soul of my Message Center delivers soul intelligence, wis-
dom, and knowledge to my heart and mind.
Soul of my Message Center delivers soul intelligence, wis-
dom, and knowledge to my heart and mind.
Soul of my Message Center delivers soul intelligence, wis-
dom, and knowledge to my heart and mind . . .

Practice three to five minutes per time, silently or aloud, the longer the better.

You may be very surprised after doing this practice. Your intelligence, wisdom, and knowledge could improve so much that it is beyond your comprehension. The way that you deal with your life, including healing, relationships, and finances, could be dramatically transformed.

Soul intelligence, wisdom, and knowledge are unlimited. The more you practice, the more you will receive from your soul.

Let me bring the teaching further. I will share the divine way to develop your soul intelligence, wisdom, and knowledge.

Prepare to receive the sixth Divine Soul Transplant offered to you in this book. Readers of the paperback edition of *Soul Communication,* the second book in my Soul Power Series, have already received this priceless divine soul:

Divine Soul Transplant of Divine Message Center

Sit up straight. Put the tip of your tongue near the roof of your mouth. Relax. Open your heart and soul.

Prepare!

Divine Soul Transplant of Divine Message Center
Silent download!

Close your eyes for thirty seconds to receive this major divine soul treasure.

> *Hao! Hao! Hao!*
> *Thank you. Thank you. Thank you.*

Thank you, Divine.

Now let me show you how to apply the divine way to develop your soul intelligence, wisdom, and knowledge.

> *Dear my divine soul of Divine Message Center,*
> *I love you, honor you, and appreciate you.*
> *Please deliver your intelligence, wisdom, and knowledge to*
> *my soul, heart, mind, and body.*
> *I am very grateful.*
> *Thank you.*

Then chant:

> *Divine Message Center transfers divine soul intelligence,*
> *wisdom, and knowledge to my soul, heart, mind, and*
> *body.*
> *Divine Message Center transfers divine soul intelligence,*
> *wisdom, and knowledge to my soul, heart, mind, and*
> *body.*

Divine Message Center transfers divine soul intelligence,
wisdom, and knowledge to my soul, heart, mind, and
body.
Divine Message Center transfers divine soul intelligence,
wisdom, and knowledge to my soul, heart, mind, and
body . . .

Practice three to five minutes per time, silently or aloud, the longer the better.

Hao! Hao! Hao!
Thank you. Thank you. Thank you.

The Divine Message Center soul has intelligence, wisdom, and knowledge beyond comprehension and imagination. Unlimited power and wisdom are within the Divine Message Center. Therefore, this practice is unlimited. The more you practice, the more benefits you will receive. Thank you, Divine, for delivering your Message Center to every reader. Can you imagine how generous it is of the Divine to give the Divine's soul treasures to humanity to develop our soul intelligence, wisdom, and knowledge? We are extremely honored. There are no words to express our greatest gratitude to the Divine.

THE SECOND SECRET SOUL CENTER OF SOUL INTELLIGENCE,
WISDOM, AND KNOWLEDGE

The second secret soul center is the abdomen. The abdomen is the foundation energy center for a human being, as it contains the Lower Dan Tian and Snow Mountain Area. It is also the foundational resource of matter for a human being, as digestion and absorption take place there.

Matter and energy constantly exchange and transform into each other. Generally speaking, matter is inside the cells. Cells are constantly vibrating, contracting and expanding. When cells contract, matter inside the cells transforms to energy outside the cells. When cells expand, energy outside the cells transforms to matter inside the cells.

The transformation between matter inside the cells and energy outside the cells is constant. Every time the transformation happens, the frequencies of the energy and the matter are transformed. Throughout history, energy and spiritual practitioners all around the world have developed conscious practices to refine the frequencies of their matter and energy. These practices, which are all part of Xiu Lian ("purification practice"), include meditation, chanting, exchanging energy with the universe, and more.

In *Soul Mind Body Medicine,* I revealed a new meditation called Universal Meditation. When you do Universal Meditation, all of the concentration and focus of your mind, any spiritual images you may see, and all the souls you invoke are placed in your lower abdomen. I did not reveal the major soul secret about the abdomen in that book because the time was not ready. Now the time is ready to tell humanity that our abdomen is the second secret soul center of soul intelligence, wisdom, and knowledge.

Why is the abdomen the second secret soul center? The abdomen has much more space than the Message Center. The abdomen is the biggest place in the body, especially for energy and spiritual practitioners, available to transform the frequencies of one's energy and matter. The goal of a Xiu Lian practitioner is to make the frequencies tinier and tinier. When this happens, power will become stronger and stronger. With proper energy and spiritual practice, rejuvenation for one's soul, mind, and body will happen naturally. One's systems, organs, cells, DNA, and RNA will improve and rejuvenate naturally. The intelligence of one's soul, heart, mind, and body will increase naturally.

Therefore, the abdomen is not only a foundation energy center and a matter center. It is also a purification and rejuvenation center. It communicates with the universe through the biggest space and with the biggest potential. Through Universal Meditation, soul communication with the universe, the Divine, and spiritual fathers and mothers from all layers of Heaven will improve one's soul intelligence one step at a time. This is why the abdomen is the second secret soul center for one's life.

The abdomen carries many soul potential messages that can increase your soul intelligence, wisdom, and knowledge. To understand this secret, you need to practice Universal Meditation. The potential for Universal Meditation is unlimited. The key is to invoke all your spiritual fathers and mothers from all layers of Heaven and also to invoke other souls to come into your abdomen. Then simply ask them to deliver soul intelligence, wisdom, and knowledge to your soul, heart, mind, and body.

Everyone has unlimited potential to increase soul intelligence. I wish you will develop your second secret soul center. Increase your soul intelligence. Heart, mind, and body intelligence will follow. Rejuvenate your soul, heart, mind, and body. Boost your energy, stamina, vitality, and immunity. Fulfill your soul journey and physical journey.

Let me share with you how to practice in this second secret soul center to develop your soul intelligence, wisdom, and knowledge:

Dear soul, mind, and body of my abdomen,
I love you, honor you, and appreciate you.
Thank you so much for being my second secret soul center.
Please deliver your soul potential messages to develop my
*   soul intelligence, wisdom, and knowledge.*
I am very grateful.
Thank you.

Then you could invoke Jesus, Mary, saints, buddhas, and your spiritual fathers and mothers in all layers of Heaven to come to your abdomen to deliver soul intelligence, wisdom, and knowledge to you. Say *hello* like this:

> *Dear Jesus, Mary, saints, buddhas, and all my spiritual fathers and mothers,*
> *I love you, honor you, and appreciate you.*
> *Please come to sit in my abdomen.*
> *Please deliver your soul intelligence, wisdom, and knowledge to my soul, heart, mind, and body.*
> *Thank you.*

Then chant, silently or aloud:

> *Deliver your soul potential messages and soul intelligence, wisdom, and knowledge to my soul, heart, mind, and body.*
> *Deliver your soul potential messages and soul intelligence, wisdom, and knowledge to my soul, heart, mind, and body.*
> *Deliver your soul potential messages and soul intelligence, wisdom, and knowledge to my soul, heart, mind, and body.*
> *Deliver your soul potential messages and soul intelligence, wisdom, and knowledge to my soul, heart, mind, and body . . .*

Practice for at least three minutes, the longer the better.

> *Hao! Hao! Hao!*
> *Thank you. Thank you. Thank you.*
> *Please return.*

You can invoke any great teacher to come into your abdomen to deliver soul intelligence, wisdom, and knowledge to you. You can invoke the souls of planets, stars, galaxies, and universes to come into your abdomen to deliver soul intelligence, wisdom, and knowledge to you.

Finally, let me share with you the divine way to receive divine soul intelligence, wisdom, and knowledge through your second secret soul center. We will use all of our divine gifts. Up to now, you have received six Divine Soul Downloads as gifts in this book:

- Divine Soul Transplant of Divine Love
- Divine Soul Transplant of Divine Forgiveness
- Divine Soul Transplant of Divine Peace
- Divine Soul Transplant of Divine Harmony
- Divine Soul Transplant of Divine Voice
- Divine Soul Transplant of Divine Message Center

Some of you may have received other Divine Soul Downloads previously. Many of my certified teachers and advanced students have received hundreds of Divine Soul Downloads.

This is the way to practice:

Dear all the divine souls I have received,
I love you, honor you, and appreciate you.
Please move to my abdomen to transfer divine soul intelli-
gence, wisdom, and knowledge to my soul, heart, mind
and body.
I am very grateful.
Thank you.

Then chant:

Divine souls deliver divine soul intelligence, wisdom, and
knowledge to my soul, heart, mind and body.
Divine souls deliver divine soul intelligence, wisdom, and
knowledge to my soul, heart, mind and body.

Divine souls deliver divine soul intelligence, wisdom, and
knowledge to my soul, heart, mind and body.
Divine souls deliver divine soul intelligence, wisdom, and
knowledge to my soul, heart, mind and body . . .

Practice for at least three minutes, the longer the better.

Hao! Hao! Hao!
Thank you. Thank you. Thank you.
Please return.

These techniques are vital. They directly come to the point. They reveal profound secrets for how you can develop your soul intelligence, wisdom, and knowledge. Most important, they reveal the top secret of how you can receive divine soul intelligence, wisdom, and knowledge.

The techniques may be too simple to believe, but these are the techniques and wisdom that the Divine is flowing through me as I am writing this book.

Grab them.

Apply them.

Benefit from them.

Thank you, Divine.

Thank you, souls in the universe.

Hao! Hao! Hao!

7

Soul Healing: Breakthrough Healing for the Twenty-first Century

ON MOTHER EARTH, there are many approaches to healing. We have modern conventional medicine, traditional Chinese medicine, Ayurvedic medicine, holistic medicine, integrative medicine, naturopathic medicine, mind-body medicine, energy medicine, Reiki, love medicine, Zhi Neng Medicine, Body Space Medicine, Soul Mind Body Medicine, and more. There are thousands of healing modalities worldwide. We honor each type of medicine. We honor each healing modality. We thank them for their contributions to help relieve the suffering of humanity, animals, and all souls.

For five thousand years, traditional Chinese medicine has emphasized *chi*, which is vital energy or life force. *The Yellow Emperor's Classic of Internal Medicine* states:

> *If chi flows, one is healthy.*
> *If chi is blocked, one is sick.*

If chi flows, blood follows.
If chi is blocked, blood is stagnant.

This top theory has guided traditional Chinese medicine for five thousand years. Traditional Chinese medicine has served millions of people in history with extraordinary results. Conventional modern medicine has also made great contributions for millions of people worldwide. Every medicine and every healing modality has made great contributions to serve humanity.

Soul Mind Body Medicine and *The Power of Soul* emphasize soul healing. Soul healing uses the power of soul to heal. Soul Mind Body Medicine gives a complete soul healing system to humanity. Many secrets, wisdom, knowledge, and practices of Soul Mind Body Medicine will continue to serve humanity. In this chapter and book, I summarize the key secrets, wisdom, and knowledge of soul healing. I will reveal a secret soul healing technique that is extremely simple yet powerful and profound.

Heal the Soul First; Then Healing of the Mind and Body Will Follow

After my whole life's study of modern medicine, traditional Chinese medicine, Zhi Neng Medicine, Body Space Medicine, and five thousand years of energy and spiritual healing secrets and wisdom, I have received divine teaching and inspiration to summarize the key secret and most important wisdom of soul healing:

Heal the soul first; then healing of the mind and body will
follow.

A human has a body soul. Every system has a soul. Every organ has a soul. Every cell has a soul. Every DNA and RNA has a soul. Every space between the cells has a soul. When an organ is sick, the soul of the organ is also sick. The soul healing secret is to heal the soul of the organ. If the soul of the organ is healed, the organ will be healed.

If a system is in disorder, the soul of the system is sick. Heal the soul of the system. The healing of the system will follow.

If the cells' function is abnormal, the souls of the cells are disordered. Heal the souls of the cells first; then the cells' function will be restored.

This is the new concept of soul healing. Why am I confident in saying soul healing is breakthrough healing for the twenty-first century? Because soul healing will bring remarkable healing for chronic pain and life-threatening conditions. Soul healing will empower humanity to self-heal. My teaching is:

> *I have the power to heal myself.*
> *You have the power to heal yourself.*
> *Together we have the power to heal the world.*

Because everything has a soul, soul healing is not limited to human beings. A company has a soul. If a company is in disorder, the soul of the company is sick. In order to improve the company's performance, heal the soul of the company. A city has a soul. A country has a soul. If a city or a country is in disorder, healing the soul of the city or country is essential for the healing of the city or country.

Soul is the boss of a human being. Similarly, the soul of a city and the soul of a country are the boss of the city and the country. Be aware of this wisdom. If you develop your spiritual abilities highly, you can directly communicate with the Divine to confirm this wisdom.

Sacred and Secret Formulas for Soul Healing

The most powerful technique for doing soul healing is the Soul Order. I explained this wisdom and its principles in chapter 4. You can send a Soul Order to yourself. Your organ can send a Soul Order to itself.

Generally speaking, do not send a Soul Order to others. You may not have the authority to send an order to others. Your spiritual standing may not be high enough to send a Soul Order to others.

To heal others, including group healing and remote healing, use the techniques I shared in my book *Soul Mind Body Medicine*. These techniques include Say Hello Healing, One-Minute Healing with the mantra *Unconditional Universal Service*, Universal Meditation, the Four Power Techniques using One Hand Near, One Hand Far, and more.

Say you want to offer healing to your sister in Canada, your uncle in Europe, and your friend in Australia. You can offer a group soul healing to these three people simultaneously and remotely. You do not have to connect with them by telephone. You do not have to see them using webcams. You can offer them a remote group healing anytime from anywhere.

Here is a simple example of how to do remote group healing using Say Hello Healing. It can serve as one basic model of soul healing for others.

> Say hello: *Dear soul, mind, and body of* (name the three people; you could also name their organs or parts of the body that need healing),
> Give love: *I love you.*
> Make an affirmation: *You have the power to heal your-selves.*
> Give an order: *Do a good job!*
> Express gratitude: *Thank you.*

Then chant a healing mantra, such as the mantra San San Jiu Liu Ba Yao Wu, Chinese for the sacred healing number 3396815 (see p. 73), for a few minutes:

> *San San Jiu Liu Ba Yao Wu*
> *San San Jiu Liu Ba Yao Wu*

San San Jiu Liu Ba Yao Wu
San San Jiu Liu Ba Yao Wu . . .

This is Sound Power.

At the same time, visualize golden light radiating in the three persons' bodies. Visualize them as being in perfect health. This is Mind Power.

Hao! Hao! Hao!
Thank you. Thank you. Thank you.

You can adapt this example to offer soul healing to a group of hundreds or even thousands of people at once. This is how simple soul healing for others can be. The other soul healing techniques of Soul Mind Body Medicine are equally simple, but they are all powerful and effective.

Soul Order is the simplest and most powerful way to do soul self-healing. If you want to heal, for example, the circulatory system, this is the sacred and secret formula for soul healing:

> *Soul Order heals the soul, mind, and body of my circula-*
>   *tory system.*
> *Soul Order heals the soul, mind, and body of my circula-*
>   *tory system.*
> *Soul Order heals the soul, mind, and body of my circula-*
>   *tory system.*
> *Soul Order heals the soul, mind, and body of my circula-*
>   *tory system . . .*

Practice by chanting like this for at least three minutes, silently or aloud, the longer the better.

This is the one-sentence soul healing secret. Chanting this mantra activates a Soul Order to heal your circulatory system. This Soul Order is given by your body soul to the soul, heart, mind, and body of your circulatory system.

How does it work? Follow the wisdom. *Heal the soul first; then healing of the mind and body will follow.*

You can practice this repeatedly until you recover. Chant many times a day and for as many days as you need. Chronic pain and life-threatening conditions may need many hours and days of diligent practice. Be persistent. Have confidence.

Many people could receive instant benefits. If you do not receive instant results, do not be disappointed. Not receiving or not perceiving results does not mean nothing has changed. It does not mean healing has not occurred. Blockages at the soul, mind, and body levels could have shifted already; you simply have not yet felt or seen the shifts in your body. Continue to practice. You could feel the change soon. However, feeling better does not mean you have recovered. You need to continue to practice until you recover completely.

This is the power of soul. This is breakthrough healing for humanity. You may not have had enough experience with Soul Power. Try it. Experience it. Benefit from it. In the last few years, I have received thousands of stories of remarkable healing results from soul healing. I share these soul healing secrets freely with humanity to empower all human beings to heal themselves. The results speak for themselves.

Soul Healing for Bodily Systems, Organs, Cells, Cell Units, DNA, RNA, and Spaces

Apply the one-sentence soul healing secret to heal any part of your body.

For systems, if you have, for example, an immune system disorder, chant:

Soul Order heals the soul, mind, and body of my immune
   system.
Soul Order heals the soul, mind, and body of my immune
   system.
Soul Order heals the soul, mind, and body of my immune
   system.
Soul Order heals the soul, mind, and body of my immune
   system . . .

Practice by chanting like this for at least three to five minutes, silently or aloud, the longer the better. Practice every day, as many times a day as you can, until you recover.

For organs, say you have a heart problem. Chant like this:

Soul Order heals the soul, mind, and body of my heart.
Soul Order heals the soul, mind, and body of my heart.
Soul Order heals the soul, mind, and body of my heart.
Soul Order heals the soul, mind, and body of my
   heart . . .

Practice by chanting like this for at least three to five minutes, silently or aloud, the longer the better. Practice every day, as many times a day as you can, until you recover.

For cells and cell units, say you have degenerative changes in your brain. Chant like this:

Soul Order heals and rejuvenates the soul, mind, and body
   of my brain cells and cell units.
Soul Order heals and rejuvenates the soul, mind, and body
   of my brain cells and cell units.
Soul Order heals and rejuvenates the soul, mind, and body
   of my brain cells and cell units.

Soul Order heals and rejuvenates the soul, mind, and body
of my brain cells and cell units . . .

Practice by chanting like this for at least three to five minutes, silently or aloud, the longer the better. Practice every day, as many times a day as you can, until you recover.

For DNA and RNA, say you have a genetic condition of your blood. Chant like this:

Soul Order heals the soul, mind, and body of my blood
cells' DNA and RNA.
Soul Order heals the soul, mind, and body of my blood
cells' DNA and RNA.
Soul Order heals the soul, mind, and body of my blood
cells' DNA and RNA.
Soul Order heals the soul, mind, and body of my blood
cells' DNA and RNA . . .

Practice by chanting like this for at least three to five minutes, silently or aloud, the longer the better. Practice every day, as many times a day as you can, until you recover.

All illnesses are due to energy blockages and spiritual blockages in the spaces in the body, both the bigger spaces between the organs and the smaller spaces between the cells. You can offer soul healing by removing the blockages in the spaces. Here is an example for healing a common cold:

Soul Order heals my cold by clearing the spaces in my
lungs.
Soul Order heals my cold by clearing the spaces in my
lungs.
Soul Order heals my cold by clearing the spaces in my
lungs.

> *Soul Order heals my cold by clearing the spaces in my lungs . . .*

Practice by chanting like this for at least three to five minutes, silently or aloud, the longer the better. Practice every day, as many times a day as you can, until you recover.

You can also boost your energy, stamina, vitality, and immunity. Here is an example:

> *Soul Order boosts my energy, stamina, vitality, and immunity.*
> *Soul Order boosts my energy, stamina, vitality, and immunity.*
> *Soul Order boosts my energy, stamina, vitality, and immunity.*
> *Soul Order boosts my energy, stamina, vitality, and immunity . . .*

Practice by chanting like this for at least three to five minutes, silently or aloud, the longer the better. Practice whenever you want a boost in energy. Practice whenever you feel you are starting to get sick. How is your energy now?

> *Hao! Hao! Hao!*
> *Thank you. Thank you. Thank you.*

Generally speaking, the technique of soul healing by using a Soul Order is very powerful. Sometimes, it does take time to recover completely.

An important wisdom I need to share here is that if you have major bad karma, you may not receive the results you wish. The Divine gave me a clear teaching. You and anybody can clear your own karma. To clear your karma, you must offer unconditional universal service. But it takes time to clear karma on your own. It could take lifetimes to clear major bad karma. The Divine gave me the honor to offer divine karma cleansing in July 2003. Since then I have offered divine karma cleansing to thousands of people worldwide. The results are heart-touching and leave me speechless. Be very clear. When I offer karma cleansing service, I do not clear one's karma. The Divine clears one's bad karma. I am extremely honored to be a servant to offer this service to humanity.

Soul Healing for Emotions

Five thousand years ago, traditional Chinese medicine stated:

> *Liver connects with anger.*
> *Heart connects with anxiety and depression.*
> *Spleen connects with worry.*
> *Lungs connect with sadness and grief.*
> *Kidneys connect with fear.*

The liver, heart, spleen, lungs, and kidneys are part of the physical body. Anger, anxiety and depression, worry, sadness and grief, and fear are part of the emotional body. You can see clearly that the physical body and emotional body are closely related. When a physical organ— for example, the liver—is sick, it is easy to be angry. On the other hand, if a person has lots of anger, it will hurt the liver. If you heal the liver, you can heal anger. To heal anger will benefit your liver. Here is how to do soul healing for emotional imbalances.

Apply the one-sentence soul healing secret to heal anger like this:

> *Soul Order heals the soul, mind, and body of my liver and*
> *   removes my anger.*
> *Soul Order heals the soul, mind, and body of my liver and*
> *   removes my anger.*

> *Soul Order heals the soul, mind, and body of my liver and*
> *removes my anger.*
> *Soul Order heals the soul, mind, and body of my liver and*
> *removes my anger . . .*

Practice by chanting like this for at least three to five minutes, the longer the better. Practice every day, as many times a day as you can, until your anger is removed.

Apply the one-sentence soul healing secret to heal anxiety and depression like this:

> *Soul Order heals the soul, mind, and body of my heart and*
> *clears my anxiety and depression.*
> *Soul Order heals the soul, mind, and body of my heart and*
> *clears my anxiety and depression.*
> *Soul Order heals the soul, mind, and body of my heart and*
> *clears my anxiety and depression.*
> *Soul Order heals the soul, mind, and body of my heart and*
> *clears my anxiety and depression . . .*

Practice by chanting like this for at least three to five minutes, the longer the better. Practice every day, as many times a day as you can, until your anxiety and depression are cleared.

If you have anxiety but not depression, just chant:

> *Soul Order heals the soul, mind, and body of my heart and*
> *removes my anxiety.*
> *Soul Order heals the soul, mind, and body of my heart and*
> *removes my anxiety.*
> *Soul Order heals the soul, mind, and body of my heart and*
> *removes my anxiety.*
> *Soul Order heals the soul, mind, and body of my heart and*
> *removes my anxiety . . .*

If you have depression but not anxiety, just chant:

Soul Order heals the soul, mind, and body of my heart and
clears my depression.
Soul Order heals the soul, mind, and body of my heart and
clears my depression.
Soul Order heals the soul, mind, and body of my heart and
clears my depression.
Soul Order heals the soul, mind, and body of my heart and
clears my depression . . .

Apply the one-sentence soul healing secret to heal worry like this:

Soul Order heals the soul, mind, and body of my spleen
and removes my worry.
Soul Order heals the soul, mind, and body of my spleen
and removes my worry.
Soul Order heals the soul, mind, and body of my spleen
and removes my worry.
Soul Order heals the soul, mind, and body of my spleen
and removes my worry . . .

Practice by chanting like this for at least three to five minutes, the longer the better. Practice every day, as many times a day as you can, until your worry is removed.

Apply the one-sentence soul healing secret to heal grief like this:

Soul Order heals the soul, mind, and body of my lungs and
grief.
Soul Order heals the soul, mind, and body of my lungs and
grief.
Soul Order heals the soul, mind, and body of my lungs and
grief.

> *Soul Order heals the soul, mind, and body of my lungs and grief . . .*

Practice by chanting like this for at least three to five minutes, the longer the better. Practice every day, as many times a day as you can, until your grief is healed.

Apply the one-sentence soul healing secret to heal fear like this:

> *Soul Order heals the soul, mind, and body of my kidneys and removes my fear.*
> *Soul Order heals the soul, mind, and body of my kidneys and removes my fear.*
> *Soul Order heals the soul, mind, and body of my kidneys and removes my fear.*
> *Soul Order heals the soul, mind, and body of my kidneys and removes my fear . . .*

Practice by chanting like this for at least three to five minutes, the longer the better. Practice every day, as many times a day as you can, until your fear is removed.

These practical techniques are priceless sacred and secret soul treasures for healing all emotional imbalances.

Apply them. Experience them. Benefit from them.

Soul Healing for Mental Disorders and Mental Blockages

Many people suffer from mental disorders and other blockages of the mind. These conditions include lack of confidence, mental confusion, lack of clarity and concentration, holding mind-sets, attitudes, and beliefs that are not beneficial, ego, ADHD (attention deficit hyperactivity disorder), and more serious mental illnesses such as schizophrenia and bipolar disorder.

Let me give you several examples of how to apply the one-sentence secret soul healing formula for healing mental disorders and mental blockages.

Here is an example to boost your confidence:

Soul Order heals my mind to boost my confidence.
Soul Order heals my mind to boost my confidence.
Soul Order heals my mind to boost my confidence.
Soul Order heals my mind to boost my confidence . . .

Practice by chanting like this for at least three to five minutes, the longer the better. Practice every day, as many times a day as you can, until your confidence is restored.

The next example is to release the mind-set of overthinking. It is very important for your spiritual journey that you release this mind-set. A spiritual being must have faith and trust in his true spiritual fathers and mothers and in the Divine. How can you commit completely to being a total GOLD and unconditional universal servant if you have doubt and overanalyze? Releasing this mind-set will have great benefits for your spiritual journey and for your physical, emotional, and mental journeys as well. Use the one-sentence secret soul healing formula like this:

Soul Order heals my mind to remove my doubt.
Soul Order heals my mind to remove my doubt.
Soul Order heals my mind to remove my doubt.
Soul Order heals my mind to remove my doubt . . .

Practice by chanting like this for at least three to five minutes, the longer the better. Practice every day, as many times a day as you can, to remove your doubt in order to become a better and better total GOLD and unconditional universal servant.

Next, use the one-sentence secret soul healing formula to heal ADHD:

Soul Order heals my ADHD.
Soul Order heals my ADHD.
Soul Order heals my ADHD.
Soul Order heals my ADHD . . .

Practice by chanting like this for at least three to five minutes, the longer the better. Practice every day, as many times a day as you can, until your ADHD is healed.

The one-sentence secret soul healing formula is the simplest soul healing technique. It is the most powerful soul healing technique available to you by using your own Soul Power. It has no side effects. It is so simple yet so powerful and profound.

I wish you will practice well.

I wish you will enjoy the benefits.

Soul Healing for Spiritual Blockages

In chapter 2 on karma, I explained that spiritual blockages, which are bad karma, are the root cause of difficulties in every aspect of life, including health, broken relationships, financial challenges, and more. I also explained that there is only one way to clear your own bad karma: offer unconditional universal service to humanity and society. The more you serve, the faster you will clear your bad karma. Only through great service, together with your greatest commitment to be a total GOLD and unconditional universal servant, can you clear your own bad karma.

You also carry the karma of your systems, organs, cells, cell units, DNA, RNA, and spaces. Their karma directly affects their health, rejuvenation, and life, which in turn directly affects your health, rejuvenation, and life.

Divine Soul Transplants for systems, organs, cells, cell units, DNA, RNA, and spaces can clear the karma of the systems, organs, cells, cell units, DNA, RNA, and spaces because these divine souls are karma free. Therefore, Divine Soul Transplants have created remarkable and heart-touching results worldwide. But Divine Soul Transplants do not clear all of your bad karma.

The soul healing techniques to remove spiritual blockages are unique. The Divine guided me at this moment to teach you *not* to send a Soul Order to clear your spiritual blockages, because *it will not work*.

Bad karma is your spiritual debt accumulated from all the mistakes you have made in this life and past lives. The Akashic Records contain all of your mistakes and all of your good service from all of your lifetimes. All of your good service in this life and previous lives will bless every aspect of your present life and future lives. All of the bad karma you have accumulated from all of your unpleasant service will block every aspect of your present life and future lives. The Divine made a clear spiritual law: Anyone who has bad karma *must* offer good service to others in order to clear the bad karma. That is why sending a Soul Order to clear spiritual blockages will not work.

People sometimes ask me if they can clear bad karma for other people. If you want to clear bad karma for someone else, you have to pay that person's spiritual debt. It is like taking out a mortgage to buy a house. If you want to own the house, you have to pay off the mortgage. Very rarely will someone else pay off your mortgage for you. You have to handle your own physical debt. Bad karma is your spiritual debt. Generally speaking, you must pay your spiritual debt yourself by learning lessons, which could be blockages in any aspect of your life.

If you want to pay another person's spiritual debt, you will carry the lessons that person was supposed to learn. Let me share two stories to illustrate this.

Several years ago, a high-level spiritual being shared her story. She had very advanced spiritual abilities. She saw her ancestors' karma. With great love, care, and compassion, she told the Akashic Records, Heaven, and the Divine, "I would like to take care of the karma of my ancestors." She willingly took on their spiritual debts. Although in apparent good health, unfortunately she was diagnosed with cancer within a year and lost her life within two years.

I heard the second story when I visited Phoenix a few years ago. The general manager of a large company shared this story. Her father was in the intensive care unit of a hospital with a serious case of asthma. He depended on a respiratory machine to maintain his breathing. While she was visiting her father in the ICU, the doctor announced that her father's lung function was so bad that his case was hopeless. Her father could die in days or even hours.

This woman understood her father's spiritual blockages. In front of her father, she connected with Heaven and the Akashic Records and said, "Dear Akashic Records, please cut my life by five years and give them to my father. Let my father live a few more years." Within a half hour, her father did not need the respiratory machine anymore. Soon he was able to leave the hospital. He lived for a few more years.

There is a divine way to cleanse one's bad karma. Since July 2003 I have traveled worldwide to many countries and cities. For example, in 2006 I traveled for six consecutive months, holding more than 140 events on four continents. Almost every evening, wherever I was, I held a workshop. At almost every workshop I offered karma cleansing for the participants.

How do I offer karma cleansing? The Divine gave me the honor to offer this service in July 2003 as a servant of humanity and the Divine. The Divine told me that when I call the Divine, the Divine will heal and bless. The Divine asked me to offer the Divine's Soul Transplants to create Divine Healers, Divine Writers, and more. The Divine told me that I could offer *the Divine's* karma cleansing. In other words, I offer karma cleansing service for the Divine. When I offer this service, the Divine goes to the Akashic Records to send an order to clear one's personal or ancestral karma. When this Divine Order for karma cleansing is given, the Divine pays one's spiritual debt by using spiritual currency, which is virtue. The Divine pays for the one who has harmed others in all of his or her lives. The one who receives the karma cleansing is forgiven his or her spiritual debt. The others who were harmed by that person also receive divine virtue to be blessed for their future lives.

Karma cleansing is not a prayer. The divine karma cleansing service is a divine payment for one's spiritual debt. Why did the Divine ask me to offer this service? The purpose is to remind humanity that if you serve well, you are blessed. If you serve unpleasantly, you will learn lessons.

Karma is easy to understand. As I said before, if you kill a person, the police have to catch you and give you the lesson that physical law requires. If you commit other crimes, you have to learn a lesson in the physical world. Otherwise, there would be no order and no peace in society and the world. It is similar in the spiritual world. If there were no spiritual law about karma, there would be no order and no peace in the spiritual world.

The Divine offers divine karma cleansing service to educate and bless humanity. I am extremely honored that the Divine chose me as the Divine's servant to offer this service. I am truly humbled.

To clear spiritual blockages for yourself, you must offer unconditional service to others. Some sicknesses are caused by energy blockages alone; these are easy to heal. Minor spiritual blockages are also easy to heal. You serve; you are forgiven. Major bad karma takes time and effort to clear. Many chronic and life-threatening conditions are related to heavy karma. It is important to understand this for one's recovery. Remember always to offer love, peace, and harmony to others. This good service will give you tremendous healing and blessing to remove your spiritual blockages.

In chapter 2 on karma, I shared a major soul secret for clearing your own karma, which is to chant the Divine Soul Song "Love, Peace and Harmony."

Lu La Lu La Li
Lu La Lu La La Li

Lu La Lu La Li Lu La
Lu La Li Lu La
Lu La Li Lu La

I love my heart and soul
I love all humanity
Join hearts and souls together
Love, peace and harmony
Love, peace and harmony

This Divine Soul Song has power beyond thought and words. It will serve your healing. It will help remove your spiritual blockages. It would be best to sit for a half hour or more and focus on singing this Divine Soul Song. The more you sing it, the more benefits you will receive.

This Divine Soul Song is a divine treasure for all humanity and all souls. This Divine Soul Song is a divine calling for humanity in Mother Earth's transition period. This Divine Soul Song is the golden key to healing and transforming life. In the last few years, I have had hundreds of students seriously chant this Divine Soul Song. The results have been really heart-touching. You *have* to try this. If you do this practice seriously, you will understand the power of this song.

Here is insight into this Divine Soul Song from one of my Divine Master Teachers and Healers, Dr. Peter Hudoba, a former neurosurgeon in Canada:

> *In September 2005 Master Sha received a new divine gift: Soul Song. He immediately offered this to all of humanity on his website with a daily healing and blessing message. One could listen to the Soul Song and then hear the message translated by one of Master Sha's students. It was a powerful and priceless new gift.*
>
> *Soul Song immediately activated my heart. I became fasci-*

nated with this treasure and appreciated it more and more as time went by. I was most captivated by the special Divine Soul Song "Love, Peace and Harmony." From the first time I heard it, I enjoyed its soothing power. I recorded onto a CD Master Sha singing this song during one of his teleclasses and listened to it frequently. This little song has such strong power over my mind that I can enter a deep meditative state in a few seconds while listening to it. I enjoyed the exquisite beauty of Master Sha's singing for a whole year as I became more and more attuned to this powerful song.

Then came the breakthroughs. The first one occurred in August 2006 while I was teaching with Master Sha in New York. I was explaining the deep meaning of this song and started to sing it. Suddenly there was a huge explosion and the universe literally opened in front of me. I was facing the soul of the universe, a huge bright star. At the moment I sang the words I love all humanity, *the question came to me: "Who is loving humanity?" The answer was: "The Divine." As I sang* Join hearts and souls together, *another question came: "Who is offering humanity to join hearts and souls together?" And again the answer came: "The Divine." Singing the words* Love, peace and harmony *was accompanied by a powerful jolt. Everything around me ceased to exist and I became part of the Source— one shining ocean of light. At that instant, I fully recognized that I was singing the Divine's Soul Song, inviting all of humanity to come and receive his blessing of love and light—how very precious and exquisite!*

Since that "aha" moment, I deeply understood the power of this Soul Song and would always sing it to bless everyone in my classes. The room would vibrate with light and it would leave a profound effect on everyone. Two months later, while teaching a Soul Mind Body Medicine Workshop in Vancouver, a second "aha" moment came to me. We had been chanting the mantra Ar Mi Tuo Fuo for twenty minutes and our hearts and minds were filled with light. As I started singing the first sentence of the Soul Song "Love, Peace and Harmony," my mind suddenly and completely opened. I realized that the words I love my heart and soul *are a precise instruction on how to practice enlightenment. We bring love to our hearts and our souls to heal them. This is an inward-oriented practice. We are bringing in love and light and increasing our purity.*

As we heal, we move toward enlightenment. But that is not enough. Once we come to this stage, we need to change our focus and move our practice outward to love all of humanity totally and selflessly. That is the significance of the next line, I love all humanity. *When we can achieve this, we can move to the next level.*

Join hearts and souls together *is a precise instruction of enlightenment. We bring the soul up from the Lower Dan Tian to the Message Center and join the heart and soul together. This is enlightenment. Then we move to the next level of joining our hearts and souls with the hearts and souls of all humanity. Once we master this, we move again to the next level of joining our hearts with all hearts in the universe and our souls with all souls in the universe. We achieve total unity and oneness with everyone and everything. We are now reaching the highest levels of enlightenment. This is our practice.*

We strive toward this for hundreds and thousands of lifetimes and millions of years until we achieve the last stage of Love, peace and harmony *with all souls. By achieving this first within and then directing it outward through the universes, we bring love, peace, and harmony to every heart and every soul in the universe.*

Since these realizations, I have not been the same. This little song completely transformed me on two occasions. In August 2006, it brought me to unity with the Source. Then, later

*in the fall, my heart opened further and I started to truly love
all souls in the universe.*

This Soul Song is the most exquisite message from the Divine. It is guidance and at the same time it is a powerful and practical tool for following and achieving the guidance. When you are able to meld completely with "Love, Peace and Harmony," you are expressing the enlightenment of the highest soul, the Divine. For me, it is still a practice. It will take some time to master this level but this Soul Song is the guidance and the tool for the goal I am striving to accomplish. It is such a beautiful gift that the Divine has given to all souls in all universes—a simple, profound truth of total love and light.

Dr. Hudoba's story shares the power and the insight of this Divine Soul Song. It is a divine mantra for the twenty-first century and the Soul Light Era.

Practice it.

Experience it.

Transform from it.

Enlighten from it.

Hao! Hao! Hao!

Thank you. Thank you. Thank you.

Soul Prevention of Sickness

$\mathcal{F}$IVE THOUSAND YEARS ago, *The Yellow Emperor's Classic of Internal Medicine,* the authority textbook of traditional Chinese medicine, stated:

> *The best doctor is one who can treat sickness before it occurs, instead of after it appears.*

When people get sick, they wish they had remained healthy. When a sickness becomes severe, people wish the sickness had been healed at an earlier stage. It is very important to prevent sickness.

The previous chapter shared the most important soul secret for healing. This chapter will share the most important soul secret for preventing sickness. Anyone who is sick wishes to know this secret. Millions of people who are healthy wish to know this secret also. I am delighted to share the soul secret of soul prevention of sickness.

Prevent Sickness of the Soul First; Then Prevention of All Sicknesses Will Follow

To really understand the power of soul, you must highly develop your soul communication channels. Therefore, my book *Soul Communication* is vital for a spiritual being to study and practice. If you have highly developed soul communication channels, you will grasp the secret I am about to share right away.

The one-sentence soul secret of prevention of sickness is:

> *Prevent sickness of the soul first; then prevention of all*
> *sicknesses will follow.*

How did I discover this secret? You might find my story very interesting. As a medical intuitive, over my whole life's practice, whenever I could see a dark shadow in someone's organ or part of the body, I would ask the person, "Do you feel anything wrong with your body?" Many times, they told me what they were suffering from. It always matched what I saw.

In 2008 I was teaching a weekend workshop in Germany for about two hundred people. I talked about soul healing. I walked down the center aisle of the lecture hall, stopped suddenly, and pointed to a man sitting on the aisle. I asked him to stand up. I didn't know his name. I had never met him before but I saw a big dark shadow at the top of his chest. I told everybody, "This man has a blockage in this area," and I pointed to the top of his chest. He immediately reported, "This is amazing. How did Master Sha know I have a blockage here? Since childhood, I have had challenges in my lungs. They have bothered me for many, many years. I even had an operation on my chest."

I offered this man a Divine Soul Operation to clear the dark shadow. A surgeon uses a scalpel to operate. A Soul Operation is not a medical service. It uses divine light to open the body spiritually and remove blockages. The Divine offers the Soul Operation. I am just a vehicle. I also offered the man a Divine Soul Transplant of Divine Lungs, which means that the Divine replaces the original souls of the lungs with new divine souls of lungs. (If you have read chapters 2, 3, and 6 of this book, you have already received six Divine Soul Transplants offered within those pages. In chapter 14, Divine Soul Downloads and Divine Soul Orders, I will explain Divine Soul Transplants in more detail.) After receiving the Soul Operation and the Soul Transplant, the man instantly felt a release and opening in his chest. He was very moved and touched.

This story shares the wisdom that I saw a dark shadow in the man's lungs, which corresponded with discomfort he had in that area for his whole life. Sometimes when I see a dark shadow in a specific part of someone's body and I ask that person if he or she has any problem there, the person may not feel any sickness or discomfort in that area at all. That was something that I was very curious about for many years. Finally, when I saw this situation again, I did soul communication. I asked the soul of the organ, "What does this dark shadow mean?" The answer was, "The soul of the organ is sick." I had this "aha" moment a few years ago. Afterward I was able to observe many other cases. They all confirmed this major secret. Now is the time to share this major secret for prevention of sickness. This one-sentence secret is:

> *Before any system, any organ, any cell, any DNA or RNA becomes sick, the soul of the system, organ, cell, DNA or RNA becomes sick.*

Soul sickness is indicated precisely by changes in the color of the soul. The normal color of the soul is gold. When the color changes to gray or dark, the soul is sick. For example, I saw a dark shadow in the liver area for a person. This person felt no discomfort at all in his liver area. A medical examination indicated that his liver function was completely normal. In conventional medicine, this is absolutely correct: his liver was normal. However, with the teaching of this chapter, you now know that his liver was not normal because the soul of his liver was already abnormal.

The soul of the liver is the boss of the mind and body of the liver. If the soul of the liver is sick, it will influence the energy flow of the liver. The energy flow of the liver will be blocked. Then sickness of the liver will occur. There are many kinds of sicknesses of the liver according to conventional modern medicine but, as Soul Mind Body Medicine teaches, they are all due to energetic and spiritual blockages. For soul healing, it does not matter what kind of sickness of the liver you have. Focus on healing the soul of the liver first; then healing of the mind and body of the liver will follow.

This chapter shares the soul secrets, wisdom, knowledge, and practices of soul prevention of sickness. To prevent sickness is to prevent sickness of the soul first, such as the soul of an organ. In my example, to prevent sickness of the liver is to remove the dark shadow in the liver. If the dark shadow of the liver is removed, the soul of the liver is healed; sicknesses of the liver are prevented. This wisdom can be used for any system, any organ, any cell, and any part of the body.

Let me share a simple technique, which may seem too simple to believe. I gave this secret in my book *Soul Wisdom*. It is called Soul Tapping.

Practice like this for soul prevention of sickness of the liver.

Put your right palm gently over your liver area and tap your liver with your palm. At the same time, chant:

> *Golden liver light prevents liver sickness.*
> *Golden liver light prevents liver sickness.*
> *Golden liver light prevents liver sickness.*
> *Golden liver light prevents liver sickness . . .*

If your Third Eye is open, you will see your liver shining golden light. If your Third Eye is not open, visualize golden light radiating from your liver.

Chant and tap for at least three to five minutes, the longer the better.

There is an ancient spiritual healing secret:

Golden light shines; all sickness disappears.

The Benefits of Soul Prevention of Sickness

The power of soul prevention of sickness is obvious. Millions of people catch colds. Millions of people suffer from back pain. Millions of people suffer from headaches. Millions of people suffer from depression and anxiety. Millions of people suffer from cancer. Preventing sickness is vital for good health. If we really knew how to prevent sickness—and did it—we could reduce the suffering of humanity beyond any expectation.

For example, let me share a soul secret to prevent the common cold:

For prevention of the common cold, there are two areas that are very important to tap. The first is the top of the back, just below the neck. Tap there for one minute as you chant and visualize:

Golden light shines in my upper back.
Golden light shines in my upper back.
Golden light shines in my upper back.
Golden light shines in my upper back . . .

Next, tap your upper chest with both hands for one minute. Chant and visualize:

Golden light clears my lungs.
Golden light clears my lungs.
Golden light clears my lungs.
Golden light clears my lungs . . .

Everybody understands the importance of prevention of sickness. If you prevent sickness, you do not need to suffer. If humanity prevents sickness, humanity does not need to suffer. The significance of this is indescribable.

How to Do Soul Prevention of Sickness for the Physical, Emotional, Mental, and Spiritual Bodies

Soul prevention can be applied to any sickness of the physical, emotional, mental, and spiritual bodies, including serious and even life-threatening sicknesses. Let me share a soul secret to prevent cancer.

To prevent cancer is to prevent sickness of the soul. The heart houses the soul and mind. The soul secret to preventing cancer is to work on the soul of the heart. Tap your heart, chant, and visualize:

> *Golden light prevents.*
> *Golden light prevents.*
> *Golden light prevents.*
> *Golden light prevents . . .*

Tapping your heart as you chant *golden light prevents* is a secret soul prevention technique for preventing not only cancer. In fact, this technique can be applied to prevent all sicknesses, whether of the physical, emotional, mental, or spiritual body.

ONE-MINUTE SOUL TAPPING TECHNIQUE FOR PREVENTION

To do soul prevention for the physical body, tap the area in which you wish to prevent sickness. For example, if you want to prevent sicknesses of your stomach, gallbladder, small intestine, and kidneys, then do Soul Tapping in each of these areas for one minute. (Note that the different colors of light in these practices are examples. In fact, they can be used interchangeably. This is divine flexibility.)

1. Tap your stomach for one minute, chant, and visualize:

   Golden light shines.
   Golden light shines.
   Golden light shines.
   Golden light shines . . .

2. Tap your gallbladder for one minute, chant, and visualize:

   Rainbow light vibrates.
   Rainbow light vibrates.
   Rainbow light vibrates.
   Rainbow light vibrates . . .

3. Tap your small intestine for one minute, chant, and visualize:

   Purple light shines.
   Purple light shines.
   Purple light shines.
   Purple light shines . . .

4. Tap your kidneys for one minute, chant, and visualize:

   Crystal light vibrates.
   Crystal light vibrates.
   Crystal light vibrates.
   Crystal light vibrates . . .

For the emotional body, major unbalanced emotions include anger, depression and anxiety, worry, sadness, and fear. Here is how to do soul prevention for these emotional imbalances:

1. To prevent anger, tap your liver for one minute, chant, and visualize:

   Rainbow light vibrates.
   Rainbow light vibrates.
   Rainbow light vibrates.
   Rainbow light vibrates . . .

2. To prevent depression and anxiety, tap your heart for one minute, chant, and visualize:

   Purple light shines.
   Purple light shines.
   Purple light shines.
   Purple light shines . . .

3. To prevent worry, tap your spleen for one minute, chant, and visualize:

   Crystal light vibrates.
   Crystal light vibrates.
   Crystal light vibrates.
   Crystal light vibrates . . .

4. To prevent sadness, tap your lungs for one minute, chant, and visualize:

   Golden light vibrates.
   Golden light vibrates.
   Golden light vibrates.
   Golden light vibrates . . .

5. To prevent fear, tap your kidneys for one minute, chant, and visualize:

Rainbow light shines.
Rainbow light shines.
Rainbow light shines.
Rainbow light shines . . .

To do soul prevention for the mental and spiritual bodies is to do Soul Tapping for your heart, because the heart houses the mind and soul.

Tap your heart, chant, and visualize at the same time:

Golden light vibrates.
Golden light vibrates.
Golden light vibrates.
Golden light vibrates.

Rainbow light radiates.
Rainbow light radiates.
Rainbow light radiates.
Rainbow light radiates.

Purple light shines.
Purple light shines.
Purple light shines.
Purple light shines.

Crystal light illuminates.
Crystal light illuminates.
Crystal light illuminates.
Crystal light illuminates.

In summary, you can do soul prevention of sickness for the physical, emotional, mental, and spiritual bodies by applying the One-Minute Soul Tapping Technique together with chanting and visualization at the same time. The technique is extremely simple. The benefits are great. You can apply this technique anytime, anywhere. You can chant silently or aloud. One minute of practice can prevent sickness. Of course, the longer you practice, the better.

I wish this soul prevention chapter will transform your health.

Hao! Hao! Hao!

Thank you. Thank you. Thank you.

Soul Rejuvenation and Longevity

Four thousand three hundred years ago, there was an ancient saint named Peng Zu. Throughout Chinese history, Peng Zu has been renowned and venerated as the *Shou Xing*. ("Shou" means *long life*. "Xing" means *star*.) This "Long Life Star" lived for 880 years. He was the teacher of Lao Zi, the founder of Taoism. Peng Zu created *Zhi Qi Zhi Tao,* which means The Tao of Qi. He created *Tao Tu,* the Map of Tao, which reveals:

- *Xu wu sheng yi qi*—Emptiness produces one *chi*. This one *chi* includes *yuan chi* (origin chi), *ling chi* (soul chi), *qing chi* (clean chi), and more. This one *chi* initiates, grows, and flourishes—like a sunrise. It represents yang, youth, and vigor.
- *Yi qi sheng yin yang*—One *chi* produces yin and yang.
- *Yin yang sheng wan wu*—Yin and yang produce everything.
- *Wan wu gui yi qi*—Everything returns to one *chi*. This

one *chi* is waste *chi*, which is heavy or turbid *chi* (*zuo chi*). Like a sunset, it represents yin, age, and decline.
- *Yi qi gui xu wu*—One *chi* returns to emptiness.

In 2002, at the Fifth World Congress on Qigong in San Francisco, I met a very powerful master, Dr. and Professor Dehua Liu. I learned that he is the only 372nd-generation lineage holder of Peng Zu and Lao Zi. I was very impressed with the profound secrets and wisdom Master Liu holds and with his healing power. I was honored to be ac-

Tao Tu, The Map of Tao

Figure 2. *Tao Tu,* the Map of Tao

cepted by him as the first 373rd-generation lineage holder of Peng Zu and Lao Zi.

I have learned profound secrets from Master Liu. Peng Zu developed many secret practices that have given me many "aha" moments. They include much great wisdom and many practices for rejuvenation and long life.

I have learned from other top Taoist masters in China. They do not want me to give their names. They want to be quiet servants. I also have learned Buddhist secrets for rejuvenation and long life from one of the top Buddhist monks in the world. Of course, I learned the most profound secrets, wisdom, and knowledge from Master Zhi Chen Guo, my adoptive father, the founder of Zhi Neng Medicine and Body Space Medicine. I have learned much secret wisdom of Xiu Lian, Zhi Neng Medicine, and Body Space Medicine from Master Guo. He taught me the integration of Taoism, Buddhism, and Confucianism with modern medicine and traditional Chinese medicine.

I started my tai chi journey at age six. I started to learn qi gong at age ten. I started to practice kung fu at age twelve. I studied the *I Ching* and feng shui at a young age. I studied modern conventional medicine to become an M.D. and traditional Chinese medicine to become a doctor of traditional Chinese medicine. My whole life's study and experience have made me understand the preciousness of the secret and sacred wisdom, knowledge, and practice of Taoism, Buddhism, Confucianism, and Master Guo's teaching for rejuvenation and longevity.

Since July 2003, when I was chosen as a divine servant, vehicle, and channel, the Divine taught me the way of divine rejuvenation. I am honored and delighted to summarize all of my life's learning from all of my masters and the Divine to share the most profound secrets of rejuvenation and long life.

Rejuvenate the Soul First; Then Rejuvenation of the Mind and Body Will Follow

After my whole life's study, practice, and mastery of energy secrets and secret soul wisdom, knowledge, and practice for rejuvenation and long life, including Taoism, Buddhism, Confucianism, tai chi, qi gong, the *I Ching*, feng shui, and Xiu Lian, as well as being a servant of the Divine, I reached a major "aha" moment only a few years ago.

The one-sentence secret for rejuvenation is:

Rejuvenate the soul first; then rejuvenation of the mind and body will follow.

In the previous chapter, I shared the secret of soul prevention of sickness. When I see a dark shadow on the soul of someone's organ, I know the soul of that organ is already sick. But the organ may or may not be physically sick. If the organ is not yet physically sick, I know that physical sickness of the organ will follow. To prevent that sickness is to heal the soul of the organ. To heal the soul of the organ is to transform the dark shadow on the soul of the organ to golden or rainbow light.

If your organ is healthy and you would like to rejuvenate it, the secret soul wisdom is to rejuvenate the soul of the organ first. Then rejuvenation of the organ will follow.

Let me directly give you a secret practice to rejuvenate your soul, mind, and body together.

To prepare for this practice, sit up straight. You may sit on the floor or on a cushion in the full-lotus or half-lotus position, if you are able, or with your legs crossed naturally. If this is not comfortable or convenient for you, you may sit on a chair. Be comfortable, but keep your back straight, and do not lean back against the chair.

Place the tip of your tongue close to, but not touching, the roof of your mouth. Contract your anus for a few seconds, and then relax it.

The placement of the tongue and the brief contraction of the anus are techniques to promote the smooth flow of energy throughout your body, which is important for maximizing the benefits of this and other practices. Gently close your eyes partially. Completely relax your soul, heart, mind, and body.

Form a little "O" with your hands and fingers, with the tips of your thumbs almost touching and with the fingers of your right hand resting on the fingers of your left hand. This is the Universal Connection Hand Position (figure 3). Place your hands on your lower abdomen, just below the navel.

Figure 3. Universal Connection Hand Position

As you practice, visualize golden or rainbow light in your entire body, from head to toe and skin to bone, while you chant.

Start:

> *Rejuvenate my body soul.*
> *Rejuvenate my body soul.*
> *Rejuvenate my body soul.*
> *Rejuvenate my body soul . . .*

Practice for at least three minutes, the longer the better. This is a Soul Order to rejuvenate your body soul. When you do this, what will happen? Your body soul will shine and vibrate. Your spiritual fathers and mothers in Heaven will pour light into your body soul to rejuvenate it. At the same time, they will pour light into your mind and body to rejuvenate them. The universe will pour light into your soul, mind, and body to rejuvenate them.

Next, visualize and chant:

> *Rejuvenate the souls of my systems.*
> *Rejuvenate the souls of my systems.*
> *Rejuvenate the souls of my systems.*
> *Rejuvenate the souls of my systems . . .*

Practice for at least three minutes, the longer the better. You will receive the same blessings from your spiritual fathers and mothers and the universe.

Next, visualize and chant:

> *Rejuvenate the souls of my organs.*
> *Rejuvenate the souls of my organs.*
> *Rejuvenate the souls of my organs.*
> *Rejuvenate the souls of my organs . . .*

Practice for at least three minutes, the longer the better. You will continue to receive blessings from your spiritual fathers and mothers in Heaven and the universe.

Continue to visualize and chant:

> *Rejuvenate the souls of my cells, cell units, DNA, RNA,*
> *and spaces between the cells.*
> *Rejuvenate the souls of my cells, cell units, DNA, RNA,*
> *and spaces between the cells.*
> *Rejuvenate the souls of my cells, cell units, DNA, RNA,*
> *and spaces between the cells.*

Rejuvenate the souls of my cells, cell units, DNA, RNA,
and spaces between the cells . . .

Practice for at least three minutes, the longer the better.

After the above steps, practice in this way for at least three minutes:

Rejuvenate my body soul, system souls, organ souls, cell
souls, cell unit souls, DNA and RNA souls, and space
souls.
Rejuvenate my body soul, system souls, organ souls, cell
souls, cell unit souls, DNA and RNA souls, and space
souls.
Rejuvenate my body soul, system souls, organ souls, cell
souls, cell unit souls, DNA and RNA souls, and space
souls.
Rejuvenate my body soul, system souls, organ souls, cell
souls, cell unit souls, DNA and RNA souls, and space
souls . . .

When you practice rejuvenating the souls of your body, systems, organs, cells, cell units, DNA, RNA, and spaces, their minds and bodies will automatically be rejuvenated. All these souls shine. Heaven responds to your practice. All universes nourish you.

The secret of rejuvenation really is this simple. The benefits are beyond comprehension.

Now let me give you an even simpler technique to rejuvenate your soul, mind, and body. You can do this anytime, anywhere. You can do it when you are lying down, sitting, walking, or jogging. Chant silently:

Rejuvenate my soul, mind, and body.
Rejuvenate my soul, mind, and body.

Rejuvenate my soul, mind, and body.
Rejuvenate my soul, mind, and body . . .

This is the one-sentence secret Soul Order for rejuvenation of your soul, mind, and body. Do this now as you are sitting and reading this book. Close your eyes and chant silently. At the same time, visualize golden or rainbow light shining from head to toes and from skin to bones. Spend a few minutes to receive the benefits.

For many of you, this is too simple to believe. But remember, as I explained in chapter 2, *Da tao zhi jian*. The Big Way is extremely simple. Remember this teaching. Most important is to put it into practice. I deliver the wisdom for the Divine and Heaven. You must take your own responsibility and make the effort to practice in order to receive the benefits. I wish you will do a good job. I wish you will receive great rejuvenation for your soul, mind, and body.

Hao! Hao! Hao!
Thank you. Thank you. Thank you.

Prolong the Life of the Soul First; Then Longevity Will Follow

In September 2007 I was in Japan to teach a workshop on Soul Mind Body Medicine. Suddenly, the Divine gave me a long-life formula for humanity. Generally speaking, when the Divine gives me sacred wisdom and knowledge, the Divine doesn't inform me ahead of time. The Divine gives sacred wisdom and practices to me suddenly, which always surprises and inspires me. On September 15, 2007, the Divine told me to teach that there are ten areas of the body that must be highly developed in order to prolong life. These ten energy centers and organs are also vital for healing, prevention of sickness, and rejuvenation. They are:

- Lower Dan Tian
- Snow Mountain Area

- Liver
- Heart
- Spleen
- Lungs
- Kidneys
- Spinal Cord
- Brain
- Small Intestine

The Divine showed me why these ten areas are vital for long life.

DIVINE LONG LIFE SECRET WISDOM

Lower Dan Tian

The Lower Dan Tian is a foundational energy center that is centered 1.5 *cun* below the navel and 2.5 *cun* inside the abdomen. (Again, the *cun* is a unit of measurement used in traditional Chinese medicine. One *cun* is defined as the width of the top joint of the thumb at its widest part. Although this varies from person to person, it is roughly equivalent to one inch.) The Lower Dan Tian is roughly the size of your fist.

The Lower Dan Tian is:

- foundational for one's energy, vitality, stamina, and immunity
- key for long life
- the postnatal energy center
- the seat of the soul for most human beings

The foundation of a one-hundred-story skyscraper must be very different from the foundation of a two-story house. The stronger your Lower Dan Tian, the better foundation you have for long, long life.

Snow Mountain Area

The Snow Mountain Area is the other key foundational energy center. To locate it, imagine a line going from your navel straight back through your body. Along this line, go two-thirds of the way from your navel to your back. From this point, go straight down about 2.5 *cun*. That is the center of this fist-sized energy center.

The Snow Mountain Area is:

- the prenatal energy center, which connects with the energy of your parents and other ancestors and holds the essence of their energy
- key to quality of life and long life
- the energy source for the kidneys
- energy food for the brain and Third Eye
- the starting point of four major meridians (Ren, Du, Dai, Chong) of traditional Chinese medicine

Snow Mountain Area is a Buddhist term. Taoists call this area the Golden Urn. Traditional Chinese medicine calls it the Ming Men area, which means the *gate of life*. In yoga, this area is known as kundalini. Developing the power of the Snow Mountain Area is vital for every aspect of life.

Liver

According to the Five Elements theory as applied in traditional Chinese medicine, the liver is the wood organ. It is a yin organ. Its paired yang organ is the gallbladder. Liver energy opens on the eyes and connects with the tendons. The liver connects with the emotional body of anger. The liver stores blood and regulates the flow of chi and blood in the body. It regulates emotions. The chi flow of the liver is closely related with menstruation in women. Rejuvenating and prolonging the life of the liver benefits all of these aspects.

Heart

In traditional Chinese medicine, the heart is the fire organ. It is a yin organ. Its paired yang organ is the small intestine. Heart energy opens on the tongue and connects with the blood vessels. The heart connects with the emotional body of depression and anxiety. The heart is in charge of blood, blood vessels, and blood circulation. The heart houses the mind and soul. Disorders of the heart can deeply affect the functions of the brain. Rejuvenating and prolonging the life of the heart benefits all of these aspects.

Spleen

In traditional Chinese medicine, the spleen is the earth organ. It is a yin organ. Its paired yang organ is the stomach. Spleen energy opens on the mouth and gums and connects with the muscles. The spleen connects with the emotional body of worry. The spleen is in charge of transportation and transformation of the food essence and body fluids. It has a key role in digestion and absorption. It also assists in metabolizing water. Rejuvenating and prolonging the life of the spleen benefits all of these aspects.

Lungs

In traditional Chinese medicine, the lungs are the metal organ. It is a yin organ. Its paired yang organ is the large intestine. Lung energy opens on the nose and connects with the skin. The lungs connect with the emotional body of sadness and grief. The lungs are in charge of chi, including respiratory chi and whole body chi. The lungs assist in metabolizing water. Rejuvenating and prolonging the life of the lungs benefits of all these aspects.

Kidneys

In traditional Chinese medicine, the kidneys are the water organ. It is a yin organ. Its paired yang organ is the urinary bladder. Kidney energy opens on the ears and connects with the bones. The kidneys connect with the emotional body of fear. The kidneys are in charge of metabolizing water. The kidneys deeply influence the reproductive system and its organs. Rejuvenating and prolonging the life of the kidneys benefits of all these aspects.

Spinal Cord

In conventional modern medicine, the central nervous system consists of the brain and spinal cord. In traditional Chinese medicine, the spinal cord plays a major role in rejuvenation and longevity.

Secret Wisdom for Long Life in Traditional Chinese Medicine

In traditional Chinese medicine, the spinal cord is named *sui*. *Sui* produces and nourishes the brain. In the secret energy and spiritual wisdom of the Xiu Lian journey, the kidneys produce *jing*, which is the essence of matter. *Jing* produces and nourishes *sui*, which is the spinal cord. *Sui* produces and nourishes the brain, which is named *nao*. Traditional Chinese medicine teaches that *nao* is the sea of *sui*. The process is:

	sheng (produces)		*sheng* (produces)	
Jing (kidneys)	⟶	*Sui* (spinal cord)	⟶	*Nao* (brain), the Sea of *Sui*
Stream		River		Ocean

This chart explains the connection of the kidneys, spinal cord, and brain. The production and nourishment referred to are at the level of energy. Do not think that the physical kidneys produce the physical spinal cord. If you think about energy production and transformation from *jing* to *sui* to *nao,* and if you understand that energy produces and transforms further and further, then you understand *jing* to *sui* to *nao* right away. There are different layers of energy. As in a factory, there is a production line to transform raw materials into a finished product, step by step.

This simple chart is a five-thousand-year-old traditional Chinese medicine secret for rejuvenation and prolonging life. This wisdom comes from *The Yellow Emperor's Classic of Internal Medicine*. This book shares many secrets of soul wisdom, knowledge, and practice. Do not think *The Yellow Emperor's Classic of Internal Medicine* is only a book about traditional Chinese medicine. This book is full of spiritual wisdom and secrets that go far beyond traditional Chinese medicine.

Secret Wisdom for Long Life in Taoism

If you know a little about Taoism, you may have heard about its most important and essential teaching, which is *jing chi shen xu tao*. However, many serious practitioners can study and practice Taoism for an entire lifetime without really understanding the wisdom and knowledge of *jing chi shen xu tao*. They may not know how to practice and achieve *jing chi shen xu tao*.

Let me reveal the secret now. *Jing chi shen xu tao* is matter, energy, and soul transformations. They carry different frequencies of matter, energy, and soul. In *jing chi shen xu tao,* matter, energy, and soul frequencies transform into finer and finer frequencies. This process of transformation is the evolution of matter, energy, and soul.

The first level, *jing,* carries the least refined matter, energy, and soul frequency. If you do not do Xiu Lian, which is energy and spiritual practice to advance your energy and spiritual journey, your frequency may stay at this level.

Therefore, to move from *jing* to *chi* to *shen* to *xu* to *tao* is to move to different layers of frequency of matter, energy, and soul, progressively finer and finer. A high-level spiritual being can immediately determine what layer your frequency is in. Only a being who does Xiu Lian can reach finer and finer frequencies. When you can move your frequency to *tao*, you have reached a very refined frequency of matter, energy, and soul. When you reach the *tao* frequency, you have reached the soul frequency.

That is not the ultimate, however. You must know that *tao* itself has layers. Soul enlightenment is the first major layer of *tao*. There are higher and higher layers of soul enlightenment. The highest enlightenment is to reach the frequency of the divine realm. Then your soul has reached the layer in which reincarnation stops. This layer carries the finest frequency. In this layer, you will serve humanity and all souls only in your soul form. You will not return to a physical form as a human being anymore. This is the divine direction for rejuvenation, transformation, prolonging life, and enlightenment. In the Soul Healing and Enlightenment retreats and Advanced Soul Healing and Enlightenment retreats that I hold regularly, I offer divine soul enlightenment and advanced soul enlightenment services for humanity.

At this moment, the Divine is giving me a completely new teaching that I only knew part of before. This new wisdom greatly enhances my previous wisdom. This is another "aha" moment!

- *Jing* is the matter, energy, and soul essence of the kidneys.
- *Chi* is the matter, energy, and soul essence of the spinal cord.
- *Shen* is the matter, energy, and soul essence of the brain.
- *Xu* is the matter, energy, and soul essence of the heart.

- *Tao* is the matter, energy, and soul essence of the soul.
- Soul enlightenment is to reach the high level and refined frequency of *tao*.
- Ultimate soul enlightenment is to reach the divine realm, which is the highest *tao* and the most refined frequency.

This is the new divine teaching that I just received. I am deeply touched and moved. For many, many years, I have not completely realized how to move from *jing* to *chi* to *shen* to *xu* to *tao*. The picture is so clear now in my heart and mind. At the same time, the Divine taught me a best practice to move from *jing* to *chi* to *shen* to *xu* to *tao*. Later in this chapter, I will share this sacred practice with you and humanity.

Brain

The brain is obviously a key for rejuvenation and long life. Aging is often accompanied by poor memory, slowed responses, difficulty thinking clearly, lack of energy, loss of flexibility, and deterioration of all bodily functions. In many cultures, these are considered to be the inevitable results and characteristics of aging. All of these behavioral changes and declines in bodily functions show that the brain is getting older. Therefore, to rejuvenate and prolong the life of the brain is vital to prolonging one's life.

According to conventional modern medicine, the brain is in charge of the central nervous system and controls and regulates all bodily functions. In particular, the functions and levels of all hormones in the body are regulated by the brain. The brain also regulates all functions in the body through the sympathetic and parasympathetic nervous systems. The brain regulates all physiological and metabolic functions in the body. Doing Xiu Lian for the brain improves not only memory and other faculties of the mind; it also improves hormonal balance, cell metabolism, and the function of every system and every organ.

We can see that to rejuvenate and prolong the life of the brain is essential to prolonging life.

Small Intestine

In modern conventional medicine, the small intestine is the vital organ for digestion and absorption. It is also emphasized in traditional Chinese medicine, where the small intestine is characterized as having the function of *fen qing mi zhuo*. "Fen" means *to separate*. "Qing" means *the essence of food*. "Mi zhuo" means *waste. Fen qing mi zhuo* means to distinguish the essence of food from the waste matter of food and transfer the waste to the large intestine for disposal. This function is very important for rejuvenation and prolonging life.

I have explained the importance of these ten areas for prolonging life. As I was flowing this chapter, the Divine gave me new wisdom. Now let me share how to practice to prolong life.

There are two ways to practice these ten areas to prolong life. The first is to practice without Divine Soul Downloads. The other is to practice with Divine Soul Downloads.

PRACTICE WITHOUT DIVINE SOUL DOWNLOADS

It is best to do this practice in a standing position. However, it is perfectly fine to practice in a sitting position (in a full lotus or half lotus, or with naturally crossed legs, or on a chair). You can even practice lying down. However, whenever you practice lying down, do not chant aloud. Chant silently; otherwise, you will drain your energy.

Let's practice.

Stand with your feet shoulder-width apart. Bend your knees a little. Keep your back straight. Put both palms on your Lower Dan Tian area, below your navel. Do Soul Tapping of your Lower Dan Tian area with both palms. At the same time, visualize golden or rainbow light in your Lower Dan Tian and chant. (You will use the same technique for all ten areas.)

Start!

Heal and boost Lower Dan Tian power.
Heal and boost Lower Dan Tian power.
Heal and boost Lower Dan Tian power.
Heal and boost Lower Dan Tian power.

Rejuvenate soul, mind, and body of Lower Dan Tian.
Rejuvenate soul, mind, and body of Lower Dan Tian.
Rejuvenate soul, mind, and body of Lower Dan Tian.
Rejuvenate soul, mind, and body of Lower Dan Tian.

Prolong life of soul, mind, and body of Lower Dan Tian.
Prolong life of soul, mind, and body of Lower Dan Tian.
Prolong life of soul, mind, and body of Lower Dan Tian.
Prolong life of soul, mind, and body of Lower Dan Tian.

Next do Soul Tapping simultaneously of your Lower Dan Tian with one palm (left palm for men, right palm for women, because left belongs to yang and right belongs to yin) and your Snow Mountain Area with the other palm (right for men, left for women). The palm that taps your Lower Dan Tian will remain there for the rest of the practice. At the same time, visualize golden or rainbow light in your Snow Mountain Area and chant.

Start!

Heal and boost Snow Mountain Area power.
Heal and boost Snow Mountain Area power.
Heal and boost Snow Mountain Area power.
Heal and boost Snow Mountain Area power.

Rejuvenate soul, mind, and body of Snow Mountain Area.
Rejuvenate soul, mind, and body of Snow Mountain Area.
Rejuvenate soul, mind, and body of Snow Mountain Area.
Rejuvenate soul, mind, and body of Snow Mountain Area.

Prolong life of soul, mind, and body of Snow Mountain Area.
Prolong life of soul, mind, and body of Snow Mountain Area.
Prolong life of soul, mind, and body of Snow Mountain Area.
Prolong life of soul, mind, and body of Snow Mountain Area.

Next do Soul Tapping simultaneously of your Lower Dan Tian (left palm for men, right palm for women) and your liver (other palm). At the same time, visualize golden or rainbow light in your liver and chant.

Start!

Heal and boost liver power.
Heal and boost liver power.
Heal and boost liver power.
Heal and boost liver power.

Rejuvenate soul, mind, and body of liver.
Rejuvenate soul, mind, and body of liver.
Rejuvenate soul, mind, and body of liver.
Rejuvenate soul, mind, and body of liver.

Prolong life of soul, mind, and body of liver.
Prolong life of soul, mind, and body of liver.

Prolong life of soul, mind, and body of liver.
Prolong life of soul, mind, and body of liver.

Next do Soul Tapping simultaneously of your Lower Dan Tian (left palm for men, right palm for women) and your heart (other palm). At the same time, visualize golden or rainbow light in your heart and chant.

Start!

Heal and boost heart power.
Heal and boost heart power.
Heal and boost heart power.
Heal and boost heart power.

Rejuvenate soul, mind, and body of heart.
Rejuvenate soul, mind, and body of heart.
Rejuvenate soul, mind, and body of heart.
Rejuvenate soul, mind, and body of heart.

Prolong life of soul, mind, and body of heart.
Prolong life of soul, mind, and body of heart.
Prolong life of soul, mind, and body of heart.
Prolong life of soul, mind, and body of heart.

Next do Soul Tapping simultaneously of your Lower Dan Tian (left palm for men, right palm for women) and your spleen (other palm). At the same time, visualize golden or rainbow light in your spleen and chant.

Start!

Heal and boost spleen power.
Heal and boost spleen power.

Heal and boost spleen power.
Heal and boost spleen power.

Rejuvenate soul, mind, and body of spleen.
Rejuvenate soul, mind, and body of spleen.
Rejuvenate soul, mind, and body of spleen.
Rejuvenate soul, mind, and body of spleen.

Prolong life of soul, mind, and body of spleen.
Prolong life of soul, mind, and body of spleen.
Prolong life of soul, mind, and body of spleen.
Prolong life of soul, mind, and body of spleen.

Next do Soul Tapping simultaneously of your Lower Dan Tian (left palm for men, right palm for women) and your lungs (other palm). At the same time, visualize golden or rainbow light in your lungs and chant.

Start!

Heal and boost lung power.
Heal and boost lung power.
Heal and boost lung power.
Heal and boost lung power.

Rejuvenate soul, mind, and body of lungs.
Rejuvenate soul, mind, and body of lungs.
Rejuvenate soul, mind, and body of lungs.
Rejuvenate soul, mind, and body of lungs.

Prolong life of soul, mind, and body of lungs.
Prolong life of soul, mind, and body of lungs.
Prolong life of soul, mind, and body of lungs.
Prolong life of soul, mind, and body of lungs.

Next do Soul Tapping simultaneously of your Lower Dan Tian (left palm for men, right palm for women) and your kidneys (other palm). At the same time, visualize golden or rainbow light in your kidneys and chant.

Start!

> *Heal and boost kidney power.*
> *Heal and boost kidney power.*
> *Heal and boost kidney power.*
> *Heal and boost kidney power.*
>
> *Rejuvenate soul, mind, and body of kidneys.*
> *Rejuvenate soul, mind, and body of kidneys.*
> *Rejuvenate soul, mind, and body of kidneys.*
> *Rejuvenate soul, mind, and body of kidneys.*
>
> *Prolong life of soul, mind, and body of kidneys.*
> *Prolong life of soul, mind, and body of kidneys.*
> *Prolong life of soul, mind, and body of kidneys.*
> *Prolong life of soul, mind, and body of kidneys.*

Next do Soul Tapping simultaneously of your Lower Dan Tian (left palm for men, right palm for women) and the back of your neck (other palm). At the same time, visualize golden or rainbow light in your spinal cord and chant.

Start!

> *Heal and boost spinal cord power.*
> *Heal and boost spinal cord power.*
> *Heal and boost spinal cord power.*
> *Heal and boost spinal cord power.*
>
> *Rejuvenate soul, mind, and body of spinal cord.*
> *Rejuvenate soul, mind, and body of spinal cord.*

Rejuvenate soul, mind, and body of spinal cord.
Rejuvenate soul, mind, and body of spinal cord.

Prolong life of soul, mind, and body of spinal cord.
Prolong life of soul, mind, and body of spinal cord.
Prolong life of soul, mind, and body of spinal cord.
Prolong life of soul, mind, and body of spinal cord.

Next do Soul Tapping simultaneously of your Lower Dan Tian (left palm for men, right palm for women) and the top of your head (other palm). At the same time, visualize golden or rainbow light in your brain and chant.

Start!

Heal and boost brain power.
Heal and boost brain power.
Heal and boost brain power.
Heal and boost brain power.

Rejuvenate soul, mind, and body of brain.
Rejuvenate soul, mind, and body of brain.
Rejuvenate soul, mind, and body of brain.
Rejuvenate soul, mind, and body of brain.

Prolong life of soul, mind, and body of brain.
Prolong life of soul, mind, and body of brain.
Prolong life of soul, mind, and body of brain.
Prolong life of soul, mind, and body of brain.

Finally, do Soul Tapping simultaneously of your Lower Dan Tian (left palm for men, right palm for women) and your navel area (other palm). At the same time, visualize golden or rainbow light in your small intestine and chant.

Start!

> *Heal and boost small intestine power.*
> *Heal and boost small intestine power.*
> *Heal and boost small intestine power.*
> *Heal and boost small intestine power.*
>
> *Rejuvenate soul, mind, and body of small intestine.*
> *Rejuvenate soul, mind, and body of small intestine.*
> *Rejuvenate soul, mind, and body of small intestine.*
> *Rejuvenate soul, mind, and body of small intestine.*
>
> *Prolong life of soul, mind, and body of small intestine.*
> *Prolong life of soul, mind, and body of small intestine.*
> *Prolong life of soul, mind, and body of small intestine.*
> *Prolong life of soul, mind, and body of small intestine.*
>
> *Hao! Hao! Hao!*
> *Thank you. Thank you. Thank you.*

This is a very practical way to heal, boost the power, rejuvenate, and prolong the life of these ten major organs and energy centers. If these ten areas are transformed, the whole body will be transformed. This is a powerful practice for prolonging life. This is the Divine Guidance that I received: share this sacred practice for prolonging life.

PRACTICE WITH DIVINE SOUL DOWNLOADS

Now I will offer the seventh Divine Soul Download in this book:

Divine Soul Transplant of Divine Lower Dan Tian

Sit up straight. Put the tip of your tongue near the roof of your mouth. Relax. Open your heart and soul.

Prepare!

Divine Soul Transplant of Divine Lower Dan Tian
Silent download!

Close your eyes for thirty seconds to receive this major divine soul treasure.

> *Hao! Hao! Hao!*
> *Thank you. Thank you. Thank you.*

Thank you, Divine.

Practice like this with your new Divine Lower Dan Tian soul:

Stand with your feet shoulder-width apart. Bend your knees a little. Keep your back straight. Put both palms on your Lower Dan Tian area, below your navel. Do Soul Tapping of your Lower Dan Tian area with both palms. At the same time, visualize golden or rainbow light in your Lower Dan Tian and chant.

Start!

> *Dear my divine soul of Divine Lower Dan Tian,*
> *I love you, honor you, and appreciate you.*
> *Turn on, please.*
>
> *Divine Lower Dan Tian heals and boosts the power of my*
> *　　Lower Dan Tian.*
> *Divine Lower Dan Tian heals and boosts the power of my*
> *　　Lower Dan Tian.*
> *Divine Lower Dan Tian heals and boosts the power of my*
> *　　Lower Dan Tian.*
> *Divine Lower Dan Tian heals and boosts the power of my*
> *　　Lower Dan Tian.*

*Divine Lower Dan Tian rejuvenates the soul, mind, and
  body of my Lower Dan Tian.*
*Divine Lower Dan Tian rejuvenates the soul, mind, and
  body of my Lower Dan Tian.*
*Divine Lower Dan Tian rejuvenates the soul, mind, and
  body of my Lower Dan Tian.*
*Divine Lower Dan Tian rejuvenates the soul, mind, and
  body of my Lower Dan Tian.*

*Divine Lower Dan Tian prolongs the life of the soul, mind,
  and body of my Lower Dan Tian.*
*Divine Lower Dan Tian prolongs the life of the soul, mind,
  and body of my Lower Dan Tian.*
*Divine Lower Dan Tian prolongs the life of the soul, mind,
  and body of my Lower Dan Tian.*
*Divine Lower Dan Tian prolongs the life of the soul, mind,
  and body of my Lower Dan Tian.*

Hao! Hao! Hao!
Thank you. Thank you. Thank you.

Now I will offer the eighth Divine Soul Download in this book:

Divine Soul Transplant of Divine Snow Mountain Area

Sit up straight. Put the tip of your tongue near the roof of your
mouth. Relax. Open your heart and soul.
Prepare!

Divine Soul Transplant of Divine Snow Mountain Area
Silent download!

Close your eyes for thirty seconds to receive this major divine soul
treasure.

Hao! Hao! Hao!
Thank you. Thank you. Thank you.

Thank you, Divine.
Invoke your new Divine Snow Mountain Area soul and practice:
Stand with your feet shoulder-width apart. Bend your knees a little. Keep your back straight. Do Soul Tapping of your Lower Dan Tian area with your left palm for men, right palm for women, and do Soul Tapping of your Snow Mountain Area with your other palm. At the same time, visualize golden or rainbow light in your Snow Mountain Area and chant.
Start!

Dear my divine soul of Divine Snow Mountain Area,
I love you, honor you, and appreciate you.
Turn on, please.

Divine Snow Mountain Area heals and boosts the power of
    my Snow Mountain Area.
Divine Snow Mountain Area heals and boosts the power of
    my Snow Mountain Area.
Divine Snow Mountain Area heals and boosts the power of
    my Snow Mountain Area.
Divine Snow Mountain Area heals and boosts the power of
    my Snow Mountain Area.

Divine Snow Mountain Area rejuvenates the soul, mind,
    and body of my Snow Mountain Area.
Divine Snow Mountain Area rejuvenates the soul, mind,
    and body of my Snow Mountain Area.
Divine Snow Mountain Area rejuvenates the soul, mind,
    and body of my Snow Mountain Area.

Divine Snow Mountain Area rejuvenates the soul, mind,
and body of my Snow Mountain Area.

Divine Snow Mountain Area prolongs the life of the soul,
mind, and body of my Snow Mountain Area.
Divine Snow Mountain Area prolongs the life of the soul,
mind, and body of my Snow Mountain Area.
Divine Snow Mountain Area prolongs the life of the soul,
mind, and body of my Snow Mountain Area.
Divine Snow Mountain Area prolongs the life of the soul,
mind, and body of my Snow Mountain Area.

Hao! Hao! Hao!
Thank you. Thank you. Thank you.

The complete Divine Long Life Package includes all ten areas addressed in the practice without Divine Soul Downloads: Lower Dan Tian, Snow Mountain Area, liver, heart, spleen, lungs, kidneys, spinal cord, brain, and small intestine. The Divine has offered two parts of this package, the Lower Dan Tian and Snow Mountain Area, in this chapter. These two divine soul treasures are gifts to offer you significant benefits for healing, boosting energy, rejuvenation, and long life.[5]

Do the practice for prolonging life without Divine Soul Downloads (see p. 174) and then do the practice with the two Divine Soul Downloads (Divine Lower Dan Tian and Divine Snow Mountain Area) you have just received as a gift. Both practices are powerful, but doing both practices will let you compare and experience the power of divine souls with divine wisdom and intelligence. The latest two Divine Soul Downloads you have received can benefit your life further

---

5. You can receive the other eight Divine Soul Downloads in any of my worldwide Soul Healing and Enlightenment retreats or remotely (see my website, www.DrSha.com).

and further. I have explained the significance of these two foundation energy centers. You must practice daily to receive great benefits of rejuvenation and prolonging life. Practice fifteen minutes or more per time, at least twice a day. It could make a big difference to your healing, rejuvenation, and longevity. If you can practice longer, you will receive even greater benefits.

Secret Soul Practice for Advancing from *Jing* to *Chi* to *Shen* to *Xu* to *Tao*

The process of advancing from *jing* to *chi* to *shen* to *xu* to *tao* has been a total secret for five thousand years. Many people are familiar with the terms but they do not understand how to practice and advance, step after step. This is the first time I am releasing this secret teaching and these special insights for practicing *jing chi shen xu tao*.

Step 1: Produce Jing

Sit up straight. It is best to sit on a cushion on the floor in a full-lotus or half-lotus position, or with legs naturally crossed. You may also sit on a chair with your back free and clear and your feet flat on the floor. Put your palms on your kidneys. Remember an energy secret: where you put your hands is where energy will go. Close your eyes gently. Put your mind in the area of your kidneys. If your Third Eye is open, enjoy the images you see. If your Third Eye is not open, visualize golden light in your kidneys.

Inhale deeply. At the same time, visualize golden light vibrating in your kidneys. Chant silently (one time only): *Produce jing*. Then hold your breath while chanting silently (four times only): *Produce jing*. *Produce jing*. *Produce jing*. *Produce jing*. Then exhale fully, while chanting silently (one time only): *Produce jing*.

Repeat this process six times, for a total of seven cycles.

Step 2: Transform Jing to Chi

Maintain your sitting position. Put one palm (left palm for men, right palm for women) over your Ming Men acupuncture point, which is on your back directly behind your navel. Put the other palm over your C-7 vertebra, which sticks out at the top of your back, just below your neck. Close your eyes gently.

Inhale deeply. At the same time, visualize rainbow light moving from your kidneys down to just in front of your tailbone, through three invisible energy holes to your spinal canal, and then up your entire spinal cord to your neck. Chant silently (one time only): *Transform* jing *to* chi. Then hold your breath while chanting silently (four times only): *Transform* jing *to* chi. *Transform* jing *to* chi. *Transform* jing *to* chi. *Transform* jing *to* chi. Then exhale fully, while chanting silently (one time only): *Transform* jing *to* chi.

Repeat this process six times, for a total of seven cycles.

Step 3: Transform Chi to Shen

Maintain your sitting position. Put one palm (left palm for men, right palm for women) over your Ming Men acupuncture point. Put the other palm over your crown chakra at the top of your head. Close your eyes gently.

Inhale deeply. At the same time, visualize purple light vibrating in your brain. Chant silently (one time only): *Transform* chi *to* shen. Then hold your breath while chanting silently (four times only): *Transform* chi *to* shen. *Transform* chi *to* shen. *Transform* chi *to* shen. *Transform* chi *to* shen. Then exhale fully, while chanting silently (one time only): *Transform* chi *to* shen.

Repeat this process six times, for a total of seven cycles.

Step 4: Transform Shen to Xu

Maintain your sitting position. Put one palm (left palm for men, right palm for women) over your Ming Men acupuncture point. Put the other palm over your heart. Close your eyes gently.

Inhale deeply. At the same time, visualize crystal light vibrating in your heart. Chant silently (one time only): *Transform* shen *to* xu. Then hold your breath while chanting silently (four times only): *Transform* shen *to* xu. *Transform* shen *to* xu. *Transform* shen *to* xu. *Transform* shen *to* xu. Then exhale fully, while chanting silently (one time only): *Transform* shen *to* xu.

Repeat this process six times, for a total of seven cycles.

Step 5: Transform Xu to Tao

Maintain your sitting position. Put one palm (left palm for men, right palm for women) over your Ming Men acupuncture point. Put the other palm over your *Ling Gong*. "Ling" means *soul*. "Gong" means *temple*. The Ling Gong, your Soul Temple, is located between the heart and the Message Center. Close your eyes gently.

Inhale deeply. At the same time, visualize crystal light vibrating in your Ling Gong. Chant silently (one time only): *Transform* xu *to* tao. Then hold your breath while chanting silently (four times only): *Transform* xu *to* tao. *Transform* xu *to* tao. *Transform* xu *to* tao. *Transform* xu *to* tao. Then exhale fully, while chanting silently (one time only): *Transform* xu *to* tao.

Repeat this process six times, for a total of seven cycles.

> *Hao! Hao! Hao!*
> *Thank you. Thank you. Thank you.*

Jing chi shen xu tao is the top Taoist secret of the process of message, energy, and matter transformation. However, many Taoist practitioners throughout history have not clearly understood *how* to transform *jing* to *chi* to *shen* to *xu* to *tao*. As I explained, the above practice was revealed to me directly by the Divine.

From *jing* to *chi* to *shen* to *xu* to *tao,* the message becomes more pure and refined.

From *jing* to *chi* to *shen* to *xu* to *tao,* the energy becomes more radiant and refined.

From *jing* to *chi* to *shen* to *xu* to *tao,* the matter becomes more nourishing and refined.

Repeat this practice from *jing* to *chi* to *shen* to *xu* to *tao* as often as you can. Each time you practice, the message, energy, and matter of your systems, organs, cells, cell units, DNA, and RNA will be refined further and further. The frequencies of your soul, heart, mind, and body will be transformed further and further. The consciousness of your soul, heart, and mind will be transformed further and further.

Divine frequency is the most refined frequency. Divine consciousness is the most pure consciousness. This practice is to align your consciousness with divine consciousness and to transform your frequency to divine frequency.

Words cannot adequately explain the significance of this sacred and secret practice.

=✷=

In this chapter, I have shared some of the most profound and sacred secrets from my whole life's study: from ancient arts and philosophies, including tai chi, qi gong, the *I Ching,* feng shui, Buddhism, Taoism, Confucianism, and Xiu Lian; to modern medicine, traditional Chinese medicine, Zhi Neng Medicine, and Body Space Medicine; and, above all, from direct teaching from the Divine. The techniques are extremely simple and practical. The results are incredibly profound.

If you want to prolong your life, it is vital to do the practices I have revealed in this chapter. Only with daily practice, consistency, and persistence can your soul, mind, and body be rejuvenated and your life prolonged. With daily practice, consistency, and persistence, your soul, mind, and body *will* be rejuvenated. Your life *will* be prolonged.

Hao! Hao! Hao!
Thank you. Thank you. Thank you.

10

Soul Transformation of Relationships

A NEWBORN BABY IMMEDIATELY starts to have relationships with parents, sisters and brothers, and others. When a child goes to school, there are relationships with classmates, teachers, and others. As an adult, you have relationships with many people. As long as you are on Mother Earth, you will have all kinds of relationships.

Relationships are a very important issue for humanity. Some of the most important relationships are those with your spouse or partner, with all family members, with colleagues and coworkers, and with friends. Each one of us is deeply affected by relationships between various organizations and relationships between cities and countries. Some other extremely important personal relationships are your relationships with your physical spiritual teachers, your spiritual fathers and mothers and other spiritual guides in Heaven, and the Divine.

There are many teachings, workshops, and seminars about relationships. This book will share the secret of transforming relationships at the soul level. The one-sentence soul secret to transform relationships is:

Transform the soul of a relationship first;
then transformation of the relationship will follow.

In recent years, I have taught this wisdom to thousands of people worldwide. They have used the wisdom and techniques that I will share in this chapter to transform their relationships with heart-touching results.

Personal Relationships

Many people have come to me seeking advice and guidance because they struggle with many blockages in their relationships with their partners. Some people have difficulties with their parents. Others have difficulties with their children. Some people have difficulties with their colleagues or their bosses. People often wonder why they have these struggles. Spiritual beings and nonspiritual beings alike often think: *I'm a good person. I'm very kind. Why are other people so mean to me? I'm very caring and loving to my partner. Why doesn't he or she like me? I give so much love to my children. Why don't they respect me?*

It is very difficult to find a person who has not struggled at some time in life with a relationship. Some people struggle their whole lives with relationships. Some people can never seem to find a true love, going through one divorce or breakup after another. Some children are abused by their parents. Some parents can be abused by their children. Other people can be cheated by their business partners. Relationship problems are very common on Mother Earth.

What is the root cause of blockages in relationships? If you have studied chapter 2 on karma, the answer will not surprise you. To answer all of the questions above, and more:

The true cause of blockages in relationships is karma.

I teach soul communication. I have trained and certified many advanced soul communicators. They can communicate directly with the Divine and the Akashic Records. They have offered spiritual guidance to many people with relationship challenges. They can share many stories that illustrate how blockages in relationships are related to karma. Therefore, clearing karma can make a big difference in a relationship.

If you have blockages with your spouse, your children, your colleagues, your boss, and your friends, it is not difficult to understand that there is a spiritual reason for these blockages. That spiritual reason is karma in your relationships from previous lives.

I will share four anonymous stories of soul readings from the Akashic Records about the true cause of blockages in relationships. These soul readings were done by my Certified Divine Direct Soul Communicators, whom I trained personally.

CURRENT LIFE RELATIONSHIP #1

We have been married for more than fifteen years and were together for nearly ten years before that. He has three children, who were young when we first got together. The two oldest lived with us. Our relationship had a lot of challenges in the first fifteen years. For me, it was a constant huge test with the children and with him. It is still a struggle with him at times.

Past-Life Soul Reading

In a temple in Egypt thousands of years ago, I see her present husband in a long white robe standing at the top of some steps. She was seated on the steps below him and he was "lording it over her." He was one of the advisors to the emperor. She was a young girl, barely of marriageable age, and a handmaiden who served him and his entire household. He bossed her around a lot. They were uncle and niece. This is the first lifetime in which they knew each other.

They were both in the aristocracy. At that time, women in the aristocracy were valued for their knowledge and wisdom, but he does not value her in this way. Her parents sent her to his household to be raised and educated with his children. However, he does not allow her into the classroom to study. She has to get her knowledge secretly. He does educate his own daughters together with his sons, but he does not expect his daughters to have any wisdom or express any opinions either.

She feels cheated by her parents, who put her into this relationship. Her uncle is not fulfilling his obligation to give her an education. She is not getting what she was promised and feels her parents should have known about her uncle's attitudes and behaviors.

She did end up having a good life, but no thanks to her uncle. She managed to get an education by standing outside the door of the classroom, bringing food and drink to the children and teachers, and assisting them in any way she could. She was very clever in finding ways to work around the limitations her uncle imposed.

In their current lifetime, she says that many times her husband has "lorded it over her." He is more than fifteen years older than she. She has to do some things secretly, on her own and without her husband's knowledge. The old karmic patterns are clearly present in their current lifetime together.

These two souls shared another past life in the Dark Ages of the eighth century in the lands near Stonehenge in England. This was the first time they were husband and wife. She was given to her husband as part of an alliance between her father's village and her husband's father's village.

She loved her husband and was happy to be married to him, although she resented that she had no choice in the decision to marry. Her new husband was somewhat interested in her but did not love her when they were wed. She was quite an independent woman during this lifetime, at a time when women were generally not independent.

The relationship was difficult in the early years of their marriage because both of them wanted to be in charge of their own lands. They were both expected to pay homage to his father, who was not a nice person at all. In this sense, the two of them formed a good unit that had to struggle against what his father created between himself and his people. Both of them were on the outside looking in. They could not be "in charge." His father would be mean to a group of people and the two of them would sneak out in the night to bring them food and comfort. It was a sense of the two of them against the world. Clearly, this pattern is repeating during their present lifetime together.

CURRENT LIFE RELATIONSHIP #2

We met more than twenty years ago. Within weeks, we were living together. I was pregnant within a few months and we married very soon thereafter. We had two more children. We had struggles and difficulties from day one. Although there was always a sense of connection and caring between us, possessiveness and jealousy intruded frequently. At times, our relationship was even abusive.

After several years, I filed for divorce. Immediately, the dynamic of our relationship changed. We set up separate households in different states, one with the children and me, the other with his business and him. His business took off, and despite the distance, we all traveled back and forth often to be with each other as a family. We enjoyed the best of times.

Five years ago, my children and I moved back in with him, with all of us living under one roof again. Last year things took a terrible turn. Although he had been a functioning alcoholic, he suddenly became very abusive, even to our two sons. I filed for an order of protection and quickly moved everyone out. A few months ago he was taken by paramedics to a "Behavioral Health" ward against his will. I visited him and continue to assist in his ongoing recovery. I am doing whatever I can to heal the wounds.

Past-Life Soul Reading

These two souls have shared seventeen relationships in the past, not only as husband and wife, but as friends, as employer and employee, and as brother and sister. Their current marital and family situation is mostly related to two prior relationships.

The first relationship was in London in the seventeenth century, where these two souls were also husband and wife. As now, he was an alcoholic then, and she was his mate. He tried to force her to become a prostitute in order to obtain money for alcohol. She refused to do this and left him, ending up homeless and living under a bridge. The river rose up in a flood and drowned her. When the husband heard of her death, he hung himself.

A second relationship was sunnier and happier. In this lifetime, she was again a woman and he a man. She owned a ranch in Mexico. Her husband died and the man who is now her husband ended up being the cowboy in care of the ranch animals. She was not easy to work for, as she was a very strict and proud señorita. He saved her life when she was attacked by a raging bull. Her personality softened and her heart opened after this event. They had a very close and intimate friendship.

In their current life together, there are karmic patterns running through and arising from both of these past-life relationships. The man paid his debt from the past life in London by saving her from the bull in the subsequent lifetime in Mexico. He is still learning lessons from his mistakes in the London lifetime. He is continuing to pay his spiritual debt in his current life. On the other hand, there are intimacy, care, and love from their relationship in Mexico. The soul guidance for both of these souls is to purify their hearts with love, care, and compassion and to offer unconditional forgiveness to each other and to themselves.

CURRENT LIFE RELATIONSHIP #3

My relationship with my mother has been a frustrating one. Growing up, I was all about feelings and their expression. My mother is not a person who "does" feelings well. When I was a teenager, I remember telling her, "I know I'm loved, but I don't feel loved." I wasn't completely ignored, but neither was I encouraged. There was often an element of correction and criticism in our interactions. At the same time, I felt many contradictions as I witnessed my mother being there for me on a daily basis with clean clothes, full-course family meals every night, and her full-time presence. However, we did not talk or otherwise connect on an emotional level, and this was painful. I struggled with acknowledging her forms of love as love, as I longed for deeper interaction.

There are still aspects of the paradox that is my mother that I have not fully come to peace with. She is emotionally very strong in some ways and yet she has let her fears determine much of her life. For example, she never learned to drive or swim. She transferred her fears to me in many ways but the one that comes to mind is when I was young and wanted to learn to water-ski. She would not allow it.

As I take care of her now at her very advanced age, those feelings come back occasionally, especially when she is in a negative, critical place and I'm tired or overwhelmed. Mostly, however, I feel privilege and gratitude for this time with her. We have reversed roles. I am very much here for her in every way, and it's been a time of healing for me. We almost always feel comfortable with each other. More than that, we laugh a lot together.

We also have the very positive effects of having Master Sha in our lives. My mother has been very supportive and encouraging of my spiritual life. We chant and practice together. My mother has Divine Soul Downloads and activates them at least once a day. It has been a great blessing to our relationship to have all that Master Sha brings into our lives to focus on and work with, as well as having the enormous physical and emotional blessings that the divine soul treasures bring. I am very grateful.

Writing this got me thinking and brought me to a greater appreciation for the love it takes to care for someone's daily needs in a consistent, reliable, and caring way. I still have to work on releasing the rest, but this is an important step in that direction.

Past-Life Soul Reading

These two souls have had many remarkable lifetimes with each other in which they shared a friendship filled with light and with many wonderful experiences. This is to be noted because at a deep soul level they share a tremendous friendship.

In their present lives, the communication blockages are indeed related to karma. They shared one particular past lifetime in which their roles were reversed. The daughter today was the mother then and the mother today was the daughter then. In this past lifetime, which took place in Europe during the Renaissance, the mother emotionally abused and abandoned her daughter. The daughter had to be removed from her mother's care because the mother was unwilling to support her. The mother went off to do her own thing. Many of the communication blockages in the current lifetime arose from this particular past-life relationship.

There was another lifetime during the Middle Ages in which their present roles were again reversed. The current mother was the disabled daughter. She could not care for herself. The mother (now the daughter) did not care for her well at all. In the current lifetime, she is to learn the lesson of unconditional love. She must learn the unconditional love that a mother should have for her children, regardless of their being disabled or anything else. This is why she has been made responsible for taking care of her mother in this lifetime. This pattern will be repeated until she is able to offer her love completely and unconditionally, without attachments, even in times when things get rough. She is to offer her unconditional love, forgiveness, and blessings for healing to occur.

CURRENT LIFE RELATIONSHIP #4

My son's father and I split after two and a half years, so I raised my son alone. However, I was absent a great deal due to my work. Because of this, as a teenager, my son did lots of "stuff" to get attention. We actually were somewhat close until he met the woman who is now his wife. Now we have no relationship.

Past-Life Soul Reading

The relationship between this mother and her son is strained by forces that seem beyond their control. However, there are many reasons why there are such large blockages. The energy and light between this mother and son have been of a very low frequency for some time. The reasons for this are primarily spiritual in nature and go back many lifetimes. The son feels he is not loved and blames this on his mother. However, his Message Center is quite closed and he is hard to reach.

The interpersonal skills of both mother and son have not been developed well enough to allow them to start even the lower levels of interaction that would lead to healing of this relationship. There is great sadness in the souls of both mother and son because of the lack of communication and connection. Each soul realizes it has been distanced from the other and from the Divine and that their soul journeys are being affected by the karma of this relationship. The mother has been very fortunate to connect with spiritual practices and a high-level master who is opening her heart and mind. The possibility of healing the painful relationship is very good.

There are several lifetimes that are significant for this current relationship. There was a lifetime in which the mother was in charge of many workers who had very little control of their work environment. They were treated poorly and worked long hours with little food or payment. In this lifetime, the son was both a worker and a son. However, this son was from a father to whom his mother was not married, so the presence of this child was not acknowledged. He was treated very poorly and worked very hard. The son was unaware of his relationship until he became an adult and discovered the truth of his father quite accidentally. The relationship between son and mother was filled with guilt, anger, and resentment. There was never an attempt to make the relationship better. Mother and son finally parted, angry and distant, and did not speak again or see each other in that lifetime. The lessons that needed to be learned, which would have brought light into this relationship and brought mother and son closer to divine presence, were not understood, and the karma from this lifetime was brought into several subsequent lifetimes.

Another lifetime in which these two were in a relationship was in the 1500s. He was a rich landlord and she was his daughter; the parent/child roles were reversed. The father was verbally abusive and excessively controlling. He was strong-willed and overbearing and the daughter suffered greatly. She was quite resentful. The relationship between father and daughter grew bitter. The daughter said very little, but planned revenge that she never carried out. However, this greatly affected her life and she saw life from a dark perspective.

This relationship was never understood at any level. The spiritual nature of the problem was never even considered. Both parties blamed each other and neither person was able to look inward and gain understanding through personal insight and prayer. The karma in this relationship deepened greatly during this lifetime and continued into many subsequent lifetimes.

The root cause is intense self-centeredness resulting in closed Message Centers of both son and mother in one lifetime and daughter and father in another. This has led to hostility, anger, and resentment. Until this lifetime there has never been a consideration of the healing nature of forgiveness. Major challenges in all lifetimes and in this current lifetime are lack of love and unwillingness to forgive.

It is strongly suggested that the mother quickly undertake a practice of forgiveness to remove blockages and bring the soul of this relationship and the soul of her son into love and light. There is an urgent need to do this before more damage is done. If this does not occur, this pattern between these two souls will be carried into future lifetimes. Many others will also be affected. Spouses and children have been drawn into this darkness and are equally lost at this time.

The significance of forgiveness between these two souls cannot be overstated. There can be no deep and lasting healing until each one has learned to forgive. It releases blockages and heals at a very deep level. Additional ways of healing this relationship are through Divine Soul Downloads, which bring immediate divine presence, and soul conferences. Consistently going to the soul of this relationship and healing at that level will have great impact on the son, his wife, and his children. The results will be dramatic and love and compassion will arise naturally. There will be an abundance of gratitude from each person in this family. The soul guidance for these souls is to undertake this healing and clear these long-standing issues.

They should also consider karma cleansing for the soul of this relationship. Karma cleansing is an act of ultimate forgiveness that would set an example for all inner and outer souls associated with this relationship. This would greatly help in removing great karmic burdens and allow the healing to progress with greater ease. However, it will be important for the mother to speak to the soul of her son and the soul of their relationship and to do forgiveness practices as well.

⁂

These four stories tell us that when there is a relationship blockage, it is no coincidence. The real cause is karma issues. I have offered thousands of karma cleansings for humanity. These many cases have deeply taught me that the true explanation for the condition of relationships is karma. Even so, you have the power to transform your relationships. The golden key to transform relationships is unconditional love and forgiveness.

Let me share a practical technique for doing this, called soul conferencing. For example, if you have real challenges with your spouse, transform your relationship at the soul level first. Do it by holding a soul conference:

Sit in a meditative posture and condition. Then sing the Divine Soul Song "Love, Peace and Harmony."

> *I love my heart and soul*
> *I love all humanity*
> *Join hearts and souls together*
> *Love, peace and harmony*
> *Love, peace and harmony*

Begin by singing for one or two minutes. Then initiate the soul conference by calling the soul of your spouse:

> *Dear soul of* _____ (name your spouse), *I love you. Please come.*

Instantly, the soul of your spouse will be in front of you. If your Third Eye is open, you will clearly see the soul of your spouse. If you have direct soul communication abilities, you will be able to communicate directly with the soul of your spouse.

The following is a suggested outline for communicating with the soul of your spouse to transform your relationship. What is important is to understand and learn the general principles. There is no exact script you must follow. Your intention, sincerity, and heart are most important.

- Thank the soul of your spouse.
- Explain your purpose in calling the soul of your spouse.
- Present the problem(s) between you.
- Offer forgiveness to your spouse.
- Ask for forgiveness from your spouse.
- Ask the divine souls of Divine Love and Divine Forgiveness that you received in chapter 2 to bless your relationship.

- Show great gratitude to the Divine, to your and your spouse's spiritual fathers and mothers in Heaven, and to your spouse for their blessings.

Let me add a few sample details to explain this soul conversation further. First call the soul of your spouse.

- *Dear soul of my spouse, I love you. Please come.*
- *Thank you for coming.*
- *I'm calling your soul to come today to have a conversation. We have some relationship challenges. I would like to create soul transformation of my relationship with you.*
- List the major challenges in your relationship.
- Offer your total forgiveness to your spouse for any wrongs your spouse has done to you. *I completely forgive you for your mistakes. Please receive my forgiveness.* Reflect and be quiet and still for one or two minutes to offer total forgiveness to the soul of your spouse.
- *May I also ask for your forgiveness? For my mistakes and wrongs to you, could I ask you to totally forgive me?* Be still for one or two minutes to receive forgiveness from the soul of your spouse.
- *Dear my divine souls of Divine Love and Divine Forgiveness, I love you. Could you bless my relationship with my spouse? I am very grateful. Thank you.*

Then chant:

Divine Love soul blesses my relationship with my spouse.
Divine Love soul blesses my relationship with my spouse.
Divine Love soul blesses my relationship with my spouse.
Divine Love soul blesses my relationship with my spouse.

Divine Forgiveness soul transforms my relationship with
   my spouse.
Divine Forgiveness soul transforms my relationship with
   my spouse.
Divine Forgiveness soul transforms my relationship with
   my spouse.
Divine Forgiveness soul transforms my relationship with
   my spouse . . .

Chant for at least three minutes, silently or aloud, the longer the better.

• Express your gratitude.

Thank you, Divine.
Thank you, divine soul of Divine Love and divine soul of
   Divine Forgiveness.
Thank you, soul of my spouse.
Thank you, my soul.
Thank you, any soul in the spiritual world who has
   blessed us.
Thank you. Thank you. Thank you.

Then respectfully return the soul of your spouse. You can say:

Gong song. Gong song. Gong song. (This is Chinese for
   "respectfully return.")

You can also simply say:

Thank you, soul of my spouse. Please return.

This is soul transformation of your relationship with your spouse. This wisdom and technique can be applied for transformation of any relationship. After doing the soul transformation practice a few times, have a physical conversation with the physical person. You could be very impressed by the profound changes following your soul transformation efforts.

To transform any relationship, there are a few very important principles:

- Always apply love and forgiveness. They are the golden key to transformation.
- Have sincerity and honesty. In ancient spiritual teaching, there is a famous statement: *Honesty moves Heaven.* Honesty can touch people's hearts deeply. Honesty is very helpful in transforming a relationship.
- Be confident. Remove fear.
- Find the right times to communicate at the soul level as well as physically with the other person. If either of you is stressed or upset, do not start either of these conversations.

These few principles will help you to transform the soul of your relationships. Then transformation of the relationships will follow.

Family Relationships

An ancient spiritual teaching says there are three kinds of children. The best kind is healthy, smart, well behaved, loving, and kind. Parents are proud of this kind of child and feel very blessed to have them.

The second kind of child presents lots of problems for the parents. This kind of child may not have good health, perhaps even suffering from chronic or life-threatening conditions. This kind of child may always argue with and disobey the parents. The parents may make great efforts to help such children. Although some of these children may appreciate it, many of them do not. They continue to fight and disobey. The parents feel very hurt. They try very hard to transform their children but have little success.

The third kind of child can also receive lots of love and care from parents. But this kind of child does not respond at all. They are often totally aloof, although sometimes they may fight back. Their unresponsiveness makes everything extremely difficult for their parents. As soon as they grow up, they leave. These children do not appear to have a close relationship at all with their parents.

Of course, there are many other kinds of relationships between parents and children. Whatever the nature of the relationship, I always like to ask why it is the way it is. I always want to figure out the underlying reason for many things. In the early stages of my life, I couldn't figure out why different parents had different relationships with their children. Many parents even have very different relationships with each of their own children—harmonious with one child but disharmonious with another child.

I finally figured out the reason for this when I highly developed my spiritual channels in 1993 and 1994. How did I figure it out? Spiritual images told me. Conversations with the spiritual world taught me. When I saw a good relationship between parents and child, I asked the Akashic Records, "Why?" When I saw a bad relationship between parents and child in some families, I also asked, "Why?" When I observed extreme challenges between parents and child, I asked, "Why?" From all of my observation, experience, and spiritual communication, I can summarize the key wisdom and knowledge about relationships in one sentence:

All relationships are related with karma,
especially the husband-wife relationship.

Think about your life. When you grow up, you find a boyfriend or girlfriend. You may have a great relationship with your boyfriend or girlfriend. You may have found your right partner right away. But many people on Mother Earth have such complicated relationships with their boyfriends or girlfriends, husbands or wives. These relationships can cause great suffering for many people. You may be with your partner for a while. Then you become unhappy with each other. You separate. Then you may decide to make up and get together again. Later you may separate again. Afterward, you can be so bothered in your mind and heart. You could be very angry. You could be heartbroken. You could be hurt for many years.

Someone else may seem like a perfect partner. You may dream of being together. Yet you never have an opportunity. Why are relationships so complicated? The answer is straightforward and clear. Your relationship with a boyfriend, girlfriend, husband, or wife in this life is related to your relationships with that person's soul in past lives. If you had very harmonized relationships in past lives, then it is very easy for you to be harmonized in this life. If you had struggles with each other in past lives, you will probably struggle with each other again in this life.

Relationships between parents and children follow the same principles. Generally speaking, you and your children were related in a past life or lives. If you have very nice children, the first kind I described above, you treated them very well in a past life. They came back to give you their appreciation as your children. Some children, such as the second kind, could come to your life and bother you so much. Generally speaking, you did something wrong to them in a previous life. Some children, the third kind, you can give such love and so much heart to, yet they do not respond. They grow. They leave. It seems they forget about you. Again, the Akashic Records and the Divine showed me that this kind of situation happens because you owe them from a past life. Then in this life they come as your children. They ignore you. You pay your debt to them in this way.

These are the insights I have learned from the Divine and from the Akashic Records. The true cause of blockages or blessings in the relationships between husband and wife, boyfriend and girlfriend, and parents and children is karma related. Therefore, you can transform your relationships. The principle is very simple. Apply unconditional love and forgiveness.

To educate the children, it is vital to not spoil them. Even if you are wealthy and can give your child many material benefits, do not spoil them. Educate them well. As parents, you must be a good example for them. Children follow the parents. If parents fight all the time, it will affect the children very much. It will deeply influence their hearts, minds, and emotions. If children do something wrong, do not think it is a small issue. If you do not correct their small mistakes, big mistakes will follow. Therefore, correct children's behavior right away. If children do something wrong, even if they speak a wrong sentence, point it out to them with love in your voice. Clearly guide them on what is wrong with their speech. Tell them how they can correct it. Tell them you forgive them and that next time they can do better.

I do not suggest that you give your children too hard a time when they make some mistake. Do not shout or yell at them. Instead, speak in a very soft and loving voice. You will receive much better results this way.

It is important to correct children when they are very small. Discipline them. At the same time, love them. Children absolutely understand your love. Love melts any blockage and transforms all life. We know karma issues. Love and forgiveness can transform karma.

Let me share a major spiritual secret. To enhance your family relationships, do it at the soul level. For example, suppose there are six people in your household—your spouse, your parents, one daughter, one son, and you. How do you do soul transformation for your three generations of family members? If you spend five to ten minutes per day doing the following soul transformation practice, you could receive remarkable results to harmonize your family.

Let me reveal this secret practice now. Sit in a meditative state.

Call a soul conference. Call the souls of your parents, your daughter, your son, and your spouse.

> *Dear soul of everyone in my family, please come here.*
> *Be with me.*
> *Let us share love with each other.*
> *Let us offer forgiveness to each other.*
> *Let us harmonize all of our relationships with each other.*

Then chant silently:

> *Love for the whole family*
> *Love for the whole family*
> *Love for the whole family*
> *Love for the whole family*
>
> *Forgiveness for the whole family*
> *Forgiveness for the whole family*
> *Forgiveness for the whole family*
> *Forgiveness for the whole family*
>
> *Harmony for the whole family*
> *Harmony for the whole family*
> *Harmony for the whole family*
> *Harmony for the whole family . . .*
>
> *Hao! Hao! Hao!*
> *Thank you. Thank you. Thank you.*
> *Please return.*

Practice for five to ten minutes per day, the longer the better.

How does this technique work? When you call the souls of your family members together, you are holding a family soul conference.

When you chant *love, forgiveness,* and *harmony,* the frequencies of these qualities will bless everyone's soul.

Soul is the boss of the human being. As you work at the soul level, many blockages in your relationships can be transformed on the spot. After this kind of soul conference, you could be very surprised at the results. Even if you have very good family relationships, you can and should do this soul conference regularly; it will help to maintain the harmonized relationships in your family. This is a simple, practical, and powerful technique for harmonizing the family.

If you have major challenges in your family relationships, invoke your divine soul of Divine Harmony (downloaded to you as you read chapter 2) to bless yourself and your family. Do the following simple and powerful practice:

> *Dear my divine soul of Divine Harmony,*
> *I love you, honor you, and appreciate you.*
> *Please turn on.*
> *Please bless and harmonize my family relationships.*
> *I am very grateful.*
> *Thank you.*

Then chant:

> *Divine Harmony soul transforms the relationships of my*
> *   whole family.*
> *Divine Harmony soul transforms the relationships of my*
> *   whole family.*
> *Divine Harmony soul transforms the relationships of my*
> *   whole family.*
> *Divine Harmony soul transforms the relationships of my*
> *   whole family . . .*
>
> *Hao! Hao! Hao!*
> *Thank you. Thank you. Thank you.*

If your Third Eye is open, you could be amazed to see your divine soul of Divine Harmony come out from your Message Center and go to the souls of your family members. It shines incredible golden light to remove the dark areas in the souls of your family members. Remember the soul secret: When dark areas of the soul are removed, transformation can be instant.

Workplace Relationships

If you would like to improve your relationships with your coworkers or your boss, you can use the same techniques I shared with you for transforming personal and family relationships.

If you are the manager or leader of an organization, or if you want to improve your relationships with all the employees, call a soul conference. Here's how:

Start by repeating the sacred healing number 3396815 three times in Chinese, pronounced *sahn sahn joe lew bah yow woo*:

> *San San Jiu Liu Ba Yao Wu*
> *San San Jiu Liu Ba Yao Wu*
> *San San Jiu Liu Ba Yao Wu*

I introduced this special mantra to you in chapter 3. I learned this number from my spiritual father, Master Guo, and first shared it in my book *Zhi Neng Medicine* in 1996. This number is a spiritual code that will serve humanity for fifteen thousand years, the entire Soul Light Era. To chant this number three times is to connect with and make a calling to the spiritual world.

Next say:

> *I am calling all souls of my company.*
> *Please come.*
> *Let us share love and forgiveness with each other.*

Let us transform our relationships.
Thank you very much.

Then chant *3396815* for three to five minutes. If your Third Eye is open, you could be surprised by what you see. You may see many buddhas, holy saints, and healing angels come right away to bless all souls in your organization. Many dark areas could be removed instantly from the souls in your organization. These dark areas are spiritual blockages among the souls of the people in your organization.

Hao! Hao! Hao!
Thank you. Thank you. Thank you.
Please return.

This technique is extremely simple. Its power is beyond comprehension.

Practice it.

Experience it.

Benefit from it.

Physical interaction and conversation with your colleagues, employees, and boss are also important. The spiritual world and physical world complement and support each other. Yin and yang join together. However, if you do soul transformation first, transformation of your relationships at work will be much, much easier. If you try it, you will really understand the teaching, wisdom, and practice that I offer here.

Relationships Among Organizations

If you would like to transform the relationship between your organization and another related organization, call their souls:

*Dear souls of _____ (call the souls of the organizations),
please come. This is what we want to accomplish today.*

Speak to them exactly as if you were in a physical meeting. Their souls will listen to your words very well. If their souls get it, their minds will get it very easily. Tell them how you want the relationships among the organizations to transform. Be specific.

Then invoke one of your Divine Soul Downloads to assist and bless the transformation you have requested. For example:

*Dear divine soul of Divine Peace,
I love you, honor you, and appreciate you.
Please turn on.
Please transform the relationships among these organizations.
I'm very grateful.
Thank you.*

Then chant:

*Divine Peace soul brings peace to all these organizations.
Divine Peace soul brings peace to all these organizations.
Divine Peace soul brings peace to all these organizations.
Divine Peace soul brings peace to all these organizations . . .*

Practice for at least three minutes per time, the longer the better.

*Hao! Hao! Hao!
Thank you. Thank you. Thank you.
Please return.*

Relationships Among Cities, States, and Countries and Among Heaven, Earth, and Human Beings

What is the final goal of the Soul Light Era? It is love, peace, and harmony for every city, state, and country. It is love, peace, and harmony for humanity, Mother Earth, and all universes.

How can we accomplish such a huge task? Let me share a soul secret for transforming the world. The Divine taught me this technique. I have thousands of students worldwide who are doing this every morning. As soon as they wake up, they spend five minutes doing this soul transformation practice:

> *Dear soul, mind, and body of every city, state, and country,*
> *Dear soul, mind, and body of every planet, star, galaxy,*
>   *and universe,*
> *Dear soul, mind, and body of every human being,*
> *Dear soul, mind, and body of every animal on Mother*
>   *Earth,*
> *Dear soul, mind, and body of every soul in all universes,*
> *I love you all.*
> *Please join hearts and souls together with me to sing the*
>   *Divine Soul Song "Love, Peace and Harmony" to offer*
>   *blessings to humanity, Mother Earth, and all universes.*
> *Dear Divine Soul Transplant of the Divine Soul Song*
>   *"Love, Peace and Harmony" downloaded to every*
>   *human being and every soul of all universes,*
> *I love you, honor you, and appreciate you.*
> *Please turn on to offer blessings to humanity, Mother*
>   *Earth, and all universes.*
> *I'm very grateful. Thank you.*

Then sing "Love, Peace and Harmony" for five minutes:

Lu la lu la li
Lu la lu la la li
Lu la lu la li lu la
Lu la li lu la
Lu la li lu la

I love my heart and soul
I love all humanity
Join hearts and souls together
Love, peace and harmony
Love, peace and harmony

Tao is The Way. There is an ancient secret: *Tao is within life. Anytime, anywhere, whatever you are doing and whatever you are thinking, meld with Tao. Tao has no time and no space. Tao is in any moment and in any place.* To do this soul transformation practice is to practice the Tao.

I have guided my students to practice and chant in this way for five minutes as soon as they wake up, and to chant anytime, anywhere during the day. I have students all around the world in different time zones. A Divine Soul Transplant of the Divine Soul Song "Love, Peace and Harmony" has been downloaded to every soul in all universes. These countless divine souls are pure servants and bless and transform every soul. In this practice, we turn on these souls to allow them to serve. As a result, this Divine Soul Song is shining on every continent, but this is only the beginning. The soul frequency of Divine "Love, Peace and Harmony" will transform humanity's consciousness.

Do not think this is a simple Soul Song. If all humanity chanted this Divine Soul Song, if all souls chanted this Divine Soul Song, no words could express the power for life transformation.

Soul Power is the power of the twenty-first century. Soul Power is the power of the Soul Light Era. Divine chanting leads Soul Power in the twenty-first century and in the Soul Light Era.

Divine mantra can transform every aspect of your life.

Divine mantra can transform the consciousness of humanity.

Divine mantra can transform all souls.

Divine mantra can enlighten all souls.

Divine mantra can enlighten all universes.

Hao! Hao! Hao!

Thank you. Thank you. Thank you.

11

Soul Transformation of Finances and Business

MANY PEOPLE WORLDWIDE want to transform their finances and business. Many people want to be wealthy. Many people dream of a successful business. What is the true reason for business success?

I received this divine teaching: *True success in business and finances is a blessing from Heaven.* Why do some people have tremendous success in finances and business? Why do others have little success in finances and business? Why are some people never successful in finances and business? The true reason is the spiritual reason. Like so much else in our present lives, success in finances and business is related to our previous lives.

If you served humanity and Mother Earth exceptionally well in previous lives, Heaven and the Divine will reward you in this lifetime. If you offered good service to humanity and Mother Earth, you will receive a good reward in this life through your finances and business. If you harmed humanity in previous lives, you could have no financial or business success in this life.

About twenty years ago, I saw a billionaire. The Akashic Records showed me that in his next life he would be a beggar. I was very shocked to see such an image and to receive that message. I asked the Akashic Records, "Why? This person is so famous in this life. Why do you show me that he will be a beggar in his next life?" The answer was that this man owned one huge company whose products were very harmful to one's health. Literally millions of people were harmed by this company. Therefore, he will have to learn a great lesson in his next life.

Then I asked the Akashic Records why this person was so successful and wealthy in this life. They told me that he had served humanity very well over his previous fifty-two lifetimes. He had been very kind. He had been the compassionate leader of a country. He had been a spiritual leader. He had been a wealthy person who was very generous, serving the poor and many others. Because of his previous fifty-two lifetimes of great service to humanity and Mother Earth, he was rewarded in this life through his finances and business.

I was really shocked by this teaching. I was shocked to see these spiritual images. I was deeply appreciative of this knowledge. When I received this information, I also heard one sentence from the Akashic Records, which I already knew: *Heaven is most fair.*

After I highly developed my spiritual abilities and learned more and more advanced spiritual wisdom from my spiritual fathers, Heaven, and the Divine, I received a very special teaching about finances that I would like to share with you.

In the physical world, human beings use money for exchange. Whether you buy a house, travel, or eat, you need to spend money to exchange for these things and services. When you work for a company, you are paid a salary. Money is the exchange for your work. You need money to support your family. If you run a business, you need money to support your employees and to expand your business. Money has vital physical value in life.

In the spiritual world, is there spiritual money that spiritual beings use for exchange? *Yes!* What is money in the spiritual world? It is *virtue*. Good virtue is expressed in dots and flowers of different colors—red, golden, rainbow, and more. This good virtue is recorded on your soul and in your book in the Akashic Records. I explained this wisdom in chapter 2.

The secret I want to reveal is that *physical money and spiritual money can exchange*. In other words, money in the physical world and virtue in the spiritual world can exchange. Physical money is deposited and stored in a bank. Virtue is deposited and stored in the Akashic Records. If you have good virtue, which is a record of your good services in all of your lifetimes—including love, care, compassion, kindness, generosity, integrity, and service to the poor, the hungry, the sick, your family, and others—this good virtue can be transformed into money in the physical world.

People who are very wealthy in this life are wealthy because they served humanity and Mother Earth very well in past lifetimes. This is the true reason. Not every wealthy person was rich from birth. Quite a few wealthy persons worked very hard to gain wealth. But it is very important knowledge to realize that no matter how hard you work, no matter how good your planning, marketing, and organizing are, no matter how high-quality your products are, you must not forget that Heaven must bless your success. Heaven blesses you if you have good virtue from past lifetimes.

Many people work very hard. Not all of them are financially successful. Many of them face constant challenges, one after another. Some of them may be very successful, but then next year, their business could fail. Business is a complicated issue.

To be successful in business, you must understand that business success is directly related to your past lives and your present life. If you did and are doing good things, Heaven can make you a success. If you have a great business and a pleasant financial situation in this life, you are blessed. But if you do very wrong things, such as harming or taking advantage of others, Heaven could stop your success. Big disasters could come to you. Improper management could lead your business to fail. You could be cheated by a business partner. You could be caught and punished for breaking physical laws. You could have major health or relationship blockages.

In summary, the success of your finances and business is directly related to your good service for humanity and Mother Earth, through past lifetimes and in this lifetime. If you want to have successful finances and business, a good physical team is important. But Heaven's support and blessing are vital. The physical team and your Heaven's Team, which includes your spiritual guides, teachers, angels, and other enlightened masters in Heaven, must be aligned to support you together. Then your finances and business will flourish. If your physical team is not right, or if either team does not support you well, it is very difficult to achieve success. Many challenges and blockages will appear.

To transform finances and business, the key is to clear your soul blockages and the soul blockages in your business. Make sure you have a good physical team. Your business absolutely should have good planning, marketing, and financial controls. It needs a good infrastructure, great customer service, and more. There are many business experts who can guide you properly on business issues. Soul secrets and wisdom are what I offer for the success of your business and finances. This wisdom tells you the real reason why a person is wealthy. It tells you what one needs to do to maintain financial success.

The key soul secrets of business success are:

- Make sure your business offers good service to humanity and Mother Earth.
- The more your business can serve, the more successful it could be.
- An effective physical team and Heaven's Team's blessing together are vital to business success.

Soul Marketing

Soul marketing is important soul wisdom that I am releasing for the first time in this book. Every business needs marketing. Very successful businesses usually have great marketing. This book does not offer any physical marketing strategies, wisdom, or techniques. There are many business experts who can offer great teaching and guidance on these topics. Instead, this book offers *soul marketing*, which very few companies have done. Soul marketing is divine wisdom. The Divine told me, "If you receive great results from this wisdom, give all the credit to the Divine." I am honored to be your servant to share this divine teaching with you.

Let me share my personal story of how I learned to do soul marketing.

In 2002 my book *Power Healing*[6] was published. Like most books, it was not a major success. In June 2004 I taught a soul retreat. The morning after the retreat ended, as I was meditating, the Divine told me, "Zhi Gang, do a book campaign for this book." I didn't have a PR person. I didn't have a marketing expert. I had no experience in doing a book campaign. I had no idea what a book campaign was!

I asked the Divine, "Dear Divine, how do I do a book campaign?"

The Divine said, "Zhi Gang, write a letter to your several hundred students. Ask each of them to buy more books to share with their loved ones. At the same time, do soul marketing for the book campaign."

I asked, "How do I do soul marketing? How does soul marketing work?"

The Divine asked me, "How many devoted students do you have?"

---

6. Zhi Gang Sha, 2002, *Power Healing,* San Francisco: HarperSanFrancisco.

My answer was a few hundred. Following Divine Guidance, I had left Canada for the San Francisco Bay Area in 2000. Every Monday for more than a year, I offered a free healing event in San Francisco. In this way, I had been able to gather a few hundred students.

The Divine said, "You have a few hundred devoted students. Write a letter to them. Ask them to support your teaching. They love you. They will support you."

The Divine then asked, "How many people are there in the Bay Area?"

I didn't know the exact number. I answered, "Probably millions."

Then the Divine asked me, "How many people are there on Mother Earth?"

I said, "Nearly six and a half billion."

The Divine said, "Correct. How many souls are there in the universes?"

I replied, "Countless."

Then Divine smiled and said, "Correct. Let me teach you, my son." He offered the following teaching:

> Zhi Gang, you have a few hundred devoted students. You love them. You teach them. They appreciate your teaching. They return your love. They will support you. They are human beings. You have the support of these few hundred people. This is a small number. There are millions of human beings in the Bay Area. There are billions of human beings on Mother Earth. You came to Canada in 1990. You came to the United States in 2000. Very few people in the world know you at this moment. Dear my son, I will teach you soul marketing. When you do soul marketing, many, many people will know you very quickly.

Then the Divine told me, "Zhi Gang, this is the formula you should follow:

Dear soul, mind, and body of every human being, I love you. Please come.

"Then tell them you published a book, *Power Healing*, which teaches people how to do self-healing. It empowers people to heal themselves and others. It shares four self-healing techniques: Body Power, Sound Power, Mind Power, and Soul Power. Ask the souls of all humanity and all souls in the universe to share this news with each other. Appreciate them. Then chant *3396815, 3396815, 3396815, 3396815* for three minutes."

The Divine told me to do this soul marketing every day for one month. I followed Divine Guidance. I wrote a letter to my few hundred devoted students to announce my first book campaign. As a result, *Power Healing* became an international bestseller.

The Divine told me exactly how to do this soul marketing technique. I cannot honor and thank the Divine enough for revealing this profound soul secret. I also deeply appreciate my devoted students for their great support. I could not have reached any success without them. I also deeply appreciate the soul marketing effort. The Divine and many souls in the universe blessed the success of *Power Healing*.

The Power of Soul Marketing

After the great success of the soul marketing efforts for *Power Healing*, I published my next two books, *Soul Mind Body Medicine* and *Living Divine Relationships*, in 2006. In 2007 the original hardcover editions of *Soul Wisdom I* and *Soul Communication* were published. In 2008 expanded trade paperback editions were published by Heaven's Library and Atria Books. For each of these books, I used the soul marketing technique the Divine taught me for *Power Healing*. *Soul Mind Body Medicine*, *Soul Wisdom I*, *Soul Wisdom* (paperback), and *Soul Communication* (paperback) became *New York Times* bestsellers, while

Living Divine Relationships, Soul Wisdom, and *Soul Communication* reached number one on Amazon.com's bestseller list.

In 2006 the Divine guided me to travel worldwide for six months nonstop to teach Soul Mind Body Medicine. I visited many cities in the United States and Canada. I also went to New Zealand, Australia, and England. I held more than 140 events in those six months. I was not a well-known speaker at that time. I did not have any professional event or speaking engagement organizers.

I did some serious planning for this tour with my business team. We asked the Divine where I should go. The Divine guided me very specifically to certain countries and cities. As I always follow Divine Guidance, those were exactly the places I included in my tour. Interestingly, we did not have any significant connections in most of those cities and countries. In many of those cities, we did not have any connection at all.

How could we make some connections, explore opportunities, and establish a presence for me in these cities? My team called local churches, universities, traditional Chinese medicine schools, nursing homes, yoga centers, shiatsu centers—whoever might have some affinity for my teaching. I called the souls of each of them. I did soul marketing to them. Then we made physical contact.

Our tour of 140-plus events was a great success. Almost literally overnight, I became an international speaker. Always following Divine Guidance, I was also brave enough to bring three or four of my students and teachers with me wherever I traveled. You can imagine the expense of doing this tour, with the costs of travel, hotels, venue rentals, advertising, and other promotion. The cost was huge but the Divine and Heaven gave me a huge blessing. People around the world gave me great support. We successfully accomplished our trip.

How to Do Soul Marketing

To do soul marketing, you need to follow a few key principles:

- Start by chanting *3396815* three times. This is very important. 3396185 (San San Jiu Liu Ba Yao Wu, pronounced *sahn sahn joe lew bah yow woo*) is a divine code. During the twenty-first century and the entire Soul Light Era, there is a big difference between chanting and not chanting this divine code. If you chant this divine code, you will receive a great response from the Soul World. If you do not chant this special number, many souls will respond by saying, "We are busy. We have no time to support you."

- After chanting *3396815* three times, then call the souls you want to call. If you are doing soul marketing only for your business or organization, call all the souls of the employees or members. Then tell them what you want, just as if you were having a physical meeting with them. If you want to do soul marketing for a city, call all the souls of humanity in the city. Ask them to support you. If you want to do soul marketing for a whole country, call all the souls in that country. Ask them to support you. If you want to do soul marketing for all humanity, call all the souls of humanity. If you want to do soul marketing for all souls in all universes, ask all souls in all universes to support you.

- After you begin by chanting *3396815* three times, the most important principle is to ask the souls you have called to support you for a good purpose and good service. You can never use 3396815 to ask any souls to support you in taking advantage of others or in any other action that is not good service for humanity. If you offer unpleasant service with soul marketing, you could learn a huge lesson. You will not receive the blessing of Heaven and the Soul World. Instead, you could receive a major blockage.

- Tell the souls you have called what you want them to do to support you. Be specific, just as though you were in a physical meeting. Then chant *3396815* for three to five minutes.
- Close with *Hao! Hao! Hao! Thank you. Thank you. Thank you. Please return.*

These are the important principles to follow when doing soul marketing. I have taught this wisdom to my students orally. Until now, I have not shared this soul secret in writing. In this chapter, I have shared my personal experiences with soul marketing wisdom and techniques. In the last few years, hundreds of my students have applied this soul marketing wisdom for their finances and business. Their results, like mine, have been remarkably successful. I wish that you too will apply this divine wisdom to benefit your finances and business.

Karma for Finances and Business

Almost all human beings have bad karma. In the last few years, about four thousand people around the world have applied for divine karma cleansing service. The Divine and the Akashic Records showed me that fewer than ten of them were already karma free. For each karma cleansing application I receive, I must check with Divine Guidance for approval. I want to emphasize that I do not clear karma by myself. The Divine clears your karma. I am a servant of the Divine to offer this major spiritual service to humanity.

Karma is the root blockage of life. Karma is spiritual debt. In the physical world, you may take out a student loan to go to college. You have to repay this debt after you leave college. Whenever you have a physical debt to others, you have to pay it back. Bad karma is the accumulation of all the mistakes you have made in this life and in your hundreds of previous lives. You have a spiritual debt to the souls of all the people you have harmed or hurt. You have to pay them back also. The way you repay your spiritual debt is by learning lessons through blockages that can appear in any aspect of your life, including relationships and finances.

To transform your business, remember to clear your own karma. Remember that there is only one way to clear karma by yourself: offer unconditional universal service to humanity, animals, the environment, and Mother Earth.

I offer karma cleansing because the Divine asked me to do it for the Divine. Through this service, the Divine offers education and divine blessings to humanity. People request. The Divine approves. People honor. The Divine blesses. I am simply a servant of humanity and the Divine.

The results of karma cleansing have been beyond words. It has saved people's lives. It has healed "hopeless" cases. It has transformed relationships and finances. In February 2008 I taught a weekend workshop with about two hundred participants in Frankfurt, Germany. It was my second visit to Germany. About fifty people in this workshop had received karma cleansing during my first visit to Germany in 2007. During the workshop, many people in this group of karma-free beings came to the stage to share their heart-touching stories of life transformation following their karma cleansings. Some of them shared how their relationships had improved. Others mentioned a major shift to success in their business. Several people experienced significant improvement in their health. Others said they felt great inner peace and inner joy, as though a great weight had been lifted from their shoulders.

Educated, moved, and inspired, about eighty other people at the workshop applied for and received karma cleansing from the Divine. In total, about 130 of the two hundred participants received divine karma cleansing. They were extremely moved and touched by the divine karma cleansing service. People thanked me deeply. I told them to thank the Divine. The Divine offered the karma cleansing. I am a servant to offer the Divine's service. I do not and cannot take any credit. All the credit belongs to the Divine and Heaven. I am extremely honored to serve.

The Importance of the Name of the Business

I want to share another important piece of soul wisdom with you: a business should have a good name. The name of a business carries messages. The wrong name will affect the business deeply.

In China, in the countryside, some parents call their child *zhu er,* which means "pig child." This is meant as a term of endearment, so the parents, family members, and others around the child affectionately keep calling the child *zhu er, zhu er.* But what happens to the child? In school, the child cannot study well at all, because the child's name links with the message of a pig, and a pig does not have high enough intelligence. Names are very important for a human being.

In the same way, names are very important for a business. How can you know whether you have a proper business name? You can open your advanced spiritual communication channels to ask for and receive guidance. If your soul communication channels are not sufficiently open, you can get a reading and guidance from someone who has opened his or her spiritual channels widely. I have trained and certified high-level spiritual beings to offer divine soul readings and guidance to humanity. They would be delighted to serve you. In the spiritual journey, people need pure, divine soul channels for guidance.

Using Soul Communication to Guide
Your Business Decisions

To make good business decisions, proper business planning, a good marketing team, a supportive and flexible infrastructure, a customer-oriented philosophy, realistic financial budgeting, solid financial controls, and more are all very important. However, Divine Guidance is also vital for business decisions. Sometimes you may think you have made a great business decision from excellent input and good analysis. You may think you have a great plan for implementing your decision. Nevertheless, success does not follow. You wonder what went wrong. What you may not realize is that this business decision did not receive support from Heaven. The decision was not aligned with the direction that Heaven's Team wants.

Therefore, it is vital to do soul communication to ask for soul guidance from Heaven's Team. If your business decision receives great support from Heaven's Team, success could come much more easily. Opening your spiritual channels in order to receive guidance from Heaven's Team and the Divine is vital for the success of your business.

Efficient and Effective Business Operations

A successful business usually has an excellent team of professionals who understand and run the business. As a business grows, it must have very capable business team members in every aspect of the business. Successful business team members are efficient and effective. In the business world, every aspect of business needs professional workers and guidance. Such people have mastered a great deal of wisdom, knowledge, and practices in every aspect of business. I honor and respect them. What I am offering are soul secrets, wisdom, knowledge, and practices for business. This does not at all mean we should ignore the physical aspects of business.

Every organization must have a proper structure and professional team members. Efficient and effective business operations are vital for success. If an organization has a great physical team, adding soul secrets, soul wisdom and knowledge, soul marketing, soul healing, soul blessing, and soul transformation to the business will bring much more success to the organization and to its team members.

Learn from the many great teachings on business in the physical world. Take the soul secrets, soul wisdom, and soul marketing techniques that I am offering you to enhance your finances and business. I wish you will have great business success!

Leadership and Management

Every business needs leadership. The leader must have the vision and ability to create and manifest the mission of the business. A great leader must be able to do the following:

- present a clear vision and a direction in which to move the company
- have great abilities to plan, market, and control
- create efficient and effective business operations
- delegate responsibilities to others
- offer great love, care, and compassion to all employees
- gather employees' hearts and motivate team effort
- be client- and customer-oriented
- be sensitive to mistakes and act quickly to correct them
- implement great systems for rewarding good work and preventing mistakes

I am not a business expert. I am learning new business wisdom and knowledge year after year, but my business team members have much more business wisdom and knowledge and know many more strategies and practices than I do. There are many great teachings about business. What I offer in this chapter is how to use the *power of soul* for business success. The key secrets and wisdom I have revealed in this chapter are:

- the power of soul marketing
- how to do soul marketing

- the relationship between karma and business success
- the need for a great physical team *and* the support of Heaven's Team
- the importance of the name of the business
- why soul communication is vital in guiding business decisions

As we move through the twenty-first century and Mother Earth's transition period, I deeply believe that the most successful businesses and the most successful business leaders will be the ones who use the power of soul in all of their business decisions and activities. These leaders will make all important decisions—hiring, compensation and incentive systems, locating and naming the business, product launches, pricing strategies, marketing strategies and initiatives, corporate structure and organization, use of technology, and more—using soul communication and soul guidance. They will implement decisions using soul guidance and soul marketing.

Every business has a soul. Every business has its soul journey. As with a human being, the physical journey and the soul journey of a business are deeply interconnected. Businesses that offer good service will be blessed and flourish. Businesses that are total GOLD servants will be extremely blessed and flourish beyond imagination.

The soul journey of your business is also related to your own soul journey. Transform the soul of your business. Clear bad karma. Transform yourself. Align your business and yourself with Heaven's direction. Great success is waiting for you.

I wish the soul wisdom in this chapter and this entire book will benefit your business. I wish your business will have great success.

Hao! Hao! Hao!

Thank you. Thank you. Thank you.

Transform Your Soul Journey

MILLIONS OF PEOPLE worldwide are on the spiritual journey now. The spiritual journey is the soul journey. More and more people are searching for soul secrets, wisdom, knowledge, and practices. Many people understand the purpose of the soul journey. Many other people may not be clear on the purpose of the soul journey. Many people are on the soul journey without realizing it. Many people do not think they are on the soul journey when in fact they are doing spiritual work. There are many soul secrets and practices and much soul wisdom and knowledge on the soul journey. I am delighted to share the essence of the soul journey.

What Is the Soul Journey?

A human being has a path from birth to death—from infancy, through childhood, education, growth, maturation, adulthood, work and career, marriage, parenthood, retirement, senior citizenship, aging, and sickness. That is the physical path and journey. For your whole life, your soul resides inside your body. Your soul has its own life. Your soul's life is related to your physical life, but your soul has its own journey.

Physical life is very short. Soul life is eternal. After your physical life ends, your soul will go to the Akashic Records, stay in Heaven for a while, and then move on to its next physical life. As I was contemplating this about twenty-five years ago, I had an "aha" moment. That "aha" moment gave me this insight. It is the one-sentence secret about the relationship between physical life and soul life:

Physical life is to serve soul life.

If one does not move one's soul life further during one's physical life, it is a great pity.

In order to understand the soul journey, we must understand where the soul comes from and where the soul is going. We must further understand the soul itself. I am delighted to release the following deep secret wisdom about the soul for the first time.

A human being consists of soul, mind, and body. In fact:

A human being has three major souls.

These three major souls are:

- Tian Ming
- Ren Xing
- Wu Shen

1. TIAN MING

Tian Ming is a soul from the Akashic Records. "Tian" means *Heaven.* "Ming" means *order.* So Tian Ming is Heaven's order. When a human being is born, Heaven and the Akashic Records send this soul to the newborn's body.

Your Tian Ming sits in your Ling Gong, or "soul temple," which is located between your heart and Message Center. Heaven sends you your Tian Ming to guide and assist your soul journey. Every person's soul is given a task from Heaven before birth. In your physical life, you have your work tasks and your family tasks. In the same way, in your soul life, you have a task given by Heaven. Your Tian Ming will guide, lead, and supervise your body soul to accomplish the task it is given by Heaven. This is "Heaven's order."

2. REN XING

"Ren" means *human being.* "Xing" means *nature.* So Ren Xing is your true nature and your true self. Ren Xing is what I have described throughout this book as your body soul. This is what most people understand as a human being's soul. Like Tian Ming and Wu Shen, Ren Xing also comes from Heaven and resides in your body. There are seven houses of the body soul in a human's body:

- just above the genital area
- lower abdomen, between the genitals and the navel
- navel area
- heart chakra or Message Center
- throat
- head
- just above the top of the head (above crown chakra)

Where your Ren Xing, or body soul, resides depends on your spiritual standing in Heaven. The higher your spiritual standing, the higher the house your body soul will reside within. Very important knowledge that I shared earlier is that if your soul can sit in the heart chakra or Message Center, your soul is an enlightened soul. If your soul can sit even higher, above the Message Center, your soul has reached higher layers of enlightenment in Heaven.

Your body soul is the soul that reincarnates. Your whole life's efforts, both good services and bad services, are recorded in your body
soul and in the Akashic Records. When people talk about a human
being's body, mind, and spirit, that spirit is the body soul or Ren Xing.
When I talk about a human being's soul, mind, and body, that soul is
also the body soul or Ren Xing.

3. WU SHEN

"Wu" means *five*. "Shen" means *souls*. Wu Shen indicates the souls of
the five major organs, which are the heart, spleen, lungs, kidneys, and
liver. The soul of the heart is named heart *shen*. The soul of the spleen
is named spleen *yi*. The souls of the lungs are named lung *po*. The
souls of the kidneys are named kidney *zhi*. The soul of the liver is
named liver *hun*. Wu Shen also comes from Heaven when you are
born. They also stay with you for your whole life.

When you end your physical life, your Wu Shen leaves you first.
Next your Ren Xing will leave. Finally, your Tian Ming will go back
to Heaven and the Akashic Records.

※

Every system, every organ, every cell, every cell unit, every DNA and
RNA, and every space inside the body has a soul. Every organ contains
millions or billions of cells. It's very hard to say how many souls there
are inside the body.

Each soul has its own consciousness, its own wisdom, its own abilities and power, and its own journey. This book reveals soul secrets,
soul wisdom, soul knowledge, and soul practices. To reveal the secret
above about the three major souls of a human being is to let you know
that your soul has a task from Heaven. If you accomplish Heaven's
task in your life, after your physical life ends your Tian Ming and the
Akashic Records will uplift your soul standing. If you make great con-

tributions to humanity and Mother Earth, your soul standing can be uplifted during your physical life. When I offer Soul Healing and Enlightenment retreats, as well as Advanced Soul Healing and Enlightenment retreats, the Divine offers his enlightenment to participants' souls in a divine way.

Now that I have shared these profound secrets and wisdom, we can answer the original question. What is the soul journey? The soul journey includes purification of the soul, transformation of the soul, and enlightenment of the soul. The soul can grow. The soul can boost its own power. The soul can gain great abilities. Jesus, Mary, Shi Jia Mo Ni Fuo, Ar Mi Tuo Fuo, Guan Yin, Pu Ti Lao Zu, and other top saints and buddhas have great soul abilities. They served humanity and Mother Earth very well through their many lifetimes. The Divine recognized this by boosting and blessing their Soul Power. As a result, they are special servants who have created heart-touching stories for humanity.

Is there a one-sentence soul secret for the soul journey? The answer is *yes*. The one-sentence soul secret of the soul journey is:

The soul journey is the journey to uplift your soul standing in Heaven until it has reached its ultimate destination, which is the realm of the Divine.

Transform the Soul First; Then Every Aspect of Life Will Be Transformed

Millions of people are searching for and dreaming of life transformation. They want to transform their health, their relationships, their finances, and much more. There are many great teachings about transforming health, relationships, and finances. I would like to share my insight as to the most important soul secret for life transformation. It is:

In order to transform every aspect of your life, transform your
soul first. Then all life transformation will follow.

Why do we need to transform the soul first? The soul is the boss for a human being. If you transform the soul of a human being, every aspect of the human being will be transformed. Similarly, a business has a soul. If you transform the soul of the business, every aspect of the business will be transformed.

To transform the soul is to cleanse karma, purify, accumulate virtue, become a total GOLD and unconditional universal servant, and uplift the soul's spiritual standing to enlightenment and further. When this is done, blockages to transformation in every aspect of life are removed.

To transform the soul, use the power of soul. Soul Power is the power of the Soul World. Soul Power connects with Heaven and the Divine. Divine Soul Power is beyond imagination. The secret of soul transformation is to apply the Divine Soul Power of the Divine Soul Song "God Gives His Heart to Me." You can listen to a sample of this Soul Song for several minutes on my website.

On November 8, 2007, while I was holding a Soul Healing and Enlightenment retreat in San Francisco, the Divine downloaded a Divine Soul Transplant of this Divine Soul Song to all souls. Chant with this Divine Soul Download for at least fifteen minutes per time, twice a day, the longer the better. To chant this Soul Song is to completely meld your soul, heart, mind, and body with the Divine. You will receive and you can offer great transformation by chanting this Divine Soul Song. The power is immeasurable.

Say *hello* first:

Dear divine soul of the Divine Soul Song "God Gives His
Heart to Me," downloaded to my soul and to every soul
in all universes,
I love you, honor you, and appreciate you.

Turn on, please.
Please transform my life—soul, heart, mind, and body.
Please transform the life of every soul of humanity and
  every soul in all universes.
I am very grateful.
Thank you.

Let me remind you of the one-sentence soul secret for chanting: You *are* the mantra. Sing!

Lu la lu la la li
Lu la lu la la li
Lu la lu la li
Lu la lu la li

God gives his heart to me
God gives his love to me
My heart melds with his heart
My love melds with his love

This Divine Soul Song soul has power that is totally beyond any words and any description. Chant with it. Sing with it. Benefit from it. Offer incredible service to humanity and all souls with it. Transform every aspect of your life.

The Power of Soul Transformation and How to Transform Your Soul

The purpose of the teachings in this book is to introduce and move humanity to *soul over matter*, which is to use the power of soul. If you heal the soul first, healing of the mind and body will follow. If you prevent sicknesses of the soul first, sicknesses of the mind and body will be prevented. If you rejuvenate the soul first, rejuvenation of the mind and body will follow. If you prolong the life of the soul first, life will be prolonged.

The teaching of this chapter is to transform your soul first; transformation of every aspect of life will follow. I will lead you in three soul practices to show you how to transform the soul of any and every aspect of your life.

You can apply the eight Divine Soul Transplants you have received so far in this book to offer soul transformation for every aspect of your life. In the first practice, I will use one of them as an example to transform our souls.

PRACTICE 1

> *Dear my divine soul of Divine Love,*
> *I love you, honor you, and appreciate you.* (Divine Love melts all blockages and transforms all life.)
> *Please turn on.* (You received this treasure when you read chapter 2. This permanent divine soul treasure resides in your body. You need to activate it.)
> *Please transform my soul in order to transform my life.* (Make your request for transformation of any aspect of your life—physical, emotional, mental, or spiritual; relationships, finances, and so on.)
> *I am very grateful.*
> *Thank you.*

Then chant:

> *Divine Love soul transforms my life.*
> *Divine Love soul transforms my life.*
> *Divine Love soul transforms my life.*
> *Divine Love soul transforms my life . . .*

Chant for at least three minutes, silently or aloud, the longer the better.

> *Hao! Hao! Hao!*
> *Thank you. Thank you. Thank you.*

In this book, I have led you to do many similar practices. You could still be wondering: *Does this really work?*

Now I am sharing with you and leading you to do soul practices for soul transformation. This first practice is a divine soul transformation technique. The technique itself is a one-sentence soul secret. Like many of the other practices and secrets in this book, it may be too simple to believe. But if you can do this one-sentence secret practice, why would you need to practice using two or more sentences? Always remember:

> *The simplest secret is the best secret.*

I have studied and experienced all of the major ancient Chinese arts. I have offered soul teaching, soul transformation of life, and soul enlightenment for many, many years. I did not know these one-sentence secrets in my early years. I have had to learn step by step. I have advanced my wisdom and knowledge step by step.

Since 1993, when I began to develop my advanced spiritual channels highly, my advancement has accelerated. Since then I have received direct divine teaching and experienced many "aha" moments. Now I am able to deliver divine secrets for healing, prevention of sickness, rejuvenation, life transformation, and enlightenment. I am delighted to offer these simplest soul secrets, wisdom, knowledge, and practices to you and all humanity.

I always say:

> *If you want to know if a pear is sweet, taste it.*
> *If you want to know the power of the soul, experience it.*

The results will confirm the true wisdom and power of the soul.

Now I am ready to offer the ninth Divine Soul Transplant in this book:

Divine Soul Transplant of Divine Compassion

Sit up straight. Put the tip of your tongue near the roof of your mouth. Relax. Open your heart and soul.

Prepare!

Divine Soul Transplant of Divine Compassion
Silent download!

Close your eyes for thirty seconds to receive this major divine soul treasure.

Hao! Hao! Hao!
Thank you. Thank you. Thank you.

Thank you so much to the Divine. Every divine soul treasure is priceless. We are receiving divine honor and we are practicing divine life transformation. This has never happened before in history. Why do I lead you again and again to practice in the simplest way? The answer is Da tao zhi jian. *The Big Way is extremely simple.* Why do we need complicated ways? Is it too simple to believe? Do it with me! You will understand further and further. Your heart and soul will be touched. You will receive more and more "aha" moments.

Now let's do the next practice together.

PRACTICE 2

Dear my divine soul of Divine Compassion,
I love you, honor you, and appreciate you.

Please turn on.
Please transform my soul in order to transform my life.
   (Make your request for transformation of any aspect
   of your life—physical, emotional, mental or spiritual;
   relationships, finances, and so on.)
I am very grateful.
Thank you.

Then chant:

Divine Compassion soul transforms my soul, heart, mind,
   and body.
Divine Compassion soul transforms my soul, heart, mind,
   and body.
Divine Compassion soul transforms my soul, heart, mind,
   and body.
Divine Compassion soul transforms my soul, heart, mind,
   and body . . .

Chant for at least three minutes, silently or aloud, the longer the better.

Hao! Hao! Hao!
Thank you. Thank you. Thank you.

Next I am delighted to offer the tenth Divine Soul Transplant in this book:

Divine Soul Transplant of Divine Honesty

Sit up straight. Put the tip of your tongue near the roof of your mouth. Relax. Open your heart and soul.
Prepare!

Divine Soul Transplant of Divine Honesty
Silent download!

Close your eyes for thirty seconds to receive this major divine soul treasure.

> *Hao! Hao! Hao!*
> *Thank you. Thank you. Thank you.*

Congratulations to you for receiving two more priceless divine life-transforming treasures in this chapter! Now ask your Divine Honesty soul to transform your relationships and finances in order to transform your life:

PRACTICE 3

> *Dear my divine soul of Divine Honesty,*
> *I love you, honor you, and appreciate you.*
> *Please turn on.*
> *Please transform the souls of my relationships and finances*
>   *in order to transform my life.* (Make your request for
>   transformation of any aspect of your relationships
>   and finances.)
> *I am very grateful.*
> *Thank you.*

Then chant:

> *Divine Honesty soul transforms my relationships and*
>   *finances.*
> *Divine Honesty soul transforms my relationships and*
>   *finances.*

*Divine Honesty soul transforms my relationships and
    finances.
Divine Honesty soul transforms my relationships and
    finances . . .*

Chant for at least three minutes, silently or aloud, the longer the better.

*Hao! Hao! Hao!
Thank you. Thank you. Thank you.*

So far in this book, I have shared the soul secrets and soul wisdom of soul healing, soul prevention of sickness, soul prolongation of life, soul transformation of relationships, soul transformation of finances, and, in this chapter, soul transformation of life. I have introduced the power of soul. The Divine has offered ten Divine Soul Transplants. Divine Soul Transplants carry Divine Soul Power. We have progressed through soul practices from using your own Soul Power to using Divine Soul Power. As you have learned and experienced, the techniques are extremely simple. It could take someone many years to fully realize and appreciate the simplicity of this teaching.

How can I offer this teaching? Why do these techniques work? The Divine guided me to offer this teaching. The techniques and practices work because the Divine and Heaven are offering these secrets, wisdom, and knowledge to us. We are practicing *soul over matter*. The power of soul can heal, prevent sickness, rejuvenate, prolong life, and transform consciousness and every aspect of life, including relationships and finances. Why does it work? The soul carries an order. A divine soul carries a divine order. The soul is the boss for a human being. The soul is the boss for our lives. If souls are transformed, every aspect of life will be transformed.

Pause for a moment. Think again about the simplicity. If the Divine guided me to share this simplest way to heal, rejuvenate, and transform our lives, let us follow this divine direction and try it.

Experience it.

Digest it.

Absorb it.

Benefit from it.

Transform our lives with it.

Hao! Hao! Hao!

Thank you. Thank you. Thank you.

13

Soul Enlightenment

MILLIONS OF PEOPLE are searching for soul secrets, wisdom, knowledge, and practices. If you are on the spiritual journey, you definitely want to know the answer to the question, "What is the purpose of the spiritual journey?" As I have already explained, the answer is straightforward. The purpose of the spiritual journey is to uplift your spiritual standing. The first step is to reach soul enlightenment.

What Is Soul Enlightenment?

Soul enlightenment is a special spiritual standing in Heaven. People who reach soul enlightenment have done great service for humanity and Mother Earth. They are committed as unconditional universal servants to offer universal love, forgiveness, peace, healing, blessing, harmony, and enlightenment to humanity and all souls.

As I have already shared, when you reach soul enlightenment, your soul will reside in or above your Message Center.

At this moment, the Divine is telling me that of the more than 6.6 billion people on Mother Earth at this time, only about 15 percent have reached soul enlightenment. For all of humanity to uplift its soul standing to the level of enlightenment is a huge task.

Benefits of Soul Enlightenment

To reach soul enlightenment is to uplift your soul standing in Heaven. Why does a spiritual being want to uplift his or her soul standing? The higher the spiritual standing a spiritual being has, the greater the blessings that being can receive. The blessings include abilities to heal, bless, and transform one's own life, as well as abilities to serve others.

As human beings, our souls reside in Jiu Tian, the realm of Heaven in which reincarnation continues. Jiu Tian literally means the "nine heavens." Each soul in Jiu Tian resides in one of nine layers or levels. The lowest layer is the ninth one, Level 9. The highest layer is Level 1. The following list will give you an idea of what souls can be found in each layer:

Layer of Jiu Tian	Souls at This Level
1	saints
2	saints
3	human beings
4	human beings
5	fish, other animals
6	bacteria, viruses, insects, birds, other animals
7	plants, forests, mountains, others
8	oceans, rivers, other inanimate things
9	stones, sand, other inanimate things

Everyone and everything has a soul. Different souls stand in different layers. The Divine made a spiritual law: *Only through service can a soul uplift its standing.* A soul must serve hundreds of lifetimes with a good record. Only then can a soul be uplifted higher and higher. If a soul offers unpleasant service, its spiritual standing can descend.

Who makes the judgment about whether a soul's spiritual standing should be uplifted, lowered, or kept the same? It is the Akashic Records. In the Akashic Records, there are different categories. Different layers of souls are recorded in different departments of the Akashic Records.

As a spiritual being, you must know this secret:

When your soul is enlightened, your soul is
instantly uplifted to Level 2.

This means:

Your soul moves to the saints' realm.

Levels 1 and 2 in the nine layers of Heaven are the saints' realm. Level 1 can be subdivided into two sublevels, 1A and 1B. Level 2 can also be subdivided into 2A and 2B. When you become an enlightened being, you are first uplifted to Level 2B. As you continue to serve, your soul standing can be uplifted further and further. It could take many, many lifetimes to uplift your soul standing from 2B to 2A alone. Generally speaking, for a normal human being whose soul stands in Level 3 or 4, it takes hundreds of lifetimes to reach the first layer of soul enlightenment, Level 2B. To uplift your soul from Level 2B to Level 1A, the top sublevel of saints in the nine layers of Heaven, it could take hundreds, even thousands, of additional lifetimes.

Therefore, the soul journey is a long, long journey. The soul enlightenment journey itself is a long, long journey. Many people think that a soul-enlightened being is one with pure love and light, a being who is very kind and compassionate. This is correct. These qualities are basic requirements for an enlightened soul. But to have these qualities does not mean your soul is enlightened. The standard for being soul enlightened is to have your soul stand at the saints' level, Level 2B or above.

In your physical life, if you have good health, a good family, good love relationships, and good finances, then you are blessed. You are satisfied. You are happy. In your spiritual life, if you are enlightened, you enjoy much greater success and blessings. Your soul is uplifted. Your soul will have inner peace and inner joy. Your soul will have great abilities to serve others. The sooner you can reach soul enlightenment, the sooner you can receive these special blessings from the Divine.

At this time, I would like Dr. Peter Hudoba to share with you part of his enlightenment journey. Dr. Hudoba is one of my Divine Master Teachers and Master Healers. I believe his experiences and insights will help you further understand the significance and benefits of soul enlightenment.

I have been studying with Dr. Sha for eight years. In those eight years, I completed my lifelong search for the Divine. I had struggled profoundly in this search for almost my entire life. From early childhood I knew I was on a journey toward something, but I didn't know exactly what I was seeking. I was like a blind man trying to find his path.

When I was ten years old, I was bullied by some schoolmates. My parents enrolled me in a martial arts school. I learned secret eastern techniques of combat that helped me put an end to the bullying very quickly. This taught me a fundamental principle: there are indeed special ways to enhance any of our abilities.

I have been guided by this principle ever since. Whenever I encountered adversity, I intuitively searched for special techniques to overcome it. I was always searching for special knowledge, for special ways of doing things, and for special techniques that would give my actions some special power. I was also searching for secret wisdom, for some set of principles that would enable me not only to overcome the adverse aspects of my life, but also to enhance the positive aspects.

From that young age of ten, I embarked on a conscious search for the principles of the Tao, the sacred and secret wisdom that evolved over thousands of years through the Taoist wizards of China. I was searching for that special wisdom that would empower me to improve every aspect of my life, including diet, sleep, sex, exercises for health, self-healing, meditation practice, interactions with others—literally every aspect of my life. I was using the I Ching, the ancient Chinese classic that offers a system of divination, to guide me in my life decisions.

Through decades of extensive study and research, I succeeded in amassing an enormous amount of knowledge. I scoured libraries in every city I visited. I studied ancient texts as a member of the British Library. After moving to Toronto, I literally spent days in the university library, and in Saskatchewan as well. I translated sixty of the nearly fifteen hundred texts compiled in the Tao Zang, the Taoist canon. I made annotation after annotation on hundreds of pages until I finally felt I was beginning to understand the true principles of life.

In the course of this deep study, I was able to discover special ways to improve many aspects of my personal life. I also came to a growing realization that there were some invisible forces shaping my life that eluded my control. Although I gradually became more and more able to manage my body, control my emotions, and clarify and purify my mind—giving me a much happier inner existence—I was still unable to go beyond that, to shape my destiny. These invisible forces were clearly unimpressed by my attempts to influence them. I knew that I had reached the limits of what I could achieve through my personal efforts.

In early 2000, once again, my life situation turned in a

direction that was very obviously outside my control. I decided to find a teacher who could teach me how to master my entire life, not just parts of it.

That October, I had the greatest honor and blessing of meeting Dr. Sha. From that moment, I knew that my search had changed its focus. Under Dr. Sha's guidance, I was empowered to go much more deeply into myself. I started to work on dismantling all of the negativity within.

Dr. Sha challenged me, and has continued to challenge me, to turn my focus in this direction. He pointed out that in order to succeed, it would not be enough to continue only to improve my physical and mental abilities; I must also discard my disabilities.

Dr. Sha taught me that the adversity in my life did not come from without, but rather from within. I myself was the cause of my difficulties! He explained that the karmic forces of my own wrongdoing from this life and all my past lives were manifesting these seemingly external adverse situations. However, Dr. Sha not only showed me how to recognize these karmic forces; he gave me incredibly powerful tools to dismantle these powers that were suffocating my life.

Within ten months of our first meeting, I was able, with Dr. Sha's guidance and techniques, to purify my soul to such a degree that I was liberated from my karmic bonds. Dr. Sha then opened my heart chakra and brought so much light to my soul that it ascended and sat in my chest. I had reached soul enlightenment and entered the realm of Buddha. That was when the real training started.

Once I became enlightened, I practiced the highest levels of spiritual teachings, following the path of the saints to achieve ascension to the highest levels of sainthood until I was finally able to approach the Divine. This fascinating journey was in-

credibly painful and challenging; yet the results were so beautiful that I persevered despite all the obstacles in my path.

Soon I realized how deeply immersed I am in the spiritual world, even as a living human being in the physical world. When my spiritual channels opened widely, my Third Eye and direct soul communication abilities reached a high level of proficiency. I was able to see saints. I was able to see the Light Side and the Dark Side. I could see clearly the forces that were shaping my life. On the one hand, I could see the Dark Side creating obstacles. On the other hand, I could see many holy beings and angels helping me to get through these obstacles. I continued to progress and analyze events in both the Soul World and the physical world. With deep insights and "aha" moments, I started to understand how the universe truly works.

After Dr. Sha received the authority and ability to transmit divine souls to humanity in 2003, my spiritual journey took another dramatic leap. Dr. Sha started to offer his students Divine Soul Downloads. Since these divine treasures first became part of my being, I have been able to enhance my spiritual evolution with breathtaking speed. Every facet of my practice has been accelerated by Divine Soul Power, bringing my practice—and me!—to totally different dimensions.

I had been practicing the ancient art of Taoist alchemy since 1996, transforming my sexual energy into bodily energy and my bodily energy into soul light. Finally, I reached emptiness and strove to go further, to be at one with the Tao. I used a system I learned from ancient Taoist manuals. As I described above, it took me twenty-five years of diligent research to find this information, and fifteen more years of deep study and analysis to comprehend what it really meant.

Once I became enlightened, my mind opened to new possibilities. I started to understand the transformation process of reaching the highest levels of sainthood. This would never have been possible without Dr. Sha. Even if I understood the process, I did not have the tools, techniques, or power. I did not have the most important ingredient: divine light. Divine light is essential for spiritual alchemy. Only divine light can suffuse and melt away all of one's karmic bonds, including one's karmic signatures from one's sexual energy, from bodily energies, from one's mind, and from one's soul. Only divine light can purify soul, heart, mind, and body completely.

Once I had the spark of divine light, the most advanced spiritual transformation described in ancient Taoist alchemy became very attainable. But Dr. Sha did not stop there. He taught me that the techniques described in ancient texts were not enough. I had to go beyond them. I had to throw out everything I had studied, analyzed, and learned. I had to take a totally new approach to spiritual transformation.

Once again, I had to reorient my entire being to a new perspective. My next major breakthrough occurred in 2006, when I gained a deep new insight into what Dr. Sha is doing. Purification of karma is vital, but it is not enough. In fact, Dr. Sha brings to us a direct experience of the process of creation, whereby one can shape one's destiny and life.

The key is to approach things from the point of view of the Creator. Dr. Sha refers to this as going into the "hero condition." Everything that Dr. Sha does is done from this perspective. He follows this fundamental Taoist principle that is so eloquently described in Lao Zi's Tao Te Jing *and that is, at heart, identical with the creation story in the Book of Genesis.*

In the Tao Te Jing:

The Tao creates one. One creates two. Two creates three. Three creates all things.

In the Book of Genesis:

First there was God. In the darkness, God said, "Let there be light." From the light came Heaven, from the darkness came Earth, and between Heaven and Earth, God created man and woman in his own image. Together, Heaven, Earth, and human being created all the possibilities and diversity we see on Earth and beyond.

Everything Dr. Sha does starts with soul. Soul gives direction. Soul gives light. Soul has power to cut through obstacles. Soul has power to create. With Divine Soul Power, Dr. Sha can create any aspect of his mission, from the minutest detail of his website to the vast direction of his entire mission.

Dr. Sha does not need to study ancient texts to teach us knowledge. He creates his own path using the soul as the leader for everything he does. Divine Soul Power, given and guided by the Divine, is the creation that Dr. Sha brings to us as a chosen divine servant.

Recently, it has become obvious to me that Dr. Sha does not even need experts to help him with any part of his mission and service. The Divine, through Dr. Sha, creates experts. Does the Divine want books to spread divine teachings? No problem! Dr. Sha will transmit divine writing power to create Divine Writers. Does the Divine want pure servants with extraordinary healing capabilities to help relieve the suffering of humanity? No problem! Dr. Sha will transmit divine healing power to create incredibly powerful Divine Healers in the blink of an eye.

Is there any limit to these realities and possibilities? No, there is none. This is true creation. This is the highest service and the best service for humanity and all souls.

Since I began to apply the principles of Soul Power in my practices, the results have been unparalleled and beyond words. The expansion of my soul and the vistas of my mind have exploded into an incredible breadth and richness. People are becoming happy and peaceful simply by being in my presence, without any such intention on my part. Spontaneous healings are occurring in my presence; all I need to do is activate the Divine Soul Healing Download that Dr. Sha so generously bestowed to me. I am able to offer my students blessings I would never have dreamt possible. I am helping them become happy and fulfilled. Their spiritual journeys are unfolding rapidly and beautifully.

It is not enough that I have become very happy and fulfilled. It is not enough that my life has been totally transformed. My transformation is shining to all who come to me. I myself can initiate the same process that I have gone through with Dr. Sha. It is as though the divine presence that shines through Dr. Sha to me is following its own direction. The process of attaining the ultimate goal of enlightening all souls is progressing further and further.

Dr. Sha's mission is enormous. The challenges may seem insurmountable, but the power of divine light and divine creation is an unstoppable force marching ever forward. What I now witness every week with Dr. Sha—instantaneous healings, divine karma cleansings, divine soul enlightenment with only two or three days of preparation, elevation of saints to new heights, and more—is absolutely incredible. All of this has happened in only a few short years. I dare not even imagine where Divine Soul Power and divine creation will take us ten years from now.

This is a new era—with new challenges, yes, but also with new possibilities and new visions. I am extremely joyful, grateful, honored, and humbled by the gifts I have received from my teacher, Dr. Sha, and from the Divine.

I wish from my heart that everyone would soon recognize this process that is unfolding. I wish that everyone will quickly open their hearts and souls to the love and light of the Divine.

⁑

The Soul Light Era started on August 8, 2003. It will last for fifteen thousand years. The divine direction for these fifteen thousand years is to enlighten all souls in the nine layers of Heaven. Even when you combine all souls of humanity and all souls in Jiu Tian, the Divine is telling me that only 15 percent of them are enlightened now. Therefore, soul enlightenment for all souls is a huge divine task.

In July 2003 I was chosen as a divine servant, vehicle, and channel. I have been extremely honored to offer Divine Soul Transplants for divine healing, blessing, and life transformation. I am also extremely honored to offer divine karma cleansing service. In 2004, the Divine asked me to hold Soul Healing and Enlightenment retreats regularly to enlighten the participants. In these retreats, the Divine sends an order to enlighten the participants. I will continue this divine service.

Advanced Soul Enlightenment

At this moment, the Divine guided me to release further divine soul secrets and wisdom to humanity. I just explained soul enlightenment and its benefits. Right away, the Divine asked me to explain advanced soul enlightenment.

I explained Jiu Tian, the nine layers of Heaven. Is there a Heaven above these nine layers? The answer is *yes*. The next layer above the nine layers of Heaven is named Tian Wai Tian, the *Heaven Beyond Heaven*. Tian Wai Tian is the divine realm. The Divine resides in his temple in Tian Wai Tian.

Souls who can be uplifted to Tian Wai Tian stop reincarnation. These souls will stay in this divine realm to do Xiu Lian and continue their spiritual journeys. They will receive direct divine teaching and blessing. They will continue to offer great service to humanity, Mother Earth, and all universes in soul form.

On August 8, 2003, when the Soul Light Era started, the previous fifteen-thousand-year era ended. In the entire fifteen thousand years of the previous era, only two souls were uplifted from Jiu Tian to Tian Wai Tian. They are Niu Wa Niang Niang and Yuan Shi Tian Zun. This tells you how difficult it is for a soul to be uplifted to Tian Wai Tian.

At this moment, the souls of Niu Wa Niang Niang and Yuan Shi Tian Zun have come to me as I am flowing this book. I am asking each of them, "How many lifetimes did it take you from your soul's first lifetime to reach Tian Wai Tian?" Niu Wa Niang Niang's answer is that it took her forty thousand lifetimes to reach Tian Wai Tian. Yuan Shi Tian Zun says it took him fifty-five thousand lifetimes to reach Tian Wai Tian. I am very grateful they shared these soul secrets with me and gave me the honor to share them with you.

Reincarnation is the spiritual path for any soul in Jiu Tian. A physical life is so short. The soul journey is forever. Can you imagine that these two top saints took forty thousand or more lifetimes to reach the divine realm? Human life is too full of struggles. If you really appreciate how long it takes to reach the divine realm, you will be very humbled. What kind of ego should we then have? What kinds of burdens should we carry? When we have conflicts, why can we not forgive?

On the spiritual journey, it is better to be farsighted, not nearsighted. If you can see the ultimate goal far, far into the future, you will have a different view of the world. You could transform every aspect of your life much more easily.

The Divine told me that in the Soul Light Era many more than just two spiritual beings will be uplifted to the divine realm. This is such fascinating news for high-level spiritual beings. You and everybody have an equal chance to move up on your spiritual journey. There is only one way: *Offer universal service unconditionally.* The more you serve, the higher you will be uplifted.

Why will more people be uplifted in the Soul Light Era? Mother

Earth is in a transition period. Because of global warming, natural disasters, conflicts, wars, sickness, and more, humans are suffering. At this special historic time, the Divine needs pure servants to stand out to offer love, peace, and harmony for humanity and for all souls. You serve. The Divine and Heaven bless. We are honored to be servants of humanity and all souls. Let us join hearts and souls together to serve and create love, peace, and harmony for humanity, Mother Earth, and all universes.

Enlighten the Soul First; Then Enlightenment of the Mind, Body, and Every Aspect of Life Will Follow

In order to enlighten your soul, you must transform your ego, attachments, selfishness, struggles for power, and more. There are many important teachings in the world now to guide you on this path. We honor and appreciate every teacher.

However, the Divine showed me the divine way to transform ego, attachments, selfishness, struggles for power, and more. The divine way is to use Divine Soul Power to transform all of them.

Now I am delighted to offer the eleventh and final Divine Soul Transplant in this book:

Divine Soul Transplant of Divine Purification

Sit up straight. Put the tip of your tongue near the roof of your mouth. Relax. Open your heart and soul.

Prepare!

Divine Soul Transplant of Divine Purification
Silent download!

Close your eyes for thirty seconds to receive this major divine soul treasure.

Hao! Hao! Hao!
Thank you. Thank you. Thank you.

Thank you, Divine.

Now ask your divine soul of Divine Purification to purify your soul, heart, mind, and body:

> *Dear my divine soul of Divine Purification,*
> *I love you, honor you, and appreciate you.*
> *Please turn on.*
> *Please purify my soul, heart, mind, and body and remove*
>   *all of their struggles, including ego, attachments, selfish-*
>   *ness, struggles for power, and more.*
> *I am very grateful.*
> *Thank you.*

Then chant:

> *Divine Purification soul purifies my soul, heart, mind, and*
>   *body and removes all of their heart and mind struggles.*
> *Divine Purification soul purifies my soul, heart, mind, and*
>   *body and removes all of their heart and mind struggles.*
> *Divine Purification soul purifies my soul, heart, mind, and*
>   *body and removes all of their heart and mind struggles.*
> *Divine Purification soul purifies my soul, heart, mind,*
>   *and body and removes all of their heart and mind*
>   *struggles . . .*

Chant for at least fifteen minutes per time, silently or aloud, twice a day—the longer the better.

> *Hao! Hao! Hao!*
> *Thank you. Thank you. Thank you.*

This is the divine way to transform all of your struggles—soul, heart, mind, and body.

I am extremely grateful for the Divine's generosity in offering this and the other ten priceless soul treasures downloaded to every reader in this book to heal, rejuvenate, transform, and enlighten our souls, hearts, minds, and bodies.

Enlighten the soul first; then enlightenment of the heart, mind, and body will follow. This divine way is the fastest way to enlighten your soul, heart, mind, and body.

To enlighten your soul is to uplift your soul standing to the saints' level.

To enlighten your heart is to have a totally loving and forgiving heart.

To enlighten your mind is to have a pure mind.

To enlighten your body is to have a healthy, strong body and long life.

There are many more secrets for enlightenment of the soul, heart, mind, and body that the Divine guided me to release in the future.

This is the most important wisdom about Divine Soul Downloads that every reader must remember: To receive divine soul treasures does not mean you are healed, rejuvenated, transformed, and enlightened. You now have eleven of these divine souls. You *must* practice with them. The more practice you do, the more you will heal, rejuvenate, transform, and enlighten your soul, heart, mind, and body.

Practice. Practice. Practice.

Heal. Heal. Heal.

Rejuvenate. Rejuvenate. Rejuvenate.

Transform. Transform. Transform.

Enlighten. Enlighten. Enlighten.

Hao! Hao! Hao!

Thank you. Thank you. Thank you.

How to Reach Soul Enlightenment

To reach soul enlightenment, one has to go through a few major steps in the spiritual journey.

- Purify soul, heart, mind, and body.
  An enlightened being must have a pure soul, heart, mind, and body. Xiu Lian, which means "purification practice," represents the totality of the spiritual journey. There have been many great teachings and practices throughout history for purification. Now, in the Soul Light Era, the Divine is offering us the divine way to do this, with the priceless gift of a divine soul of Divine Purification.

- Pass spiritual testing.
  Spiritual testing is part of the purification process. Passing spiritual testing is necessary for moving forward on your Xiu Lian journey. In your enlightenment journey, the higher your spiritual standing, the more seriously Heaven will test you. Testing can be very severe. Unfortunately, many spiritual beings cannot pass their tests. They quit their spiritual journey. Their spiritual standing goes up, down, up, down. They must reincarnate more times to continue their spiritual journey.

  If you cannot pass your spiritual tests in this life, Heaven and the Divine will give you the same tests in your next life. If you cannot pass the tests in your next life, you will continue to receive the tests again and again until you pass.

  Do you really want to move further on your enlightenment journey by passing your spiritual tests in this life? If you are a spiritual being, consider this question seriously.

  The spiritual journey is a painful journey. But at this special time, the Divine has given eleven priceless soul treasures in this book to transform and enlighten our souls, hearts, minds, and bodies. This has never happened before.

I cannot emphasize enough that you must spend time to practice. Activate the treasures. Follow the techniques and do the practices I have presented. Remember, Niu Wa Niang Niang and Yuan Shi Tian Zun spent forty thousand and fifty-five thousand lifetimes, respectively, to reach the divine realm. If you want to move to that realm, can you not spend fifteen minutes or a half hour twice a day to apply your divine soul treasures to transform and enlighten your soul, heart, mind, and body?

Think about the honor and privilege we are being given. Why are we receiving such a huge honor now? I have already explained it very clearly: Mother Earth is in transition. The Divine and Heaven urgently need enlightened beings to serve during Mother Earth's transition. That is why the Divine is offering his treasures in this book. You are given the divine way to heal, rejuvenate, transform, and enlighten your soul, heart, mind, and body. If you are grateful, inspired, and feel the honor, please do the practice. To do the practice is to respond to the Divine's calling. To do the practice is to benefit your soul journey and your physical journey. To do the practice is to stop your reincarnation sooner. I believe you will do it. I believe you will do it well.

- Serve humanity, Mother Earth, and all souls unconditionally.

Whenever you serve others, never think that you have gotten lost. Some participants in my workshops have told me that they served for many years, but they felt they got lost because they still faced many struggles in their lives. I smile. I say, "If you served a lot but your life is still full of struggles, do not complain. If you had not served a lot, you could have even more and even bigger struggles in your life."

Service must be unconditional. Study the lives of the holy saints, buddhas, and all major spiritual teachers. Every one of them went through a big struggle. Every one of them went through major spiritual testing. They were tested not just in one life, but in hundreds of lifetimes. When the Divine chose me as the Divine's servant to transmit divine soul treasures, the Divine told me the Divine had tested me for hundreds of lifetimes. In this lifetime I went through tremendously heavy testing. Remember: no testing, no growth. Pass tests, grow further. Pass big tests, grow even further.

- Make a vow to the Divine and Heaven.
  I already shared this vital soul secret for enlightenment in chapter 1. *If you are ready*, I suggest that you silently make a vow to the Divine and Heaven. Tell them you want to make a total commitment to serve humanity and all souls.

  After you make a vow, the Divine and Heaven will test you more. Therefore, you must be ready. Make a little vow and do it well; make a little progress in your enlightenment journey. Make a big vow and do it well; make big progress in your enlightenment journey. If you are not ready to make a vow, do not do it.

I welcome all to my Soul Healing and Enlightenment retreats and my Advanced Soul Healing and Enlightenment retreats. The Divine will send an order to enlighten your soul or to further enlighten your soul. These retreats will first give you soul healing and intensive soul purification and blessing in order to prepare you to receive the Divine Order given near the end of the retreat.

The Divine is telling me at this moment that this is his calling. If you are inspired and touched by the teachings of this book, I welcome you to join me. If you are ready, I am ready to serve you. I am ready to assist you to uplift your spiritual standing and to reach soul enlightenment and advanced soul enlightenment. I am honored to be your servant. I am honored to be a servant of humanity and the Divine.

Enlightening your soul is part of the beginning of the journey of soul enlightenment in the Soul Light Era. At this time, only 15 percent of humanity has reached enlightenment. The other 85 percent are waiting for enlightenment. Beyond humanity, there are countless souls in Jiu Tian. Only 15 percent of them are enlightened also. The other 85 percent of these souls are also waiting for soul enlightenment.

Soul enlightenment for humanity and for all souls in Jiu Tian is the Divine's calling and direction for the soul journey of humanity and all souls. It is the Divine's calling and direction for the Soul Light Era. We are honored to receive the Divine's calling and to move in the direction to which the Divine is guiding us.

To transform the consciousness of humanity and all souls is to move humanity and all souls to the soul enlightenment journey. The Divine guided me to create the Soul Power Series of books to offer soul healing, soul prevention of sickness, soul rejuvenation, soul prolongation of life, soul transformation for relationships, soul transformation for finances, soul transformation for all lives, and soul enlightenment for all souls. The Divine guided me to spread these teachings, wisdom, knowledge, and practices further through Soul Healing and Enlightenment teleconferences, workshops, radio programs, audio and video podcasts, the Internet, and other media to offer service to humanity. Join me. Allow me to serve you more. I dedicate my life to serve you, all humanity, Mother Earth, and all souls in all universes. I am honored to be a servant to all.

I love my heart and soul
I love all humanity

Join hearts and souls together
Love, peace and harmony
Love, peace and harmony

Hao! Hao! Hao!

Thank you. Thank you. Thank you.

14

Divine Soul Downloads and Divine Soul Orders

Up to now, I have explained the power of soul, including soul healing, soul rejuvenation, soul transformation, and soul enlightenment. I have also explained karma and Soul Orders. I have shared many soul secrets and practices and much wisdom and knowledge. I am honored that the Divine has offered many one-sentence soul secrets. I am extremely honored that I am flowing this divine book. The Divine is always above my head as I flow this book. Thank you, Divine.

In this chapter I will explain Divine Soul Downloads and Divine Soul Orders.

In July 2003 the Divine chose me as the Divine's servant and as a servant of humanity. The Divine told me that when I call the Divine, the Divine will offer blessings. When I ask the Divine, the Divine will offer the Divine's soul downloads. As I mentioned in the first section of this book, the first Divine Soul Download the Divine offered was the soul treasure of Divine Liver to Walter. Two and a half months later, Walter had recovered from his liver cancer. A CT scan and MRI showed no sign of cancer in Walter's liver. In May 2008 I met Walter again. He was still cancer-free after nearly five years.

In the last five years I have offered countless Divine Soul Downloads to humanity, animals, organizations, houses, oceans, mountains, planets, galaxies, and universes. I am extremely honored to be a servant of the Divine to offer the Divine's soul downloads to serve humanity, Mother Earth, and the universes.

What Are Divine Soul Downloads?

The Divine is the creator. The Divine is a soul. The Divine is the top leader of all souls. Whatever power you can imagine, the Divine has. The Divine can directly offer healing, blessing, transformation, and enlightenment anytime, anywhere, to anyone and any soul the Divine wishes. In July 2003 the Divine created a new way to express the Divine's power and offer divine service. This new way is Divine Soul Downloads, which are Divine Soul Transplants. Divine Soul Downloads are divine creations. The Divine creates new souls from the Divine's heart to be downloaded (or transmitted) to recipients. The Divine creates new souls to carry the Divine's power to serve—to heal, bless, transform, and enlighten.

You have received eleven major Divine Soul Downloads as gifts from the Divine as you read this book. You have experienced the power of Divine Soul Downloads for healing, preventing sickness, rejuvenating, prolonging life, purifying soul, heart, mind, and body, and transforming every aspect of life, including relationships and finances.

Divine Soul Downloads are Divine Soul Transplants. These new divine souls are created on the spot from the Divine's heart. Generally speaking, the original souls that the divine souls replace are small. For example, the original soul of a bodily system is about four to five inches tall and two to three inches wide. The original soul of a bodily organ is typically about two to three inches tall and one to two inches wide. Different things have different-sized souls. Souls have different colors also. Generally speaking, divine souls are golden-, rainbow-, purple-, and crystal-colored souls. These different-colored souls carry different divine frequencies and different powers. The Divine can download any and all of them. New divine souls could be hundreds or thousands of feet tall and wide. New divine souls could also be countless feet tall and wide.

When these huge souls created from the heart of the Divine are transmitted to humanity, animals, Mother Earth, and the universes, it usually takes several days for the new divine souls to condense to the proper size, depending on the recipient. The size varies. When one's Third Eye is fully open, one can witness what I just explained.

The color of a soul indicates its level in the following order:

- golden
- rainbow
- purple
- crystal
- beyond crystal

The frequencies of these five layers of divine souls are different. As you progress from the golden layer to the beyond crystal layer, the vibration becomes tinier and tinier. The power and abilities increase. The golden layer has the lowest power and the least refined frequency. (Nevertheless, all divine souls carry Divine Soul Power, which is beyond comprehension.) The beyond crystal layer has the highest power and the most refined frequency. In the last few years, I have offered these five layers of Divine Soul Transplants to humanity, Mother Earth, and all universes.

Now let me reveal an important secret:

Top holy saints, Taoist saints, buddhas, lamas, gurus, and other top spiritual leaders can offer spiritual blessings only through their golden and rainbow light. Only the Divine can offer blessings of purple, crystal, and beyond crystal light. Generally speaking, a recipient of a Divine Soul Transplant receives a Level 1 golden light soul. Recipients should practice regularly with these divine soul treasures for at least three months to integrate and transform their own frequencies to the Divine Level 1 golden light frequency. Regular practice means at least fifteen minutes of practice per time and at least two times per day.

After transforming your frequency to the Divine Level 1 golden light soul frequency, you can then apply for a Level 2 Soul Transplant, which is a rainbow light soul treasure. Remember, receiving Divine Soul Transplants does not mean you are healed or transformed. Receiving Divine Soul Transplants only means you have received permanent new divine soul treasures. These soul treasures have the power to heal, bless, and transform your health and every other aspect of your life but you *must* practice with them.

There are no limitations to practice. The more you practice, the more blessings you receive from the divine soul treasure. There can be no overpractice. There are no side effects. There are only full divine benefits of healing, rejuvenation, blessing, and transformation waiting for you when you practice.

The Significance of Divine Soul Downloads

Divine Soul Downloads or Soul Transplants are directly created from the Divine's heart. These new souls carry divine frequency, with divine love, forgiveness, compassion, and light. The following one-sentence secrets explain the power of Divine Soul Downloads or Soul Transplants:

> *Divine Frequency transforms the frequency of humanity,*
>   *Mother Earth, and all universes.*
> *Divine Love melts all blockages and transforms all life.*
> *Divine Forgiveness brings inner peace and inner joy.*

Divine Compassion boosts energy, stamina, vitality, and immunity.
Divine Light heals, prevents sickness, rejuvenates, and prolongs life.
Together they transform all lives for humanity, Mother Earth, and all universes.

From the above explanation of the power of Divine Soul Downloads, we can deeply understand why a person needs Divine Soul Downloads. These are the major benefits of Divine Soul Downloads for human beings:

- transformation of human consciousness to divine consciousness
- healing, including self-healing and healing others
- prevention of sickness and other imbalances
- rejuvenation
- prolongation of life
- transformation of relationships
- transformation of finances and business
- purification of soul, heart, mind, and body
- passing spiritual testing
- transformation of the soul journey
- opening and developing soul communication channels
- opening and developing soul intelligence
- physical and spiritual safety and protection
- transformation of all souls of humanity
- promoting love, peace, and harmony
- and more

Why does an animal need Divine Soul Downloads? These are the major benefits of Divine Soul Downloads for animals:

- transformation of the animal's consciousness to divine consciousness
- healing, including self-healing and healing others
- prevention of sickness and other imbalances
- rejuvenation
- prolongation of life
- transformation of relationships
- purification of soul, heart, mind, and body
- transformation of the soul journey
- physical and spiritual safety and protection
- transformation of all souls of animals
- promoting love, peace, and harmony
- and more

Why do Mother Earth, other planets, stars, galaxies, and universes need Divine Soul Downloads? These are the major benefits of Divine Soul Downloads for them:

- transformation of their consciousness to divine consciousness
- healing
- prevention of imbalances
- rejuvenation
- prolongation of life
- transformation of relationships
- purification of soul, heart, mind, and body
- transformation of the soul journey
- opening and developing soul communication channels
- opening and developing soul intelligence
- physical and spiritual safety and protection
- transformation of all souls of planets, stars, galaxies, and universes

- promoting love, peace, and harmony
- and more

In the last five years, we have received thousands of heart-touching and heart-moving stories from all over the world that tell of the healing, prevention of sickness, rejuvenation, and life transformation received from Divine Soul Downloads. You can read many of them on my website.

Dr. Peter Hudoba and his research team have completed studies on the effects of Divine Soul Transplants on human beings. I will invite him now to share the essence of the research on Divine Soul Transplant of Divine Heart.

In 2005 a research team of Sha Research Foundation conducted a short double-blind randomized crossover study to investigate the effects of the Soul Power of Divine Soul Transplant of Divine Heart on the mental and emotional states and the spiritual standing of recipients. Forty-five spiritual practitioners were randomized and received this Divine Soul Transplant via a distance blessing from Zhi Gang Sha at one of two different times, one month apart, in a blind fashion. The team observed improvement in empathy, egotism, and mental and emotional well-being, and improvement in the quality of meditative states. Some remote viewers were able to document changes in the soul image of participants between the blessed and control groups. The results of this study document the effects of the remote use of Soul Power on the mental, emotional, and spiritual well-being of recipients, opening a wide range of potential applications in spirituality and health management.

To date, these and other research results have been presented and well received at more than ten research conferences and symposia worldwide. Divine Soul Power will continue to spread in the academic world and to all humanity.

Types of Divine Soul Downloads

Whatever a human being has, the Divine has. The Divine can download a new divine soul to replace any soul in a human being or an animal. The Divine can also download a new divine soul to replace the soul of a house, a building, a business, or an organization. The Divine can further download a new soul to replace the soul of a city or a country.

The Divine is the creator. Whatever we can think of, the Divine can create a new soul for it. Divine Soul Downloads or Soul Transplants are instant divine creation and manifestation.

The Divine asked me to start offering Divine Soul Downloads in July 2003. So we have only a few years of history with Divine Soul Downloads. Since then I have personally experienced Divine Soul Power and divine creation and manifestation every day. I have received "aha" moments many times. Many people worldwide have been moved to tears of joy by the healing and life-transforming results they have received from Divine Soul Downloads. Every person and every soul who has received Divine Soul Transplants is extremely grateful. No words can express our greatest gratitude to the Divine. This is the first time in history that the Divine is offering his Soul Transplants or Soul Downloads to all humanity and all souls in the universe.

As I have explained, Divine Soul Downloads are unlimited, but here are some major categories of Divine Soul Downloads that are available at this time:

- Divine Health
- Divine Relationships
- Divine Safety and Protection
- Divine Pets

- Divine Finances and Business
- Divine Spiritual Journey

I will discuss each of these categories briefly.

DIVINE SOUL DOWNLOADS FOR DIVINE HEALTH

Health concerns cover a wide range of issues. These include:

- alleviating chronic health conditions
- dealing with sudden illness or other emergencies
- boosting energy, stamina, vitality, and immunity
- maintaining good health in bodily systems, organs, and cells
- preventing future health problems before they arise
- fostering rejuvenation and prolongation of life

Through the generosity and compassion of the Divine, every aspect of the health spectrum can receive a Divine Soul Download. Divine Soul Downloads can be tailored to whatever your health concerns may be. Therefore, every person can find Divine Soul Downloads appropriate for his or her healing journey.

Divine Soul Downloads for health include:

- Divine Soul Transplants for Bodily Systems (for example, cardiovascular system, endocrine system, musculoskeletal system, reproductive system, or respiratory system)
- Divine Soul Transplants for Organs and Parts of the Body (for example, heart, liver, brain, pancreas, knees, eyes, teeth and gums, or blood)
- Divine Soul Transplants for the Cells, Cell Units, DNA, RNA, and the Spaces between the Cells of a Bodily System, Organ, or Part of the Body

- Divine Soul Transplants for Energy Centers (for example,
  Lower Dan Tian or Snow Mountain Area, which you received when you read chapter 9)

DIVINE SOUL DOWNLOADS FOR DIVINE RELATIONSHIPS

We often wish our relationships would improve. We want friction and
conflict to be removed. We want love, care, and compassion at all
times. Divine Soul Downloads for relationships are available to help
make such wishes a reality.

Everything has a soul, including all forms of relationships. Divine
Soul Downloads can offer a new divine soul for a relationship, including relationships with family members, friends, coworkers, and others. They can also assist in healing relationships with those who have
transitioned.

Divine Soul Downloads for relationships include:

- Divine Soul Transplants for Divine Relationship Between
  Two Family Members
- Divine Soul Transplants for Divine Relationship Between
  Two Friends
- Divine Soul Transplants for Divine Relationship Between
  Two Business Colleagues
- Divine Soul Transplants for Divine Other Relationship
  (for example, your relationship with a pet, a musician's
  relationship with his or her instrument, or an informa-
  tion technology worker's relationship with his or her
  computer)

DIVINE SOUL DOWNLOADS FOR DIVINE SAFETY AND PROTECTION

Three very important Divine Soul Downloads for safety and protection are available at this time. They place special signals on the recipi-

ent's soul to alert the Divine and the Akashic Records that this one is protected. The significance of this special attention from the highest levels of the Soul World is beyond words and physical value, particularly in the transition time of Mother Earth.

The Divine Soul Downloads for safety and protection are:

- Divine Soul Transplant of Divine Protection
- Divine Soul Transplant of Divine Light Wall
- Divine Soul Transplant of Divine Prevention and Healing of Communicable Diseases

Divine Soul Transplant of Divine Protection protects your life from physical harm in situations such as hurricanes, earthquakes, tornados, floods, and other natural disasters, as well as automobile accidents, turbulence in air flights, crossing busy intersections, and other potentially life-threatening situations. This special divine soul places a mark on your soul that tells the Akashic Records that your life is to be guarded and protected at all times. You can obtain this protection for yourself and for your loved ones. It does not, however, release you from exercising a prudent and respectful approach to life.

Divine Soul Transplant of Divine Protection is available to all, from an unborn child to an elder. The Divine is making it possible for humanity to be protected in every way during these difficult times on Mother Earth. Divine Protection is an expression of the unconditional love and compassion the Divine has for each one of us.

Divine Soul Transplant of Divine Light Wall holds you within the embrace of divine light to protect you from unwelcome or troubling souls who would want to disturb or harm you. Divine Light Wall allows you to experience serenity, peace, and tranquillity on your soul journey. If any unpleasant souls pass through the Divine Light Wall, they will be transformed to light or you can invite them to become part of the light. They will choose either to do that or leave.

Divine Soul Transplant of Divine Prevention and Healing of

Communicable Diseases places a mark upon your soul that tells the souls of communicable diseases that you are protected, from both existing diseases and diseases that will emerge in the future. Your frequency is brought to a much higher level than the frequency of the souls of communicable diseases, thereby protecting your physical health. With this divine soul, it is possible to remain calm and confident in the face of reports of spreading illnesses or outbreaks of new diseases as the transition of Mother Earth continues and intensifies.

DIVINE SOUL TRANSPLANTS FOR DIVINE PETS

Whatever Divine Soul Downloads are available for human beings could also be available for your beloved pets. The Divine has great tenderness and unconditional love for your pets also. Your pet could receive Divine Soul Transplants for health, for safety and protection, and more.

DIVINE SOUL DOWNLOADS FOR DIVINE FINANCES AND BUSINESS

Divine Soul Downloads for finances and business are new divine souls. They can replace the soul of a business with a divine soul, which is karma free. They can give you a soul of a Divine Professional, as I illustrated with the story of the opera singer in chapter 3. They can give you virtue to increase your account in Heaven's bank. This spiritual currency then can be manifested on Mother Earth as greater financial success. As I explained in chapter 11, spiritual currency can exchange for physical currency. However, do not expect physical money to come running to you. You must practice with your divine soul treasure or treasures and you must offer good service. Then your spiritual fathers and mothers, Heaven's saints in charge of money, and the Divine will bless you more and more. Your spiritual currency in Heaven's bank will be converted more and more to physical currency.

DIVINE SOUL DOWNLOADS FOR DIVINE SPIRITUAL JOURNEY

Every Divine Soul Download can benefit your spiritual journey. However, in this category there are specific Divine Soul Transplants for the energy centers (with the Message Center and the Third Eye being the two most important spiritual energy centers; a Divine Soul Transplant of Divine Message Center is included in *Soul Communication,* the second book in my Soul Power Series), for opening and developing one's soul communication abilities (for example, Divine Soul Transplants for opening Soul Language and for translating Soul Language, both of which are included in *Soul Wisdom,* the first book in my Soul Power Series), for purification, and for divine qualities such as love, forgiveness, peace, and compassion. You have received several of these Divine Soul Transplants as you read this book.

How to Apply Divine Soul Downloads

I have explained how to apply Divine Soul Downloads in the specific practices that I have led you to do throughout this book. The essence is to sincerely request the Divine Soul Download to offer healing, prevention of sickness, rejuvenation, prolongation of life, transformation of any aspect of life, and purification of soul, heart, mind, and body. Always offer your pure love, total gratitude, and highest respect and honor to these divine souls that were created specifically for you. They are pure divine servants but just as with physical beings, the more love, gratitude, honor, and respect you give them, the more they will multiply, magnify, and reflect this back to you through their divine service.

What Are Divine Soul Orders?

In June 2006 the Divine asked me to offer a new divine soul treasure for healing, blessing, and life transformation. This new divine service is named Divine Soul Order.

Three years after being chosen as a divine servant, I received the higher honor to send the Divine's Soul Orders. When I meet a person with a very serious or even life-threatening health condition, I check with the Divine. The Divine will tell me if I should send the Divine's order for healing. For example, for one person with very serious arthritis, the Divine told me to send the Divine's order: *Heal knees*. Newborn twins in Los Angeles had a genetic sickness that was life-threatening. I was asked to offer a divine blessing to them. I asked the Divine what kind of blessing the Divine wished to give. The Divine said, "Send my order: *Save the life of these two babies*." The babies survived and are doing very well; they received benefits beyond comprehension.

In fact, every time I offer divine karma cleansing service, the Divine asks me to send the Divine's Soul Order to the Akashic Records to cleanse one's karma. I am extremely honored to be a divine servant to offer Divine Soul Orders.

Like a Divine Soul Download, a Divine Soul Order also carries a new divine soul for healing, blessing, and life transformation. How does a Divine Soul Order work? The recipient of a Divine Soul Order has the original soul of the system, organ, thing, or situation that is the subject of the order replaced with a new divine soul. The new divine soul carries divine frequency with divine love, forgiveness, compassion, and light. It can transform all the unhealthy and unbalanced conditions of the system, organ, thing, or situation. All of the souls around that system, organ, thing, or situation will follow the Divine Soul Order and assist the Divine Soul Order for healing, blessing, and life transformation.

After receiving a Divine Soul Order, one needs to chant the order repeatedly. Generally speaking, chant a Divine Order three to five minutes per time, three to five times per day, the more the better. You may chant for yourself if you have received a Divine Soul Order. You may chant for a loved one if he or she has received a Divine Soul Order. For example:

Divine Order heals my knees.
Divine Order heals my knees.
Divine Order heals my knees.
Divine Order heals my knees . . .

Another example:

Divine Order restores the health of my mother's kidneys.
Divine Order restores the health of my mother's kidneys.
Divine Order restores the health of my mother's kidneys.
Divine Order restores the health of my mother's kidneys . . .

In 2006 I spent six months traveling worldwide on my Love, Peace and Harmony Tour. I held more than 140 events within these six months in many cities in North America, Europe, Australia, and New Zealand. In each of these 140 events, I sent at least one Divine Soul Order for healing. The results left the recipients and me speechless. I am extremely blessed that the Divine gives me the honor to send the Divine's order for healing, blessing, life transformation, and saving life. I am extremely humbled. All the heart-touching and moving results belong to the Divine. I am a servant of the Divine and humanity.

The Power of Divine Soul Orders

I have explained the significance of Divine Soul Downloads or Soul Transplants earlier in this chapter. All the power of Divine Soul Downloads applies to Divine Soul Orders.

Divine Soul Orders are the next step beyond Divine Soul Downloads. Generally speaking, a Divine Soul Order is sent only for very serious health issues, for saving life, or for major transformation of any aspect of life.

The power of Divine Soul Downloads is beyond comprehension

and thought. The power of Divine Soul Orders is beyond even that. I am extremely honored and humbled to be a servant of the Divine and humanity to offer Divine Soul Downloads and Divine Soul Orders to serve humanity, Mother Earth, and all universes.

> *I love my heart and soul*
> *I love all humanity*
> *Join hearts and souls together*
> *Love, peace and harmony*
> *Love, peace and harmony*

Hao! Hao! Hao!

Thank you. Thank you. Thank you.

Conclusion

$\mathcal{I}$ WOULD LIKE TO offer my total GOLD—total gratitude, total obedience, total loyalty, and total devotion—to the Divine. I am deeply honored and appreciative. The Divine gave me the entire contents of this book to simply flow out. All credit goes to the Divine.

In this book the Divine shared soul secrets, wisdom, knowledge, and practices. The Divine offered eleven Divine Soul Downloads, which are priceless divine soul treasures. The Divine revealed the new divine way for healing, rejuvenation, life transformation, and soul enlightenment for the twenty-first century and the entire Soul Light Era.

This book can be summarized as follows:

For healing: *Heal the soul first; then healing of the mind and body will follow.*

For prevention of sickness: *Prevent sicknesses of the soul first; then prevention of sicknesses of the mind and body will follow.*

For rejuvenation: *Rejuvenate the soul first; then rejuvenation of the mind and body will follow.*

For long life: *Prolong the life of the soul first; then long life for the mind and body will follow.*

For consciousness: *Transform the consciousness of the soul first; then transformation of the consciousness of heart, mind, and body will follow.*

For relationships: *Transform the soul of the relationship first; then transformation of the relationship will follow.*

For finances and business: *Transform the soul of finances and the business first; then transformation of finances and the business will follow.*

For life transformation: *Transform the soul first; then every aspect of life will be transformed.*

For enlightenment: *Enlighten the soul first; then enlightenment of the heart, mind, and body will follow.*

Souls have the power to do all of this. The Divine and divine souls have divine power to do all of this. Divine Soul Transplants are permanent divine soul treasures for doing all of this.

This book teaches and practices *soul over matter.* This book reveals Soul Power, including soul secrets, wisdom, knowledge, and practices to heal, rejuvenate, transform, and enlighten all life.

This book is a divine gift to humanity. I am extremely honored to be a servant of the Divine, you, humanity, and all souls.

This book, *The Power of Soul,* shows you "the way to heal, rejuvenate, transform, and enlighten all life."

Take it.

Use it.

Benefit from it.

> *I love my heart and soul*
> *I love all humanity*
> *Join hearts and souls together*
> *Love, peace and harmony*
> *Love, peace and harmony*

Love you. Love you. Love you.

Thank you. Thank you. Thank you.

Afterword

by Dr. Peter Hudoba

$\mathcal{I}$T IS MY great pleasure and honor to share some of my personal experiences and insights.

Over the eight years I have studied with Dr. Sha, I have witnessed an explosion of Soul Power, right in front of my eyes. I can think of no better testimony to the power of soul than what I have personally seen and experienced.

When I first met Dr. Sha in 2000, he was teaching mainly Chinese healing arts, which he practiced masterfully and advanced significantly by introducing and incorporating Soul Power. This is how Dr. Sha created Soul Mind Body Medicine, a simple yet very effective soul healing system. Thousands of people around the world, including my family and me, have benefited greatly from its powerful techniques.

I have seen Dr. Sha grow incredibly in every dimension. For example, as he joyfully admits, he could never sing. Yet by applying Soul Power to bring out his Soul Song, he has been able to record ten extremely beautiful Soul Song CDs.

How has Dr. Sha been able to do this? It is very simple. Dr. Sha applies Soul Power to everything he does, including healing, teaching, singing, writing, and even the practical necessities of life. He is guiding his students and readers to do the same. For Dr. Sha and his team, every teaching, every project, and every endeavor, down to the minutest details of website design, for example, follow Divine Guidance and are supported by Divine Soul Power.

Allow me to share some personal examples. I never imagined I would be writing books. Yet Master Sha transformed that mind-set easily. Since he transmitted the necessary Soul Power to me, writing books has become child's play. Although my schedule is incredibly busy, I have written eight books in the last two years. Similarly, when I prepare a presentation or class, I connect with the soul of the presentation and receive a complete outline for it. Now I am even composing a libretto for an opera, a *soul* opera, with the assistance of a Divine Soul Download tailor-made for that purpose!

I use Soul Power in every aspect of my life. This has completely transformed my life. Existence is now incredibly rich, satisfying, and most enjoyable. I no longer rely on my intellect or memory or information from others. Through Soul Power, I can not only receive Divine Guidance for any issue; I am literally able to shape the events of my life.

I cannot honor and thank Dr. Sha and the Divine enough for the gifts they have given to me. I am very pleased that Dr. Sha is bringing all of these gifts, and more, to humanity in this inspiring and invaluable book.

The Power of Soul does not discuss whether there is such a thing as a soul. *The Power of Soul* is not merely an attempt to describe the soul. In this book, Dr. Sha is offering sacred wisdom, simple yet very effective techniques, and, most amazingly and generously, transmissions of Divine Soul Power to each reader. Dr. Sha is giving us all of the tools we need to completely develop our own souls so that we can liberate our own existence.

In this book, you have learned what the soul is. You have learned how to develop the total potential of your soul. You have learned how to apply the power of your soul to any aspect of your life, empowering you to resolve your difficulties and discover possibilities beyond your imagination and dreams.

You have realized that the highest aspiration of your soul, which is to become one with the Divine, is very attainable. You have learned how you can attain this oneness. With the teachings in *The Power of Soul*, Dr. Sha has gone far beyond any other spiritual leader in the history of humankind.

The Power of Soul is a masterpiece that will open the door to a new era for humanity and Mother Earth. It will serve humanity for many years to come. Clearly, at this particular time, we are facing challenges that cannot be resolved by the intellect alone. After all, our intellect created these challenges in the first place. There is no time to continue with the old approaches. Humanity must make a radical change and enter fully into the dimensions of the soul. In my humble opinion, our very survival depends on Soul Power.

Soul Power is present everywhere, anytime, for everyone. Soul Power is inexhaustible. We simply need to learn how to access it and apply it. *The Power of Soul* teaches us the way.

The Way is the Tao. I have searched for the Tao all my life. After many years of committed pursuit, I finally feel I am coming to the Tao. Better said, it is Master Sha who is bringing me to the Tao.

The Power of Soul teaches the Tao in a way that anyone can understand. This book reveals and demonstrates that the Tao is not complicated. This book gives you clear guidance on how to reach the Tao.

Be with the Tao. Live the Tao. Apply the teachings of *The Power of Soul* to reach the Tao. The benefits for transforming and enlightening every aspect of your life are beyond comprehension. I wish you will receive the same benefits that I have, and even more.

Dr. Peter Hudoba
British Columbia, Canada

Acknowledgments

THE POWER OF SOUL offers the soul way and the divine way to heal; boost energy, stamina, vitality, and immunity; prevent sickness; rejuvenate; prolong life; and transform every aspect of life, including relationships and finances. It reveals to humanity Divine Soul Downloads or Divine Soul Transplants, Divine Soul Orders, divine karma teaching, divine healing, divine blessing, and divine life transformation for every aspect of life.

I cannot appreciate and honor the Divine enough for choosing me as the Divine's servant, vehicle, and channel to be a total GOLD servant for humanity and all souls. I cannot honor the Divine enough for the divine abilities given to me to heal and serve. I cannot honor the Divine enough for constantly standing above my head to guide me as I flowed this entire book. I am extremely grateful to the Divine.

I cannot appreciate and honor my most beloved spiritual father, Master Zhi Chen Guo, and beloved Mama Guo enough for teaching and training me to be a total GOLD servant for the Divine, humanity, and all souls. The secret wisdom that they taught me is priceless. Without their teaching and training, I could not have grown fast enough to be a divine servant. I am extremely grateful for them.

I cannot appreciate and honor all my Taoist, Buddhist, Confucian, tai chi, qi gong, kung fu, *I Ching*, and feng shui masters and teachers in my life enough. The ancient soul secrets, wisdom, knowledge, and practices that they delivered to me are priceless. Without their teaching and training, I could not have grown fast enough to be a divine servant. I am extremely grateful to them.

I cannot appreciate and honor Rev. and Dr. Michael Bernard Beckwith enough for writing a foreword for my entire Soul Power Series of books. I cannot appreciate and honor Dr. C. Norman Shealy enough for writing a foreword for this book. I also cannot appreciate enough their endorsements and work and the endorsements and work of other great teachers and authors. They include Dr. John Gray, Marianne Williamson, Dr. Wayne Dyer, Rev. Dr. Barbara L. King, Sri Rani Kumra, Debbie Ford, Dr. Larry Dossey, Dr. Masaru Emoto, Dr. Bernie Siegel, and Dr. Walter Semkiw. I am very grateful for their recognition of my service.

I cannot honor and appreciate enough the members of the Founding Committee of the World Soul Healing, Peace and Enlightenment Movement. They are Rev. Dr. Barbara L. King, Dr. C. Norman Shealy, Dr. Kofi Kondwani, Sri Rani Kumra, Rev. Darlene Strickland, Renee Morgan Brooks, Dr. Peter Hudoba, Marilyn Smith, and Allan Chuck. I am very grateful for their joining hearts and souls with me to offer the service of this movement to help accomplish the divine mission.

I cannot appreciate and honor all my Certified Master Teachers and Healers of Soul Healing and Enlightenment enough. They are Marilyn Smith, Dr. Peter Hudoba, Allan Chuck, Joyce Brown, Shu Chin Hsu, Patricia Smith, Francisco Quintero, Michael Stevens, Lynne Nusyna, and Peggy Werner. They have made great contributions to the divine mission. They travel worldwide to teach soul healing and enlightenment. I could not accomplish the divine mission without their total support and contribution. I am extremely grateful to them.

I cannot appreciate and honor my key dedicated business team members enough. Their tireless work and total commitment deeply touch my heart. They have made great contributions to the mission. They include Donna Schmidt, Allan Chuck, Ximena Gavino, Francisco Quintero, Kara Jewell, David Lusch, Shu Chin Hsu, Patty Baker, Robert Liu, Wei Fu, Ye Yu, Diana Gold Holland, Gloria Kovacevich, Sher O'Rourke, Jurg Muhlebach, Isabel Love, Elaine Ward, Angee Jenkins, Sande Zeig, Barbara Howard, Irene Stevens, May Chew, and more. I could not accomplish the divine mission without their greatest efforts. I am extremely grateful to them.

I cannot appreciate and honor my hundreds of Divine Healers and Teachers enough. I also cannot appreciate and honor all my Divine Writers and Divine Editors enough for their total commitment to serve humanity. They have done service beyond words. I could not accomplish the divine mission without their greatest efforts. I am extremely grateful to them.

I cannot appreciate and honor my final editor of this book, Allan Chuck, enough for his great contribution of editing this book and my other books. He is a total GOLD servant for the divine mission. He is responsible for training our Divine Writers and Divine Editors. He has made great contributions to Heaven's Library publications and to our entire mission. I am extremely grateful to him.

I cannot appreciate and honor my literary agent for this book and the two preceding books of the Soul Power Series, Cathy Hemming, enough. She has made a great contribution toward establishing Heaven's Library's partnership with Atria Books/Simon & Schuster. I am extremely grateful to her.

I cannot appreciate and honor all of the key personnel at my publishing partner, Atria Books/Simon & Schuster, and at Simon & Schuster Canada enough. They include Judith Curr, Johanna Castillo, Gary Urda, Christine Saunders, Christine Duplessis, Kitt Reckord, Ghenet Powell, Amy Tannenbaum, Sandy Moore, Mike Noble, Lourdes Lopez, Craig Dean, Amy Cormier, Felicia Quon, Melissa Ong, Dominic Stones, and many more. I am extremely grateful for them. Judith, the publisher of Atria Books, has given me the greatest support and love in bringing the Soul Power Series to the world. I am extremely grateful to her and her team.

I cannot appreciate and honor all the hundreds of thousands of people I have met worldwide enough. They have given me the opportunity to serve them. They have given me the opportunity to improve my service and myself. I have learned a great deal from all of them. I have received incredible love and support from them. I am extremely grateful to all of them.

Finally, I cannot honor and appreciate my beloved wife, children, parents, and parents-in-law enough for their great love and great support of my mission. I deeply appreciate them. I am extremely grateful to them.

Mother Earth is in a special period of time now. It needs millions of pure servants to serve humanity. I am delighted to be a servant of humanity and all souls and to make a spiritual calling to all humanity and all souls through the first Divine Soul Song I received from the Divine on September 10, 2005.

> *I love my heart and soul*
> *I love all humanity*
> *Join hearts and souls together*
> *Love, peace and harmony*
> *Love, peace and harmony*

With love and blessing,

Zhi Gang Sha

A Special Gift

*I*N EARLY 2008 the Divine guided me as follows: "Zhi Gang, this is the time for you to sing Soul Songs for healing and rejuvenation for humanity. Because you are my servant, vehicle, and channel, your Soul Song carries my love, light, and compassion. I will also download many divine souls to your soul. When you sing a Soul Song, these souls will come out to serve humanity and other souls."

I was deeply touched and moved. After receiving transmissions of new divine souls from the Divine every day for a week, I invoked these new Divine Soul Transplants and recorded a number of Soul Songs for Healing and Rejuvenation of various organs, systems, parts of the body, and emotional imbalances.

The Divine guided me to offer Soul Songs for Healing and Rejuvenation to all humanity. You can sample them at www.Master ShaSoulSong.com. People have already reported hundreds of heart-touching stories of remarkable healing and life transformation they have received by listening to my Soul Songs. My heart is deeply moved. I cannot honor the Divine enough for the Divine's guidance, blessing, and Soul Power.

As a special gift for you, I am including a sample CD of my *Soul*

Song for Rejuvenation in this book. This is an abbreviated version of a full-length CD that is available on my website. If you wish to rejuvenate your soul, mind, and body, I recommend you listen to this often, even continuously. You could have it playing constantly at low volume in your home or office. This Soul Song could offer you great benefits for rejuvenation.

When you listen to this Soul Song, do not forget to say *hello* first:

> *Dear Soul Song for Rejuvenation,*
> *I love you, honor you, and appreciate you.*
> *Please rejuvenate my soul, mind, and body.*
> *I am very grateful.*
> *Thank you.*

A soul healing wave of divine love, light, compassion, vibration, and frequency will pour into your body and soul to serve you. This divine wave will stimulate cellular vibration, promote energy flow, and assist the souls, minds, and bodies of your systems, your organs, your cells, and the spaces between your cells to rejuvenate. Of course, you must also use normal approaches, including getting adequate sleep, following a proper diet, reducing stress, and exercising regularly, for best results. These yang methods will work together with the yin method of this Soul Song. Yin and yang support and nourish each other.

My Soul Song is your servant. I wish you will receive great benefits from this Soul Song.

Thank you. Thank you. Thank you.

Dr. Sha's Teachings and Services

Books and Audiobooks

Power Healing: The Four Keys to Energizing Your Body, Mind & Spirit (HarperSanFrancisco, 2002)

Soul Mind Body Medicine: A Complete Soul Healing System for Optimum Health and Vitality (New World Library, 2006)

Living Divine Relationships (Heaven's Library, 2006)

Body Space Medicine by Dr. Zhi Chen Guo (foreword by Dr. Sha) (Heaven's Library, 2007)

Soul Wisdom: Practical Soul Treasures to Transform Your Life (revised trade paperback edition, Heaven's Library/Atria Books, 2008; also available as an audiobook)

Soul Communication: Opening Your Spiritual Channels for Success and Fulfillment (revised trade paperback edition, Heaven's Library/Atria Books, 2008; also available as an audiobook)

Multimedia eBook

Soul Mind Body Medicine: A Complete Soul Healing System for Optimum Health and Vitality (Heaven's Library/Alive! eBooks Network, 2008; www.HeavensLibrary.com). Includes one hour of new audio content and one hour of new video content with Dr. Sha.

Healing, Blessing, and Life Transformation

Divine Remote Group Healing, Rejuvenation, and Transformation Teleconference Session with Master Sha, Sundays, 5:00–6:00 p.m. Pacific Time.

Divine Sacred Soul Song Singing Teleconference for the World Soul Healing, Peace and Enlightenment Movement, Tuesdays, 5:45–6:15 p.m. Pacific Time. Register one time at www.DrSha.com for this ongoing weekly Soul Song singing service.

Divine Soul Downloads, Karma Cleansings, Divine Soul Orders, and Other Divine Blessings (www.DrSha.com).

CDs and DVDs

The Voice of the Universe: Power Healing Music (Qi Records, 2002). Four powerful universal mantras for the Soul Light Era recorded by Dr. Sha:

- *God's Light*
- *Universal Light*
- *Shining Soul Light*
- *Follow Nature's Way*

The Music of Soul Dance (Institute of Soul Healing and Enlightenment, 2007). A ten-CD boxed set of Heaven's music to inspire and help guide your Soul Dance.

Blessings from Heaven (Institute of Soul Healing and Enlightenment, 2007). Divine Soul Music by Divine Composer Chun-Yen Chiang and Dr. Sha.

Love, Peace and Harmony (Institute of Soul Healing and Enlightenment, 2007). The first Soul Song given by the Divine to Dr. Sha and humanity.

God Gives His Heart to Me (Institute of Soul Healing and Enlightenment, 2008). The second Soul Song given by the Divine to Dr. Sha and humanity.

Soul Songs for Healing and Rejuvenation (www.MasterShaSoulSong .com, 2008). Divine Soul Songs for various organs, systems, parts of the body, emotions, and weight loss.

Power Healing to Self-Heal Ten Common Conditions (Institute of Soul Healing and Enlightenment, 2004). On this DVD, Dr. Sha teaches the Four Power Techniques to self-heal:

- Anxiety
- Back pain
- Carpal tunnel syndrome
- Common cold
- Constipation
- Energy boosting
- Headache
- Knee pain
- Menopause
- Weight loss

Dr. Sha also offers personal blessings for each condition.

Power Healing with Master Zhi Gang Sha: Learn Four Power Techniques to Heal Yourself (Institute of Soul Healing and Enlightenment, 2006). This four-DVD set offers a comprehensive teaching of the wisdom, knowledge, and practices of Power Healing and Soul

Mind Body Medicine. All aspects of Body Power, Sound Power, Mind Power, and Soul Power are covered in depth. Dr. Sha reveals and explains many secret teachings and leads you in practices.

www.DrSha.com
www.HeavensLibrary.com
1.888.3396815
DrSha@DrSha.com

Soul Power Series

SOUL WISDOM

Practical Soul Treasures to Transform Your Life

NEW YORK TIMES BESTSELLER
DR. ZHI GANG SHA

"Heal and transform the soul first; then healing and transformation of every aspect of life will follow."
– Dr. Zhi Gang Sha

Soul Power Series

SOUL COMMUNICATION

Opening Your Spiritual Channels for Success and Fulfillment

#1 NEW YORK TIMES BESTSELLING AUTHOR
DR. ZHI GANG SHA

"Soul communication can benefit every aspect of life. Soul communication can serve you anytime, anywhere, for anything."
– Dr. Zhi Gang Sha

New York Times Bestsellers

www.HeavensLibrary.com